Youngblood
of the
Peace

The authorized biography of Father Emile Jungbluth, OMI

Shirlee Smith Matheson

Detselig Enterprises
Calgary, Alberta

Canadian Cataloguing in Publication Data

Matheson, Shirlee Smith
Youngblood of the Peace

ISBN 1-55059-033-2

1. Jungbluth, Emile, 1908- 2. Oblates of Mary
Immaculate — Missions — Peace River Region (B.C. and
Alta.) — History. 3. Missionaries — Canada, Northern
— Biography. 4. Oblates of Mary Immaculate — Canada,
Northern — Biography. I. Title.
BX4705.J85M38 1991   266'.2'092   C91-091349-8

Detselig Enterprises Ltd.
P.O. Box G 399
Calgary, Alberta
T3A 2G3

Printed in Canada   SAN 115-0324   ISBN 1-55059-033-2

Dedication

Men of the North, we're a dwindling race;
Things travel too fast for our plodding pace;
We've played our parts, and with God's grace,
We served our purpose well.

This book is dedicated to the people of the Peace.

"Men of the North," *Beneath these Waters*
Earl K. Pollon, Hudson's Hope, B.C.

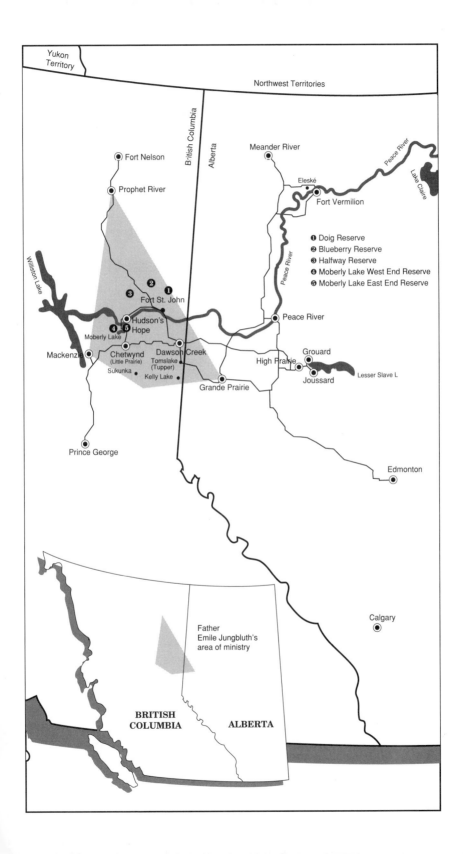

Yukon Territory

Northwest Territories

British Columbia

Alberta

Fort Nelson

Prophet River

Meander River

Eleské

Peace River

Lake Claire

Fort Vermilion

❶ Doig Reserve
❷ Blueberry Reserve
❸ Halfway Reserve
❹ Moberly Lake West End Reserve
❺ Moberly Lake East End Reserve

Williston Lake

❷
❸ Fort St. John
❶

Peace River

Hudson's
❹ ❺ Hope
Moberly Lake

Peace River

Mackenzie

Chetwynd
(Little Prairie)
Sukunka
Kelly Lake
Tomslake
(Tupper)

Dawson Creek

High Prairie

Grouard

Joussard

Lesser Slave L

Grande Prairie

Prince George

Edmonton

Calgary

Father
Emile Jungbluth's
area of ministry

BRITISH COLUMBIA   **ALBERTA**

Acknowledgements

I would like to thank the following individuals and organizations for their assistance during research and writing of the manuscript:

Canada Council, Explorations Program and Hudson's Hope Arts Council for grants received.

Ministry of Provincial Secretary and Government Services, Victoria, B.C., for their interest in acquiring tapes of interviews.

Immaculata - Pole et Tropiques, Strasbourg, for permission to make use of their published material concerning Father Jungbluth's mission.

Archdiocese of Grouard for material published in *La Voix*.

Hudson's Hope Museum and Historical Society for permission to make use of files and unpublished manuscripts, and for reproduction of photographs.

Hudson's Hope Public Library for procurement of books relative to my research.

Father Emile Jungbluth, OMI, for participating in weekly interviews over a three-year period, for taking me to his various missions, introducing me to his parishioners, providing copies of stories, photographs and articles that give depth and immediacy to the manuscript; for tireless proofreading of the various drafts; for encouragement of my work and complete candidness in answering myriad questions pertaining to his life.

Don Stanley, PhD, Vancouver, B.C., for editing the first four drafts of the manuscript.

Chris Carmeliet-Vanstone, Hudson's Hope, B.C., for French translations.

Eva Maria Stuntz, Hudson's Hope, B.C., for German translations.

Father Césaire Mariman, OMI, for valuable details of the Fort Vermilion era.

Sister Gemma (Barbara Kernick), Sister of St. Joseph's, for getting the project off the ground.

Residents of Kelly Lake, Fort St. John, Doig Reserve, Hudson's Hope, Moberly Lake and Chetwynd, B.C., for submitting themselves to untiring interviews.

Father Allan Noonan, OMI, and Father T. Lobsinger, OMI, Provincials, St. Paul's Province; Bishop Fergus O'Grady, OMI, Bishop of Prince Rupert; and Father R. L'Henaff, OMI, for their support and encouragement.

Note: Conversations have been recreated and dramatized in the interests of narrative.

Detselig Enterprises Ltd. appreciates the financial assistance for its 1991 publishing program from Alberta Foundation for the Literary Arts and Canada Council.

Table of Contents

Prologue

The soft summer wind agitated the dusty patches of couch-grass that carpeted the clearing, and teased the efforts of the young man who sat in quiet contemplation. The folds of his heavy black cassock almost hid the sculpted Oblate cross tucked into a wide belt of folded cloth cinched around his waist. As he wrote, head down, the papers of his writing pad flipped sporadically with the notions of the breeze. Beside him on the ground were several notebooks weighted down with stones to keep them from skipping away on the wind.

It was early evening. The day had been very hot and the settlement was unusually quiet. Even the dogs rested, flopped over on their sides in the shade of the tents, uninterested in the still red bones of two deer scattered over the baked ground. The coals of a campfire flickered dully as the breeze brushed them. Someone had lately feasted, and the smell of cooked meat haunted the air. Lazy flies buzzed about the man's head. With an impatient flick of his hand he brushed them away and continued writing.

On this July day in 1936, Father Emile Jungbluth, Oblate of Mary Immaculate, was 27 years old. He had fine sandy hair, a straight delicate nose, smooth skin and a wide expressive mouth. But his eyes drew one's attention: of a rare light blue, they sometimes took on a hooded appearance that camouflaged his inner amusement, disdain or meditation. His eyes were often discussed by the Beaver Indians, the parishioners of his northern Alberta mission. They could not read such eyes, and preferred his mouth, whose easy laugh transcended the frontiers of culture and language. The young priest had only to smile, and the Indians would instantly break into laughter. Sometimes, quite by accident, he caused them to laugh over his attempts to learn the complex Beaver language.

He already knew many languages from his home country: French because he was from France and was still a French citizen; German, learned in school until 1918; and Alsatian (a kind of low German mixed with Yiddish, Italian and French), because he had been born in 1908 in Strasbourg, in the Lower Rhine region of Alsace, when Germany was in possession.

He paused to look up. Several children were advancing, hesitant, shy, moving quietly in their bare feet over the dusty grass of the settlement. He smiled and beckoned them to sit beside him. He knew what they wanted, but first he would practise with them some of his newly learned Beaver words.

"It is warm," he said hesitatingly in Beaver. But they were shy, and just looked down at their brown knees and wiggled their toes in the grass. He smiled and reached deep into the pockets of his cassock to bring out some

1

pictures. Three little hands reached out. He smiled at the contrast of their brown hands, with knuckles shaded a darker hue, small fingernails chewed and broken, reaching for the colored pictures of the ivory-skinned Holy Virgin, whose blue eyes were cast upward toward her ethereal halo as were those of the curly-haired blonde child she held. Beneath the Latin verse inscribed on the back of the card was the advice that its recitation was worth five years indulgence.

As the children raced off to show their silent and uncomprehending parents the new decoration that would adorn their tent, Father Jungbluth watched the dust fly up from their brown heels in energetic puffs and then subside again into the zigzag waves of the afternoon's heat. It had been a good day. He had enjoyed a good visit with the Chief, and had learned six more words to add to his dictionary. He closed his writing pad and let his eyes travel from east to west across the forest that surrounded the clearing. Poplar bluffs and red willows skirted stretches of prairie that bottomed out in muskeg or encircled alkali sloughs rimmed in great white circles. This place, known officially by a statute in Ottawa as "Child's Lake Reserve," was locally called Eleské, meaning "White Mud Land" for the white alkali mud that lay to a depth of 15 centimetres beneath the tufted grass.

The Indians used this mud to chink the walls of their cabins, smearing it on with moose-hide lathes. These rude log huts, leaning and sagging at odd angles under the dirt roofs that sprouted weeds and grass, seemed to be a part of the landscape, as if they had grown as naturally as mushrooms. The faded canvas of the tents pitched among the cabins harmonized with the browns and grays and deep topazes of the surrounding bush.

The Father's black cassock flapped in the wind. Tucking it around his legs, he began again to study the papers upon his lap. He had written a letter (in German) to the periodical *Redaction Immaculata* of Strasbourg:

Dear Readers,

Summer in the Ice Missions is a beautiful time! The sun comes out of its long winter sleep and moves across the heavenly sky not only the whole day but right through the night. Only at midnight does it vanish from the horizon, but even then there is still a glow so that one can write or read all night long without using artificial light. This continuous warmth enables the grass to grow quickly and there are flowers everywhere.

Father Mariman left me two weeks ago to collect the mail and purchase food supplies in Fort Vermilion. He was supposed to be back within five days, but a fortnight has passed already. In the North, however, there are different laws of time and planning, and I spend my time very well indeed alone here with the Indians. It is already ten o'clock in the morning, and strangely nobody seems to be up in Eleské. Yesterday the young men killed two deer and all the Indians feasted right into the morning. At the moment, everyone seems to digest, so I take the opportunity and, with notebook in my hand, take a walk outside to practise some Beaver words.

It is rather nice to walk through the middle of an Indian camp and watch man and dog in sleep. Very nice indeed, with the burning sting of the millions of mosquitoes! Remembering the dear Alsace mosquitoes back home, I must admit they are really harmless in comparison with these grim enemies over here which seem to suck my "young blood" to the last drop. Within minutes I am completely surrounded by them and require a dozen hands to keep them from face and neck. When such an intensive attack occurs it is best to retreat, and so the brave missionary escapes quickly into the tent of his new "professor."

It is Beaver etiquette to pick a handful of grass, creep into the tent without knocking, throw the grass into the middle of a small fire to enlarge its smoke, and then sit down on a bear hide and watch to see what will happen. Not far from me, lying on the ground in full length, is my professor, clad in a torn pair of pants, his only clothing. The professor wakes up when I approach, but politeness demands that he wait for some minutes before he speaks to me. His visitor has first to feel completely at home, and must be given a chance to become familiar with the surroundings.

Towards evening I'll visit with some other Indian families. Everyone will be gathered outside the huts, sitting in the fresh grass, talking. Everywhere the Man of Prayer is welcome, and is given the best place at the campfire, there where it is smoking severely, as the smoke repels the mosquitoes. The children in great numbers ask for a small picture, which I give to each only after they have made a fine sign of the cross . . .

Father Jungbluth sat back, remembering the conversation with the Chief. In fine Beaver language the Chief had lamented, "What a heat! I'd rather freeze to death in winter than melt in the summer. Don't you think so too, Man of Prayer?"

"Yes," Father Jungbluth had answered, concentrating strenuously upon making the correct tongue clicks, thereby pleasing his professor. He took a deep breath and surged on: "That is the reason why it is not cold but so hot in Hell, so hot that one burns there."

"Burning! Hey! Hey!" The professor leaned back on his elbows to digress on Hell and, in almost untranslatable language, began to scold those ignorant people who would throw themselves into the eternal flames.

Father Jungbluth quickly was writing the words into his notebook. But, right in the middle of making plans for his "Hell" sermon, a thick drop of blood fell onto his notes from the meat above his head. He raised his head, wondering if it would happen again. The professor laughed.

"The meat is smiling at you, because you are hungry. I am too." Then, springing up, he tore a piece of meat from above and scurried out of the tent, where he lit a fire and hung the roast at one end of a green sapling rod. On another rod he fastened a tin pail filled with water for making tea. After ten minutes the meat was ready. Father Jungbluth made the sign for prayer as the professor sat back on his heels. With the roast in one hand and a huge knife in the other, he made a great cross-sign with the knife. Then with the knife still in his hand, the professor showed the priest how one eats according to the Beaver rules: the meat is cut in long strips, stuffed into the mouth, and cut off right at the lips as one eats.

"*Ot'ie udjon*," he had murmured, his black eyes blinking rapidly in the smoke from the fire. "Very good, just like I do."

The breeze was dying now in the late afternoon. Father Jungbluth again bent to his writing.

"And so a beautiful summer day passes into twilight in Eleské."

As the cool of the evening settled, the people began emerging from their tents to gather around the campfires to visit and to prepare their evening meals. He could understand bits of conversation, and noted with interest comments on the berries that were fast ripening down by the riverbank.

The horrors of his first winter in the North were now past, the strange new language posed fewer problems each day, and his system was adjusting to the strange customs, food and climate into which he had been so suddenly thrust late last fall. He had come across an ocean, across a time-span in civilization, and the thought of the future among these people filled him with exhilaration.

THE CONTINENT

1

Alpha

*E*mile was born at five o'clock in the early dawn of September 2, 1908, in Strasbourg, Bas-Rhin, the youngest child of Georges Jungbluth and Monique Barth Jungbluth. His sister, Madeleine, was three years older, and his brother, August, two years older than him. Another son had died at birth.

Father Jungbluth dimly remembers visiting his brother August, a chronic patient in a hospital for crippled children. He can only recall August coming toward him supported by crutches, but he cannot remember what misfortune crippled his brother. When August died, "sometime after the age of 10," he cannot recall if he even attended his funeral. The Jungbluth children did not live together as an ordinary family. Their father, Georges, died in America after fleeing with his brother from impending prosecution.

Georges Jungbluth died on July 3, 1910, when Emile, his youngest child, was not quite two years old. Monique and her children turned to the hospitality of Georges' mother, who was not wealthy. Monique despaired over what would become of the family. Her will, strong through the death of one son and the chronic illness of another, broke completely.

The family agreed that Emile should continue to stay with his grandmother. His sister Madeleine was to live with an aunt and uncle where she could help tutor the younger cousins to pay for her schooling. Then, as August was a chronic hospital patient, Monique was able to seek work in one of the *herchaffs*, the rich estates in the Rhineland, where the money she earned helped pay for her children's keep.

When Emile was five years old he contracted diphtheria which raged in epidemic proportions, striking young and old. At first it seems only to be a cough, a cold, a fever, but as the grey membrane forms deep inside the throat it chokes off the breath, burns the body with fever, paralyzes its victim.

Emile was hospitalized in Strasbourg, about 32 kilometres from Wolxheim, in a ward with other young diphtheria victims, isolated from the rest of the hospital. When a message was sent to the ward that the children had visitors, a nurse would carry them to the window, allowing them to wave to relatives or friends who stood below on the lawn. Some-

Emile's mother, Monique Barth Jungbluth (wearing national
headgear of the time in Alsace), Emile's sister, Madeleine, and Emile age 2½ years.

times they were allowed to call out, but that was exhausting and not often permitted.

Later, when the child had passed the crisis point and needed to build up his muscles, the nurses encouraged him to jump on the beds; each child was urged to jump higher than the next to strengthen the affected limbs while the children also had some fun.

After a year in the Strasbourg Hospital, Emile emerged walking, but his legs were a burden all his life, and the vocation he followed taxed them to their limits.

Emile's mother had secured employment as a governess in Wolxheim, where she could supervise his growing years, even though she resided in the house of her employer. Many times Emile accompanied her on visits to her friends throughout the village and these friends later became supportive benefactors to his missions in the far North. A constant visitor to the Jungbluth house was a family friend, the very pious Monsieur le curé Alphonse Sensenbrenner. It was he who acquainted Emile with the advantages of entering a college of a religious order, where higher education might be obtained at minimal cost, not to mention the honor of a religious vocation.

The school Emile attended in Wolxheim taught up to the eighth grade; it was a one-room village school with one teacher for all students. It was customary then in that area for priests to come to these small schools to show slides of and speak about the mission schools.

Alsace at that time exported almost as many vocations to the missions as it did bottles of wine. Mission schools, novitiates and seminaries dotted the Alsatian landscape, with their goal to spread missionaries abroad "as the four winds of the heaven." The missionaries recommended books to the students, including the beautiful compelling stories of Karl May. Emile read these stories, as did most other young boys and girls, and for him they stirred a great longing. He loved best the story of Winnetou, the brave young Apache chief who befriended the white man. The Indians were so manly and brave, yet not cruel, for in Karl May's books violence was occasioned only when the Indians had no other choice but to retaliate. And always emphasis was placed on the great potential of the Indians to become Christians.

Karl May's exciting narratives brought Emile visions of romance and adventure:

> Winnetou, his knife between his teeth, flew toward the enemy
> like a flat stone skipping over the surface.

Even when Winnetou was finally defeated and lay dying, his honor prevailed. With his last breath he asked the white man to sing for him the song of "the Queen of Heaven":

Virgin, hear our prayer
We lay it at your feet;
Guard us from despair
That our lives may be complete.
Ave Maria!

Winnetou, a symbol of natural human innocence, had been destroyed by western civilization. Emile could hardly wait to get over there and help set things right. He imagined himself a black-robed priest befriending a Winnetou; the two of them would ride horseback over the plains, share wisdom, learn of each other's culture. His Winnetou would take him to the Indian council where they would listen quietly and attentively to his inspirational messages. Such were the dreams of a young boy, fed by the imaginative writing of a man who had never set foot on the North American continent.

"Don't I laugh inside now!" Father Jungbluth related many years later. "When I came to Canada I found it quite different from the descriptions of Karl May. His Indians are much more noble. There are no beer parlors in his stories."

During World War I, families were evacuated from Strasbourg, so the house of Emile's grandmother in Wolxheim became filled with cousins, uncles and aunts. Emile's favorite relative was his Uncle August, the godfather of his crippled brother. Uncle August was also crippled, but by his own hand. He had learned the trade of a butcher and was to have taken over the family business. Then he had his misfortune: he cut himself badly in the foot with his own butcher knife and the foot had to be amputated above the ankle. But he got an artificial foot — a good one too — that allowed him to even climb trees, an ability he exercised flamboyantly in 1918.

The German army had been defeated and the French were in hot pursuit on horseback. While the Germans still swarmed throughout the village, chased by the French, Uncle August climbed to the top of a big tree in the centre of Wolxheim and there he placed the French flag. Even though the country had been under German rule since 1871, the Jungbluths were completely Frankish.

Uncle August's next feat was to organize a French celebration in the town. He was now learning the trade of a tailor, and he made all the boys *kepis*, little French hats, and they paraded through the town carrying lighted torches.

When Uncle August first came to live with Emile's grandmother, he was unmarried. In his tailor shop, adjoining the house, he would sit cross-legged at a wide cutting table, cutting the cloth and then stitching the pieces together by hand before the final sewing on the machine. Emile often sat in the shop reading, listening to his stories, or looking at his pictures.

Emile completed his schooling in Wolxheim in 1921, when he was 13 years old. His entry into the Jesuit college was a matter of circumstances: among the missionaries who visited the little school in Wolxheim was a priest from L'Ecole Apostolic in Florennes, Belgium. At the encouragement of his grandmother, Emile asked to have an interview with the priest. He found that the college gave grants to those who stated that they wished to become missionaries.

Emile gained an intense interview with the Father Superior of the Minor Seminary of the Missions, and assured the Father Superior of his dedication to become a missionary. "I feel it is my vocation," he said.

"A man's life is meaningless unless he has some kind of vocation" the priest answered. "'I am the Alpha and the Omega,'" he quoted, "'the beginning and the end, the first and the last.' That is the Revelation of Saint John the Evangelist."

He smiled at the eager young boy. "You will be contacted by the college regarding the success of your application."

On September 23, 1921, just after he had turned 14, Emile Jungbluth entered L'Ecole Apostolic, operated by the Jesuit Fathers in Florennes, Belgium, to begin his secondary studies.

2
The Jesuits

Emile's desire for adventure was further stimulated by the many books available to him at the Minor Seminary of the Jesuits in Florennes. Here he read Father Ortolan on northwest British Columbia, tales of the Indian missions in the early 1900s. He read Father Buillard's *Inuk* about the Eskimos, and watched a film showing these strange wonderful people, with Father Buillard among them, mushing dogs, building snow houses, preaching the gospel. He later discovered the ultimate treasure, *Aux Glace Polaires* (Amidst Ice and Snow), by Father Pierre DuChaussois.

The potential in the far North was exciting. A missionary could make incredible advances. Emile would look out through the ivy-wreathed stone windowcasings of his school, hear the perfect intonations echo through the walls, and think how uncompromisingly civilized was his country, how old and ordered. And so Emile was understandably elated when he heard the announcement that Father DuChaussois was coming to visit the school.

Emile sat spellbound throughout the presentation, and afterwards he asked if he might talk personally to the great man.

"How might I ever get to your people, to these Eskimos?" he asked. "It is such a long way."

"I would suggest the Order of the Oblates," Father DuChaussois advised. He explained that the Oblates send young men to these far missions, where life is never easy. The natives do not come to the missionaries begging to be taught. The missionary must first learn to live with them, said Father DuChaussois, to learn their languages, to hunt and eat with them, and only when they feel the missionaries have come up to their mark do they begin to listen. They have their own civilization, fitted to the climate and the food supply. "They have gods too, and we must never belittle them, although many use that approach," Father DuChaussois conceded.

Emile read everything on the North that the Jesuit school library contained. He discovered Bishop Emile Grouard's *Sixty Years Among the Indians*, and later in the year the Bishop himself came to talk to them.

He was 80 years old and leaning on a cane. He couldn't hear. But he could tell stories that made you laugh and cry at once. He told, for example, of his visit with the Pope. The Pope had said to him, "Do you say you eat mostly rabbits?"

"Yes," Bishop Grouard had replied, and right there he showed the Pope how to make a snare, how to skin a rabbit and make it ready for the big pot over the fire.

The Oblates sent their French-language magazines to the school, and Emile was the first to reach for the newest issues. All the orders sent their magazines, but the Oblates were the most faithful: every month they showed pictures of missions from around the world. He read about Africa and Ceylon, but he was never interested in those hot countries. He wanted Eskimos in the ice missions.

The years following World War I were hard years. Emile was the only member of his family to receive such a high education, although it was a constant struggle since his common background provided no treats, no luxuries. He found sanctuary in the Jesuit training that was aimed at the mind over the heart. The Jesuits taught one to think for oneself, to rely on a formed intellect and practical habits.

Emile eventually decided on the priesthood, a decision dictated by poverty and by the influence of the visiting missionaries and their promises of adventure. During his six years at Florennes, Emile was home only for short vacations, and even then he did not pursue an active social life. Once he had made up his mind to become a priest, he was not supposed to take out a girl, or attend dances. "Fear is the beginning of wisdom," was the lesson they were taught, and his natural shyness kept his path straight.

To become a priest was one thing, but the choice of order was another. There were hundreds of orders. He studied them all: the Trappists were severe, their members ordered to rise around two o'clock in the morning to say the Office and the chant, and thus earn a few more hours rest. (In some Trappist monasteries no dishes were provided, just holes in the table, indentations). The Carthusians were presented with little shovels with which to dig their own graves. The Benedictines observed a rigorous order of prayer, study, meals, manual labor and exercises. The Spiritans were strictly opposed to materialism. Well, that was fine, he didn't have much, but he loved his books. And he liked doing things: playing music, taking part in plays, learning motor mechanics and photography, tinkering.

His choice lay with either the Jesuits or one of the Oblate orders.

He respected the Jesuit teachings. Their goal was to turn out scholastics, coadjutors, and professed. They looked for constancy of character, virtue, prudence, and, if one were to become a priest, learning. But would that take him to his Eskimos? The Jesuits had one mission in Alaska, but there was a great chance he might not get it. The Oblates had many Northern missions.

The missionaries he most admired, Father DuChaussois and the spirited old Bishop Grouard, belonged to the Order of the Oblates of Mary Immaculate. Emile did not want a parish in a city or prosperous village, as did some of his companions. He wanted Eskimos. He admired their versatility, their ability to scratch a livelihood from what seemed to be nothing. He too could make things from nothing: he could scavenge parts of old watches, radios, car motors, and assemble them to make one good item. Perhaps the Order of the Oblates of Mary Immaculate could make some use of these talents.

3

The Oblates and the Army

On August 30, 1927, Emile Jungbluth entered the Novitiate of the Oblate Fathers of the Province of Strasbourg, at St. Ulrich, Moselle, France. He had one year to choose an order, and the school had likewise one year to decide if he were suitable.

After his second week as a postulant, he became a novice and was presented with his cassock, a long black woollen affair that touched down on the tips of his black boots. A novice was presented with two cassocks: an everyday one for work and for play (even football), and the better one for dressing up. He was at once proud and self-conscious. Cassocks were common attire around the school, but he wondered what the reaction would be when he first ventured out onto the street. The cassock made him look short and small. His dreams of seeing himself running behind a dogsled in the Far North were taking on an alteration. Well, he would just have to tuck it up somehow. Father DuChaussois had managed.

He took his first vows at St. Ulrich on September 8, 1928, and gained his lifelong Oblate number: 4,810. This day would be, throughout his life, the anniversary of his profession, the day of his first vows. The clock started now.

Immediately after taking his vows, he was sent to study directly for the priesthood at the Scholasticate of the Oblate Fathers in Liège, Belgium. There he delved into philosophy courses geared to divinity students. They studied the Greeks, Socrates and Plato. They studied Karl Marx — for refutation purposes. Most enjoyable to Emile was their study of the teachings of Jacques Maritain, a famous philosopher and a member of the Academy of France who often spent his summers near Ernolsheim in a little village called Kolpsheim.

Some years later when Father Jungbluth was home from his mission on vacation, the parish priest of Ernolsheim asked him to give Mass at the castle of M. Klotz, where Jacques Maritain stayed. After Mass, Emile informed M. Maritain that they had studied his philosophies in school and that the complexities of his ideas had made them sweat.

"Yes, I can understand that," he said.

"You have done a great service, a great work, for the Church," Emile said.

The philosopher looked at him for a moment. "Not half what you do," he replied.

On April 25, 1930, Emile's studies were interrupted by the French government. He was inducted into the army.

Many young men from the seminaries were conscripted and it was said that France was taking in every citizen who could walk. (He could have stayed in Belgium but he would have been considered a deserter).

The change in Emile's outlook and practical education was phenomenal. Always protected, first by the confinements of his illness and later by cloistered schools, he had not yet met with the real world.

He was sent to Strasbourg for his medical, where the examining doctor noted his weakened limbs. Spared from walking over France's prepared roads (only to tackle the wind and snow and knee-deep mud of his mission land a few years later), Emile was assigned to a supply unit in Nancy, Moselle.

He was given basic training in combat duty and he learned, with some surprise, that he was a good marksman. So good, in fact, that others always asked to borrow his gun. He must have an excellent gun to be able to shoot so straight, they reasoned, so Emile would hand over his gun and then be relegated later with the laborious job of cleaning it. The next few competitions he aimed to one side of the mark, and no one asked to use his gun. "You're learning," his comrades told him. "You'll get it yet."

When the seminarists were inducted into the army, they were given temporary release from their vows. They were set free to spend their money and to do their duty with good conscience. But while they were free canonically, they were expected to behave "as one who prepares himself to the priesthood." That meant no women. So when Emile had arrived first at Nancy, straight from the seminary at Liège, he didn't know how to behave. All the men talked of was women. Emile felt his face flush time after time as jokes and stories were recounted in agonizing detail.

The gulf between Emile and his mates was all too obvious the first Sunday he attended Mass. He discovered a church which offered Mass at seven o'clock Sunday morning. He invested in a small alarm clock, a cheap one with two bells on top, supported by little legs, to wake him at six.

The dormitory in which Emile slept consisted of one long hall shared by 15 men from his platoon. Few had come in before midnight Saturday. Punctually at six o'clock the next morning the little alarm clock rang. Fumbling to turn it off, Emile became aware that one after the other of the men was being blasted awake by the strong insistent ringing.

Emile knelt upon his bed, his offensive investment hidden beneath the pillow. All eyes were on him, eyes red with anger, mouths calling him names he'd never before heard.

"I wanted to go to Mass," he whispered. With muttered oaths the men turned away, pounded on their pillows, and tried to regain sleep.

Emile dressed and quickly left the *caserne*, still smarting from the rebukes. Outside he opened his small black book and read from the Book of Judges: "The Philistines took him and put out his eyes, and brought him down to

Gaza, and bound him with fetters of brass, and he did grind in the prison house."

"Philistines!" he hissed, wiping out the humiliation. "Oh Lord God, remember me, I pray thee, and strengthen me, I pray thee, only this once, O God, that I may be at once avenged of the Philistines for my two eyes." (Judges 16:28)

Later, Private E. Jungbluth was transferred to the *20e Regiment du Train* at Strasbourg. Because he knew Strasbourg so well, he was made group postmaster. His job, riding a motorcycle equipped with a little side-car, took him all over Strasbourg collecting mail and purchasing supplies. He met people who worked in commercial as well as military offices. And he met women.

He notified his Provincial of his new duties, and the Provincial wrote back hurriedly, congratulating him but warning, in Latin so if it were read by outsiders there would be no understanding, *nequam puellae* (no women).

Emile lived with another helper on the top floor of a two-storey *caserne*; below them lived a family, the Thomases. Mr. Thomas's job was to maintain the large trucks and reserve army vehicles contained in the big sheds so they could be mobilized at 48-hours notice. Mrs. Thomas was an excellent cook and pastry-maker, and it was not difficult to encourage the young soldiers to come down for dinner with their family, a young son and a daughter, Jeanne, who worked as an office clerk in the barracks. Emile often played the mandolin, or would join in with Jeanne and her brother for a game of *à la marelle* played with nine white buttons and nine black buttons. Emile always won (or so he remembers).

Miss Jeanne Thomas was a good-looking girl of 17, with dark shining hair and a happy smile. A slight limp from a childhood illness provided a common bond between her and Emile; although he did not limp, he often had to favor his legs after a hard day.

On his days off, Emile often took Jeanne Thomas on excursions around Strasbourg; together they explored the famous old cathedral adorned with statues in every portal. They went off to the mountains to visit the shrine of St. Odile, a pilgrimage which took them 64 kilometres from Strasbourg, high into the mountains. From there they could see stretching on each side the green hills and valleys surrounding the city. Emile's conduct was proper, in keeping with that of a seminarist.

The Church thought otherwise.

A Military Chaplain in Strasbourg assumed responsibility for all the seminarists who were then in the military within the city. When one's military duty was completed, this man was charged with giving out a Certificate of Good Conduct. Because Emile had his Provincial House close by, he never visited with the Military Chaplain, not once. In his words, "I just ignored the whole outfit."

As his 18-month tour of duty drew to a close, he received a letter from his bishop, whom he had never met, asking Emile to send in his Certificate of Good Conduct. "Without it," wrote the bishop, "a seminarist is not allowed back." Emile went to see the Military Chaplain.

Emile remembers well the ominous and aggressive chaplain's response. "How can you expect that I would give you this certificate?" the chaplain demanded, very irate. "I don't even know you! I never saw you before in my life!"

Emile was stunned. His vocation seemed impossible. He decided to ask the advice of his Provincial House. Happily, they laughed off the ominous threats of the chaplain and interceded on Emile's behalf.

He was released three months early, on September 1, 1931, after serving in the army for 15 months. He had begun as a private and was emerging as a corporal. "They just called me a *Courier-du-Poste* — nothing so very great in the French army," he says.

Stopping at his usual supply houses, he bid farewell to the clerks whom he had come to know in his sojourn with the motorized division. The women in a certain stationery store had always been friendly, and one in particular had usually hurried to serve him. One of the clerks would call back, "Bertha! Bertha! He's here!" and from the back would emerge the smiling young woman who usually filled his order. Often he tarried, visiting with her; she was so much fun, and with her and Miss Thomas he had become more at ease with women. He could see that his wit pleased them, and so therefore he couldn't help complimenting them when they looked especially nice, just to hear them laugh and see their eyes sparkle.

The day of his last visit, after he told her he was leaving, she wheeled about and ran to the back of the store, into a storage room behind the wall. He looked to the other women for an explanation, but they were busy. He stood for a moment, embarrassed and not knowing what to do. Then he turned and went back out into the sunlight. He started his motorcycle, his thoughts tumbling about, trying to pinpoint a time in the past year when he had seen anything more in her manner that might indicate deeper feelings. He had never asked her out nor hinted at anything. He had thought the reason she chose to wait on him was because she knew more about the army forms he needed than did the others. What a fool he had been! She had admired him, and he was too blind to notice.

"Perhaps," he mused as he returned to the barracks, "that's what a Guardian Angel is for, to keep one ignorant of things one has no business knowing."

He had seen many of his comrades fall since their induction into the army. They were not now going back to the Scholasticate. The freedom had captured them.

Seminarists who were in the army wrote to the students back at the school. They were read, in a slightly censored form, in the refectory during meals, and the students were encouraged to write back to them. It kept the alliances alive. But when the soldiers stopped writing it was assumed that they were faltering in their vocations. Finally no letters would be exchanged, and the soldier was a free man. It had been said that the two main causes for a man to lose his vocation were "Punch and Judy." Emile was not inclined to drink to any extent, and here, when a chance had presented itself for the other, he had been too ignorant to recognize it.

"It looks like I've been chosen after all," he thought to himself.

With Jeanne Thomas it was a different matter.

"We can write each other," he said to her on the eve of his departure, "and remain friends forever."

"Yes," she agreed. "I will write. I will be with you in your heart when you are in the Far North with your Eskimos. I want to be a part of it, to hear from you all about your life there."

He looked at her. Her eyes were shining, her manner quiet and controlled. He placed his hands on her shoulders and kissed her.

His army days were over.

4

The Seminary

*O*n September 8, 1931, Emile renewed his vows. It was hard to shroud the pride of a mature soldier under the black cassock of a restricted seminarist. Gone were his iron helmet and his gun. The high stiff army boots and spurs had been replaced by short black leather boots that seemed to whisper and not shout as he strode down the halls. Gone were his days of riding a motorcycle down the busy main streets of Strasbourg, stopping to chat here and there with the shopkeepers; gone were his evenings with the boys, once feared, but now remembered with nostalgia; gone were the cafe evenings, drinking beer and singing boisterous songs of adventure and bravery and lost love.

By 1931 the Strasbourg Oblate House had abandoned their college at Liège and had built a new Scholasticate of Christ the King in Burthécourt, diocese of Metz, Lorraine. Barely two days after his army discharge, Emile once again settled into a routine of supervised studies of philosophy, geology, theology, some English and music. In four short years, if he progressed well, he would be an ordained priest and sent out to a mission. He would be self-sufficient, secure in his knowledge and in his beliefs. There would be no superior to turn to for consultation, no other judgement but his own.

He wrote to Jeanne Thomas, telling her of his new location, his roster of studies, the new friends he was meeting, but could not tell her of the confusion that had sprung into his heart. The Oblate superiors did not understand that a man who has just spent two years in the army has some readjustments to make, that this is normal, and this time should be given.

"When a horse is brought in from the plains," Emile mused, recalling the adventure stories he had read, "one does not immediately put him into a small stall, throw on a saddle, and expect him to carry the weight without objection. No! First he is corralled; only when he is used to a restricted range is he approached, caught, and rope-trained. The discipline is energized when the main objections and fears are overcome, and the freedoms forgotten."

He received tonsure just before the Orders, on February 25, 1932, by Bishop Cenez. The tonsure, a shaved circle on the back of the head about the size of a silver dollar, gave witness that he was now consecrated to God. Emile sat still and quiet as he felt the warm wetness of the soap being lathered onto the top of his head; he watched the cutter pick up the straight razor, and then shivered involuntarily as he felt the cold blade shave off a round hole, right on top. It was a sign of distinction, and was shaved again as soon as the hair reappeared. (Emile kept the tonsure until he came to Canada, but then let it grow back. Had the Church not changed, this procedure would still be observed. "In those days we didn't think it unbecoming," he reminisced, "but now I have to laugh at it too.")

Under the guidance of the priests at the seminary, and because of his army experience, Emile learned how to socialize. His friend, Alfred Bruckert, who was one year behind him in his studies, remembers that "Father Jungbluth ('Junki' as we called him) was very well liked for his great sense of humor, his good character, his readiness to help in any project. Though he was a little awkward in the motion of his limbs, his gestures and his particular accent in French and in German, he fulfilled all kinds of jobs. One year he was 'Minister of the Interior,' responsible for the weekly housecleaning which, at that time, we had to do ourselves. He was also for a time 'Minister of Public Works' in charge of the upkeep and improvement of the roads and the cleanliness of our great park."

Emile's social life broadened considerably at the Scholasticate. He recalls life in the seminary:

> There were all kinds of committees. They say for every three German men there must be a half-dozen committees — they are very organized. We had at the school what you might call a Glee Club, the *Comité de Fete*, or just C.D.F for short, to which one had to be elected. I was a member for about three years. We met together quite often. Whenever something was coming up, some celebration, everybody got frantic — we had to prepare! We had to make up something to perform, a skit or a song. With others, I, who was kind of the boss, would go to the Superior to see if a piece we had decided on might be considered a little touchy or controversial.

The dramatic arts were not Emile's only talent.

Father Bruckert remembers:

> I shouldn't bypass the fact that he was well-known for repairing watches. I remember one day I was looking for a book in the drawer of his desk. To my great surprise I found there was a horrible pell-mell of books, scribblers, notes, pencils — a Roman collar — and God knows what. And, from underneath all that *capharnaum* came the soft ticking of a bunch of watches.

Emile's ordination took place on a fine summer day, July 8, 1934. After three years of theology, with one year still to go, Emile could now say the Mass.

After Ordination, the routine completely changed. Instead of being housed in dormitories, the young men found themselves honored by the unaccustomed privacy of double rooms. Emile's roommate, Petrie, also "wanted Eskimos." Together they made a pact that, in the dead of winter, they would sleep with the windows wide open and with only one blanket covering them, in order to inure themselves to the cold they would suffer in the North.

From that point on, they knew true misery. Each night seemed colder than the one before, allowing only intermittent sleep. One night Emile awoke to find that Petrie also seemed to have trouble sleeping. He was tossing about and making a sound like crushed paper. Petrie was caught in the act, busily shoving newspapers between the thin blanket and his body. The paper gave the warmth of a good blanket. With a yell Emile flew at Petrie, ripping at the papers, scattering them about the room. And then they began to laugh. (Petrie eventually quit the Order).

Looking over a photograph of the seminarians taken at St. Ulrich at the end of their year's probation, Father Jungbluth's eyes get a faraway look and his voice becomes softer. "This is Petrie here," he says. "He was still with us then. He later became a diocesan priest. This one here was sent to Rome, an intelligent man. He later had a nervous breakdown, and was sent back. He was not permitted to say Mass for a long time, couldn't hear confessions or anything, but that's because he studied so hard and it went to his mind. He shouldn't have been sent. This one here is a good fellow, very, very conservative. This one died shortly after this picture was taken. He got pneumonia. This one left the Order too and is now a parish priest.

Seminarians at Novitiate of the Oblate Fathers of the
Province of Strasbourg at the end of their year's probation, 1928.

This one here got into quite a bit of trouble. Do you recognize me, here on the end?"

A few months before the end of his studies, in January of 1935, Emile was invited to write to Rome to the Father General (Labouré) telling him what kind of Obedience (mission) he would prefer, and his reasons for it. He asked, of course, for Eskimos.

"They didn't send a reply, nothing at all," Father Jungbluth remembers, as he sifts through the papers that lie folded in a thick pad in his black leather case: his Jurisdiction to hear confessions; his "celebret" (meaning "may he celebrate"), a card that shows that Father Emile Jungbluth, OMI, is in good standing as a priest. It was issued in Burthècourt, written in Latin, signed by Father Resle, OMI, the Director of the Seminary. May he celebrate.

Then, on June 7, 1935, he received his Obedience for the Diocese of Grouard in northern Alberta, Canada. The bishop in Grouard could then send him wherever he wanted within that diocese. He was overjoyed when he received it. "I might have been more joyous if I would have been given Eskimos," he says, "but Indians are good enough. I didn't know the difference too much anyway."

Emile's ordination took place on July 8, 1934, at the
Scholasticate of Christ the King in Burthécourt, Diocese of Metz, Lorraine. (Emile on left).

Celebration of Father Jungbluth's first mass (Strasbourg)
Flower girl in the background is his cousin, now Sister Damien, Little Sisters of Jesus,
Fairbanks, Alaska.

TRANSITION

5
To the Ice Missions

Paris. The greatest city in all France, perhaps in all the world. On the train, enroute from Strasbourg to Paris, Emile had time to consider what he was leaving behind. He might never again see his family and friends from Strasbourg and Alsace. If he did come back many years later, all would have changed. He had seen the older missionaries return from their faraway fields to their homeland and look about in bewilderment, searching for familiar landmarks.

The biggest change was often within themselves. What would he be like when he returned? Would he have a long beard like the older Oblates? Would he be hobbling about on a cane like a younger version of Bishop Grouard? With his legs, it wasn't unlikely.

He put his face to the train window to watch the lights of the small villages twinkle as they flashed past. It was never totally black outside; people were everywhere, the villages only a few kilometres apart. But in the North, he was told, one could go for miles — he would have to get used to that term of measurement — without seeing another human soul.

He was not met at the train station, but he had the address of the Oblate House in Paris where he would be staying until he sailed for Canada on the *Normandie*. There were four Oblates sailing together, but he had not met any of the other priests nor did he know their names. One, he had heard, was also being sent to the *Vicariate Apostoli* of Grouard, Canada. He would be sharing accommodation with him on the boat, and likely be living with him during the training period in the mission. He hoped the other man would be agreeable but, if he wasn't, that was not so important. He would still have his Indians. He hoped they would like him.

He arrived at the priests' house in the morning and was introduced immediately to the others, all quick intelligent men who felt the same excitement and zeal as he to be sent to the far North. One of the Fathers, Jean Dessey from Brussels, announced with great satisfaction that he was destined for the Northwest Territories to work among the Eskimos. Emile felt a twinge of envy, but the other laughed and said Emile's mission would likely be just as interesting.

But it was Father Césaire Mariman to whom Father Jungbluth devoted his attention, for this energetic man was to be his companion for the entire trip to Grouard, and for some time thereafter. Emile did not know then that their friendship was to last a lifetime, and at first Father Jungbluth viewed Father Mariman with awe and some amount of scepticism.

"Whatever gave you the notion to grow such a thing as that?" Emile asked, before he hardly knew him at all, pointing to Father Mariman's great brown beard.

Father Mariman laughed, and said that all of his Belgian graduating class who received appointments for faraway missions had decided to grow beards as a common badge of identification. "It is good for protection in cold weather. My brother, a missionary in Africa, also has a beard. It is good protection for the hot weather."

Father Mariman

He smiled benignly at Father Jungbluth, who stood back and said abruptly, "You do not make sense all the time."

Thus was formed the lifelong pattern of their relationship.

After a two-week delay (which caused them to lose their booking on the *Normandie* and necessitated their travel to LeHavre to board the *Isle de France*) the four young men — all in their mid-20s — boarded the ship on August 15, 1935. There they found a surprise awaiting them. Piled high in their allotted room were wardrobes and great fancy suitcases. They called the cabin boy.

The priests looked around, embarrassed, hoping their excitement would not bring a crowd. The cabin boy was having a hard time understanding. Yes, they had tickets allotting them to this cabin, but so did the luggage emblazoned with the name "Mlle. Leclercq."

The situation was evolving to high drama when the woman whose name was written upon the offending wardrobes arrived. She was beautiful, with soft fair curls and a sultry Americanized accent, and she was accompanied by two others whose appearance and demeanor could only indicate that they were entertainers. Indeed, they were members of a theatrical group that had been on a tour of France and were now heading back to Montreal.

"This is a bad fault," stammered the embarrassed Father Mariman.

"No, no!" Mlle. Leclercq stamped her little foot. "Not a 'fault,' monsieur, a 'mistake'. It is different. A mistake has been made here. Our room is down the hall, 10 numbers different."

She explained hurriedly to the cabin boy that he must move the trunks of theatrical costumes and dance dresses; they did not belong to these poor priests. As there was no room to step inside while the transfer was made, the priests stood in the hallway, pressed against the women while the cabin boy struggled past them with the great boxes.

Mlle. Leclercq took it upon herself to become the priests' tutor in English during the voyage. She seemed especially committed to Father Jungbluth, whose mistakes she repeated in a loud laughing voice that could be heard throughout the dining room and right out to the deck.

"No, no, dear Father," she would say. "It is not a 'scale' you advance upon to climb to your bed, it is a 'ladder.'"

The chastened priests opened up their small grammars and studied voraciously.

At the dock in New York they were met by Father Lucas, an Italian priest from that city. He recognized his charges immediately, since not many people disembarking were clad in foreign-cut long black coats, but he must have wondered why they were saying farewell to a group of showgirls.

The priests spent their time in New York visiting the sights and learning to cope with the North American culture. Father Jungbluth visited with his sister, Madeleine, and when it came time to venture to Canada by train, he was truly on his way North.

The immensity of their new land unfolded as the train carried the three priests in one straight line farther than they could believe possible. It was golden autumn, the first week of September. The Canadian train was rough compared to the smoothness of European trains; the cars clanged and bashed about without heed to their jostled passengers. And Canadian trains used bells instead of whistles. Every locomotive had a bell, and during the night the bell would clang, clang, clang. The priests, conditioned after so many years at the seminary to awaken to the sound of a bell, were shocked out of their sleep at hourly intervals during the night. They absorbed the shifting landscapes — dark forests that nearly brushed the windows and sweeping prairies silvered and shimmering under the harvest moon.

They arrived in Edmonton, Alberta, on September 6, 1935, and were taken to the House of the Oblate Fathers on 110th Street and 99th Avenue. It was hard to imagine such a small city being a capital; yet the province of Alberta covered more land than all France's holdings put together.

When they arrived at the Oblate House, they learned that one of the priests from their new diocese had passed away just that morning. Their first duty in Canada was to bear the coffin to the cemetery.

Before the funeral the young priests were taken to view the body, and were then told the history of deceased Father Petour, OMI. He was called

"The Red Fox," and true to his epithet, even in death, his striking red beard flared out from the casket.

Father Fahler silently examined Fathers Mariman and Jungbluth from head to toe. "Two will not be too many to replace that Father who just died," he grunted. "He was a very great missionary, and many stories could be written about him."

Only Father Fahler had been able to come down from Grouard to attend the funeral. Mail service was poor and there was not yet telephone nor telegraph to Fort Vermilion, where the Red Fox had been stationed. When the young priests arrived at Fort Vermilion three weeks later, it was they who brought the first news of his death.

During their stay in Edmonton the priests were to hear of many of his exploits. Each anecdote evoked an unfamiliar sense of ambiguity that Father Jungbluth would learn was central to the North. "He travelled on horseback when there were no bridges over the rivers," Father Fahler told them. "At some places he had to cross high railroad bridges, with spaces between the ties where one could look down and see the churning water below. Although horses are usually wary of crossing such a bridge, once they can be persuaded to begin they are usually very sure-footed, stepping exactly from tie to tie. Perhaps the Red Fox pulled the bridle a little bit, distracting the horse for a moment. Suddenly it took a false step and before anything could be done all four feet fell between the ties, leaving the horse suspended by its belly. It lay there, eyes rolling in fright, breath coming in short heaves. As he tugged with all his might trying to pull up the horse, the Red Fox suddenly remembered the purpose of this bridge: when was the next train due?" Father Fahler sat back, chuckling quietly, remembering Father Petour telling him the story.

"But how did he remove the horse?" Father Jungbluth asked, leaning forward in his seat.

The old priest waved his hand, flicking back his wrist in a gesture that showed a casual indifference to the solution. "Oh, I don't remember if he got help or how he did it, but somehow he managed to solve it."

Father Jungbluth felt somewhat bewildered as he contemplated what was necessary knowledge to the North — horses and dogs (he had heard that dogsleds were used in Fort Vermilion), preparing food in the coldest weather, learning the many Indian languages.

Father Fahler looked for a moment at the two young greenhorns who would be replacing the Red Fox. "Have you a coat?" he said abruptly, addressing himself to Father Mariman.

"Well, yes, the coat I was wearing. Is it not good enough?"

"For the North? I should say not! You'd freeze to death in an hour. Come. You have carried the Red Fox to his resting place, and you will be expected to carry on at least part of his work. It is fitting that you should carry his coat upon your shoulders also."

He went to the back recesses of the house and brought out a big fur coat, covered with long curled hair. Father Mariman looked at the thing in amazement. "What kind of hair can that be?" he asked timidly.

Again the old priest made the same unconcerned upward flick of his wrist. "I don't know," he answered. "Probably dog." With that he walked away.

Father Mariman stood still, holding the great mass of curled hair in his outstretched arms. He stared in silence at Father Jungbluth, whose light blue eyes twinkled with barely held mirth.

"Do you think it was really a dog?" whispered the astounded Father Mariman.

Father Jungbluth gave a flick of his wrist. "How should I know?" he asked. "To me it looks like a black sheep."

6

Homebase

*O*n September 9, 1935, they boarded an unfamiliar sort of train, this time heading north to Joussard, named for a well-known bishop who once served in Fort Vermilion. The coaches of the train were small and made of metal, and rocked like ships on a stormy sea. The rails, affected by extreme winter temperatures of 50 or 60 degrees below zero, had warped to become crooked and bumpy. The Lesser Slave Lake area was severely flooded, and two train personnel wearing high rubber boots walked in front of the engine looking for the rails. The trip took a long time and the priests wondered whether they could have made it more quickly on foot.

They arrived in Joussard on September 10 around one o'clock in the morning. The mission car was waiting for them. The highway was a muddy muskeg trail. They slipped from one ditch to the other.

Uphill they had to get out to push, and downhill the car slid on its own. The wheels became clogged with clay and no longer turned. In the eerie darkness the roadside seemed a black vacuum. Shouts and barks resounded through the stillness, seeming to come first from one side, then from the other. A hooting resounded again and again like a nervous insane laugh. The car slid alarmingly close to the water lapping at the road's edge.

"That there's the lake," the driver commented. He told them that the lake had been flooding so much that in some places the railroad tracks were just floating. "Sometimes they have to get the passengers to run ahead and press the rail lines down and hold them steady until the train gets its weight on them. You came at a good time." The two priests exchanged glances.

When they arrived in Joussard they were given a warm welcome by Father Serrand. (Many years later Father Mariman changed his opinion of Father Serrand when, as a joke, he set fire to Father Mariman's beard. "He committed arson," the offended Father Mariman said, "right there in my beard!") The young priests made themselves comfortable inside the mission house and learned a bit about the history of the little mission.

The St. Bernard Mission in Grouard was opened by Bishop Grouard in 1894 to serve all the surrounding Indian settlements. However, the Indian people living on the far side of the lake said it was too far away to send their children and they refused to attend. A smaller mission, called St. Bruno's, was then built 29 kilometres away in Joussard, between Sucker Creek and Driftpile reserves. By the end of 1917, enrollment included 76 pupils, but this number fluctuated wildly as an influenza epidemic whipped through the reserves, killing many and severely weakening the rest. Entire families were stricken. It was then that the school requested the children board continuously at the school — even through the Christmas and Easter holidays — to avoid further contamination. The parents agreed, and the epidemic was halted.

Father Serrand spoke at length about the uneasy relationship between the mission schools and the Indians. There were mixed ideas about the residential schools, Father Serrand told the new priests. In Europe it was not considered unnatural for children to be separated from their families to attend boarding school — in fact it was often an option afforded only to the rich — but in Canada the concept was sometimes looked upon negatively, especially by the Indians. They said the white population was trying to rob the children of Indian ways; the children returned home and were disrespectful to their elders who didn't know how to read or write or speak English. The children no longer liked the Indian fare.

Father Serrand sat back for a moment, studying his clasped hands. And perhaps they had a point, but so did the Church who saw children often sadly neglected, some with constant colds and throat infections and discharging eyes, worms and lice. Often the parents were taken by illness or death, and an old grandmother had to look after them. Food was scarce and uneven in a bad year when there was no game. Also, he added, Indians are not known to be great budgeters. They would give their last piece of dried meat to a friend.

Father Jungbluth could not help but interject. "They seem then to follow high principles," he said.

"I know, it sounds fine," Father Serrand went on, "but once you are here a while you won't be viewing the situation through your rose-colored glasses. There's beauty and generosity, yes, but there's also untold poverty and ugliness, superstition and malice. We hope to ease these peoples' burden by teaching them the ways of God; and also to teach them hygiene and give them enough education so they aren't forever at the short end of the deal. The North attracts many traders and some, I'm afraid, are not what you'd call honorable."

The next day Father Jungbluth wrote the first of many letters to the *Mission Revue Immaculata* of the Eastern Province, the communication link to his benefactors in the old country. The foreign missions would be powerless if it was not for the support of the people back home. From their generous donations churches, halls and rectories were built, proper windows and doors installed, Mass supplies replaced, clothing and food supplied.

"*Scheiden tut weh* . . . it hurts to say farewell," he began, writing in his native German. Outside the window the endless rippling waters of the Lesser Slave Lake stretched like a small sea. He turned back to his page:

> Thus I felt when I had to depart by train from my beautiful Alsace on August 4th. Yet my heart was filled with joy, for my deepest wish has come true: I am a missionary, entrusted now to

look after the souls of the poor and forlorn North American Indians.

He stopped writing, distracted by shouts and laughter from outside. He could see some Indian children playing outside on the wide expanse of grass. They looked happy, cheerful, well-fed. They spoke in a strange language, likely Cree, with the odd English word thrown in. He looked down at what he had written, and concluded the letter:

> We arrived happily at the Mission. Now I have to wait here until I get to know the final destination, most probably Fort Vermilion, several hundred kilometres further north.
> Thanks to all dear friends and supporters back home for their presents and prayers assisting our Ice Missions. You will hear again from me. Until next time!

On the morning of September 10, 1935, Father Mariman and Father Jungbluth were driven by car to a destined meeting place, where they stood on a peninsula of dry land and watched the little motorboat, propelled by a two-horsepower engine, come toward them through the tricky brush-filled channels. In the boat were the Secretary to the Bishop and the Reverend Brother Bossé. They cached their few personal belongings in the back of the boat (the major portion was to be shipped up later) and the four men then made their way across the southwest corner of Lesser Slave Lake. The water, black and forbidding, slapped against the little boat; white-capped waves swelled and ebbed. In the oarlocks rested a rifle ("Ducks," said the Brother), but although they could hear the haunting calls and see the odd quick flutter in the tall rushes bordering the lakeshore, no shots were fired.

The brilliant blue September sky framed the cathedral of the St. Bernard Mission which towered above the steep banks of the lake at Grouard. In front of the cathedral was the well-kept cemetery. Behind the cathedral were the Sisters' building and the Bishop's house. Father Fahler, once the Superior of Grouard, said that the priests who chose this setting were "artists of topography." Wide golden prairies shimmered around the pastoral settlement. Sparkling creeks tumbled through the far valleys beyond; and encircling this complete picture was the great churning Lesser Slave Lake, stretching 160 kilometres to the eastern shore.

Father Mariman recalled that first landing at Grouard:

> We arrived with lots of love for the Indians, lots of sentiment, and it was increased by the sight of the crowd of Indians who stood on the dock to greet us on our arrival. I had my beard and one Indian seemed to take a liking to me; perhaps I looked like Father Fahler, who also had a beard. So one of the old Indians, old Giroux, came up to me holding his pipe upside down, show-

ing me there was no tobacco in it. I could not speak Cree. He spoke a few words and, seeing I could not understand, he tapped his inverted pipe a few times to show me it was empty. He wanted tobacco. So he put out his fingers like that, rubbing his thumb against the side of his forefinger, and that I understood. I had some cash left over so I gave him a little.

The Fathers sure teased me afterwards. It hadn't taken me long to get fooled by the Indian. "That man has fooled all the priests and he has even fooled Bishop Grouard," they said. Then they told me the story of Bishop Grouard's meeting of him:

"Monsignor," old Giroux said, "Monsignor, one of your little calves, your little steers from the mission, got died. Could I have the meat?"

"Well," said the bishop, "of course if it is dead, you can have the meat."

What old Giroux failed to tell was that he had killed it.

And another Father, LeTreste, who traveled also all over this area, was once taking care of the little mission store. Father LeTreste liked going trapping too, and he had a few snares in the bush. One day old Giroux came into the store with a few snares and traps to sell, and Father LeTreste immediately bought them from him. When the Father next went out to his trapline to check his other traps and set the new ones, he looked, blinked his eyes, and looked again. No traps anywhere. He had bought his own traps from old Giroux! Oh, he was an old crook, that one. Everyone at the mission got to know him, but he still managed to play some tricks on the newcomers.

The first question asked by the priest at Grouard was, "Did you get any ducks?"

With this equivocal welcome, the two priests settled in at Grouard to await the return of the bishop, who was to give them their orders. Twelve days later, Bishop Guy sent a letter: Father Jungbluth and Father Mariman were being sent to the same mission of Fort Vermilion. Their prime purpose there was to acclimatize themselves to northern conditions and to learn the complex Beaver Indian language.

Their belongings arrived while at Grouard and the morning of their departure everything was loaded onto a big truck to be transported to Peace River Crossing. There they had to wait for the Hudson's Bay Company riverboat, the *Weenusk*, and then travel north down the Peace River 400 kilometres to Fort Vermilion. The engine boat pushed two scows, one in front and the other tied at the side, which made it easier for unloading and for landing.

They embarked near dusk on Saturday evening, and were assigned to a little cabin right over the engine. The rhythmic throbbing of the engines

helped the Fathers fall into a deep
sleep. The big boat glided through
the night down the Peace, taking
them to their long-wished-for northern wilderness.

There were three priests now
traveling together: an old French
priest, Father Floc'h from Grouard,
had also received an appointment
for Fort Vermilion. This poor man
viewed the journey from a different
angle. Father Mariman and Father
Jungbluth watched, embarrassed, as
the old man stood on the deck, tears
running down his cheeks while the
steamboat carried him relentlessly to
his dreaded destination. He had always been in Grouard, had nearly
been made bishop along with Father
Fahler, and later held the capacity of
Vicar General to the Bishop. Now
they were sending him north to take
over the work of the Red Fox.

*Father Floc'h, Brother Allie and
Father Jungbluth*

Also on board was Reverend Brother Allie, a well-known builder of
northern mission churches and schools. The mission at Fort Vermilion had
experienced a fire and he was being sent up to help rebuild. The three priests
and the Brother said their Holy Mass at the vibrating kitchen table above
the engine room, as the Mass wine rippled in the trembling chalice.

The rich Peace River landscape swept by them on either side. They saw
a moose drinking at the river's edge, and a bear wander up from the bank
to disappear among the trees. And they made their first acquaintance with
the vicious northern mosquitoes. They passed dry mud banks, held back
from eroding by willows clustered along the river's edge, which also
provided food for moose and deer. From time to time they heard shotgun
blasts resound across the valley.

The boat stopped frequently to unload freight and passengers. They
reached Carcajou (Wolverine) Point in a day's travel and saw the cabins of
a small Indian settlement, called East Bank, scattered over the grassy flat.
Almost opposite Carcajou was the storehouse at the old Keg River landing.
At Stony Point they stopped to let off a young Protestant girl who had been
sick and was just returning home from a stay in the hospital at Peace River
Crossing. As she stood on the deck beside Father Jungbluth and Father
Mariman, awaiting the boat to tie up, she mentioned that her father worked
at the Dominion Experimental Station at Stony Point. She could see her
family standing on the dock, her mother and father, brothers and sisters.

She was young, just 14 or 15, and as the boat came nearer to shore she jumped up and down, waving excitedly, calling out to them. It seemed the boat was taking forever to tie up. Father Jungbluth, whose English was still almost nonexistent, turned to the girl and made swimming gestures with his arms. She looked at him quizzically, then burst into laughter. Her parents saw too, and they began laughing, mimicking Father Jungbluth's suggestion that it would be faster to swim ashore. Suddenly he did not feel strange among these people after all.

Down in the cabin, Father Floc'h read his breviary by rote, as his teary eyes clouded his vision.

7

Fort Vermilion

Fathers Jungluth and Mariman arrived at Fort Vermilion near dusk on Wednesday, September 24, 1935. When the boat arrived in town, a large gathering met them on the shore, including the two priests of the mission, Fathers Habay and Deman, 10 Sisters of Providence, and the children of the mission school.

The mission priests were somewhat at a loss as to how to accommodate their guests; they had not much room and little bedding. As Father Habay led Father Mariman into the little room where he was to sleep, he bent down over the bed to see, by the light of his little candle, if it were suitably made up.

"I thought there were no sheets," he said, "but I see there are some here."

Father Mariman bent to look. There were no sheets, only a couple of grey blankets. Later he learned that the rough grey flannelette blankets were indeed used as sheets in the northern missions. Only in more settled areas to the south would one find starched white cotton or linen.

"I spent a horrible night," Father Jungbluth whispered to his companion as soon as they were alone together the next morning. "I thought I would freeze to death."

"Perhaps I am better prepared for the coldness . . . with my warm beard," Father Mariman said.

Father Jungbluth shot him a piercing look. "We will see," he said. "There must be a reason. I am not exactly a weakling, you know." It didn't take long to discover what made the difference in their comfort: Father Mariman's room was located just above the furnace. Only a single ineffective pipe ran near Father Jungbluth's room. The next morning, Father Jungbluth did not shave.

Father Jungluth and Father Mariman undertook their first duties, as assistants to Father Habay in a Requiem Mass for the Red Fox. After the Mass, Father Floc'h left to begin his new missionary duties with the Cree Indians: the two young Fathers were left to acquaint themselves with the area. They each wrote a letter home, and Father Habay told them to hurry to the post office before the Hudson's Bay Company steamer departed if they wanted to post them.

Given a chance to see the little town, the two men set off eagerly, striding purposefully the 100 metres to the mission gate. There they inquired the way to the post office.

"You go to the foot of that hill there, then you ask again," they were told. "It's not far."

Again they walked, and stopped to ask. And again. When they finally arrived at their destination, both men were exhausted. "And they say that's not far," Father Jungbluth puffed. "Over in France we would have taken a street car and not thought we were wasting the fare."

The people of the town were friendly, volunteering local news and information, but the priests' poor knowledge of English prohibited lengthy conversations. Father Mariman had picked up a few Cree words — "I am hungry. It is difficult." — but he was too shy to practise them on any of the Indians he saw.

The Fathers were impatient to begin learning the Beaver language. The third priest of the mission, Father Quemeuner, would be the one to give them their first lessons in the Beaver Indian language. He had invented a method so that one could learn the syllabic system in a couple of hours. He knew Beaver, Slavey and Cree, English, a bit of German, French, and his own language from Little Brittany in France. Fathers Jungbluth and Mariman now awaited Father Quemeuner's return from his outlying mission at Meander River.

Father Quemeuner was a man whom Father Jungbluth later described as "one of these Frenchmen . . . *qui se glorifier dans sa misère*" (who glorifies in his misery). He was small, with a soft voice caused by a problem in his throat which made his words scarcely audible. He was extremely devout, very humble, and assumed a workload that would have daunted a man half his age and twice his size. By 1934 he had begun to worry about the effect of his faltering voice on his mission work. By the time Fathers Jungbluth and Mariman met him, it was difficult to hear half of what he said — and this was their prime professor of lessons in northern survival skills and in the Beaver Indian language.

Father Quemeuner

The young priests had been in Fort Vermilion nearly a month when the first snowfall occurred. Father Quemeuner gave them a lesson in running dogs, using a team owned by the mission. "You run, run, run!" he said, and away he went. The priests barely kept up with him as he ran behind the sleigh in ever-widening circles, demonstrating turns and stops.

For the better part of a day Father Jungbluth practised running behind the sleigh, jumping onto the runners, hopping off to continue his trot with unbroken stride.

He decided that the two lead dogs should be named Castor and Pollux after the twin sons of Zeus and Leda.

"Gee Pollux!" he called out, and the dogs would obediently turn to the right. "Haw! Haw!" and they'd swing to the left. So simple, it seemed.

The day was bright and cold, and the trip out went smoothly. He decided to head back in the early afternoon, so if he encountered problems he would not have darkness to contend with as well. He first checked the harnesses and the sleigh, and double-checked the long training rope which dragged behind the sleigh for 15 metres. Although this rope was often a nuisance, tangling with the sleigh's runners or in one's feet, or snagging around a tree, it was a lifeline if the dogs should happen to get away. Even if you suddenly found yourself lying on your back in the snow, you still had a chance to grab the rope.

Running along the trail, homeward bound, one of the dogs gave a sudden sharp bark. The others, catching the excitement, immediately gave a great lunge forward and Father Jungbluth found himself in the brambles. Muffled through a layer of soft snow that covered him, he heard the excited howling of his dogs as they thrashed off in search of a moose or a bear, whose scent on the wind was likely responsible for their erratic behavior. He could hear his sleigh crashing from tree to tree, see the long rope slapping along after it, but there was nothing he could do except brush the snow from his face, find his lost mitts, and begin the 16-kilometre trudge home. He remembered Father Quemeuner's warning that dogs are like horses: they know what kind of driver they have, if he is good or green. It hadn't taken them long to figure him out.

A torn line had freed the sleigh about 100 metres down the road and Father Jungbluth added to his humiliation by wrapping the rope around his waist and pulling it himself. Luckily it was the beginning of winter and the snow was not more than five centimetres deep, for he had no snowshoes.

He could hear the mad barking of dogs off in the distance, and he cursed them vehemently. They would eventually come home when they tired. Sadly he trudged up the trail, picking up a piece of harness here, a broken trace there. The dogs' arrival at the mission preceded his by half a day.

As Father Quemeuner was not intending to stay long in Fort Vermilion, the priests had to learn quickly. Father Quemeuner began the language lessons by outlining a "four position turning sign," as he called it, actually the invention of a Wesleyan missionary named Reverend Evans, developed in the mid-nineteenth century. The first part, structured in the form of a cross, taught them the vowel sounds, beginning in the centre.

They first learned nouns and verbs one by one. Father Mariman, knowing he eventually had also to learn Cree, made a big dictionary using Latin as the basic language: beside the Latin word he wrote the Beaver Indian word, then planned to add a Cree word, then maybe an English, Ukrainian

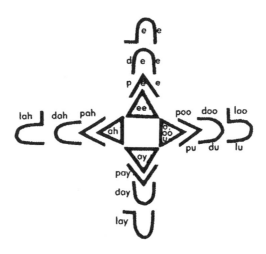

The four position turning sign

or German word, from all the languages spoken in that part of the country. His big sheet of paper, measuring 43 x 56 cm, was headed up:

LATIN BEAVER CREE ENGLISH UKRAINIAN GERMAN

They were given study notes that once belonged to Fathers Grouard, Leserrec and LeTreste. They also had an incomplete dictionary that Bishop Joussard copied, when he was 70 years old, from the notes of others. And finally they had the syllabic writing method taught by Father Quemeuner.

"There is no passive in the Beaver Indian Language," Father Mariman noted. "There are up to 12 persons that can be the subject of a verb. Then, not only that, the person changes the verb, so there are up to 12 persons that can change the conjugations of the verb. Then their verbs are so complicated, like the verb "to give," which is so easy in English. The beginning of the verb changes according to the person to whom you give something; the centre of the verb changes according to the person who gives; the ending of the verb changes according to the object you give. So there are three different things that you have to pay attention to. It took me at least three days for that one verb, with at least 1,000 forms."

The Fathers wrote furiously in their books, noting the words phonetically. Father Jungbluth's spelling differed from that of Father Mariman, because the former based his notes on German sounds, the latter on Flemish sounds.

The time came for Father Quemeuner to leave again for his outlying mission. Who could continue the lessons? They asked Father Habay if he would tutor them. He declined, but suggested they approach a Metis, Petit-Jean Lizotte, who was in a hospital in Fort Vermilion.

Father Quemeuner agreed. "Petit-Jean will be a fine professor. Although he is now full of rheumatism and he walks on crutches — his legs are so bent that they cross each other — he will be a good teacher on the days when his pain is not too bad. He is a real holy man, always praying." The young Fathers envisioned a haloed light shining from the black hair of an old Indian they had not yet met.

Petit-Jean Lizotte was very patient with his new students. The nurses would bring him downstairs to the little rectory dining room where the men who were rebuilding the burned-out portion of the hospital ate their meals, and there he would sit with his young students, hour after hour. He knew French and this served as their *linga franca*, although he spoke Metis French, containing a lot of slang. Best of all, he knew both Beaver and Cree.

The priests attended their lessons daily, taking notes, questioning Petit-Jean constantly, pointing to things, asking "What is that? How do you say that?" The old Indian would slowly and methodically mouth the strange syllables that seemed to change with every utterance.

Petit-Jean's health was failing, and the priests were reluctant to pressure

Fathers Mariman and Jungbluth with their first "professor" of the Beaver Indian language.

him. The school was not interested in helping them; most did not know the Beaver language very well, because the Sisters forbade the children to speak their native language. It was thought that it would interfere with their learning of English. Father Jungbluth and Father Mariman came to the conclusion that there was little hope of learning the Beaver Indian language at the mission. Then, through Father Habay, they made the acquaintance of several Beaver Indians from Eleské; among these was a man named Albert Ollivier (not his real name) who could speak both Beaver and English.

"I spent five years at the university," he said, in response to their inquiry as to where he had learned his English.

"You must not believe everything you hear," Father Habay warned. "Albert has just come back from five years in prison . . . that is where he got his English."

So Albert Ollivier became their professor and through his suggestions they began to think seriously of moving out to Eleské. A trader suggested they make a little room upstairs in the church at Eleské; then they could go to visit the Indians, or invite them over for tea to gain language lessons, instead of relying on the Indians' irregular trips into town. They could easily make living quarters upstairs in the attic of the church by adding a cookstove or a bit of furniture. The Indians would be glad to come and drink tea, eat with them, or perhaps receive tobacco for their pipes in return for teaching them.

They made the trip out to Eleské on December 15, a Sunday, for the baptism of a baby. Father Jungbluth had the honor of performing the rites, for, as Father Mariman conceded, he was the elder.

The church at Eleské was a bare structure, hardly adequate for the cold climate. An Indian named Beauchè had helped Father Habay build it the previous winter when the temperatures were so cold that, in order to keep their hands warm enough to pound shingle nails, a bucket of burning coals was hauled up onto the roof for a heater. The building had no sanctuary and no belltower, but its solid 6 x 4.5 metre frame was constructed of top quality unplaned British Columbia spruce purchased from a bankrupt sawmill. Father Habay named the church after St. Bernadette.

The interior of the church couldn't have been more plain. Boards resting on stumps of firewood served as pews and a wooden kitchen table served as an altar. An elevated platform, one step up from the altar, became the choir stand or makeshift sanctuary.

"Oh what a fine church," cried Father Mariman, looking around at the ice-frosted boards. Father Jungbluth surveyed the room in silence. Father Habay, off in a corner talking with an old Indian man, seemed not to mind if he was inside or out, for indeed there was not much difference.

"We will say the Christmas Mass here," announced Father Habay, rubbing his hands as he walked briskly toward the two priests. "By then you may know enough Beaver Indian to be able to follow along. I'll make it simple — a catechism about Adam and Eve, the Christmas Story, and perhaps a few songs and hymns with French melodies. You can assist me in the service. It will give you a good chance to meet everyone before you move here."

With that, Father Habay hurried out to the front of the church, knelt a moment in silent prayer, then began to talk rapidly to the old Indian man in a language that seemed to combine every language spoken on earth. The young priests recognized English, Cree, French and even some German *achts*.

As they walked toward the sleigh, the whistling wind flapped the folds of their cassocks and penetrated through their protective layers of underclothes. The cold whipped around the corners of the unpainted church, sending a burst of snow crystals stinging against their faces.

8

Eleské

*T*he two Fathers made the move to Eleské in January of 1936 to begin their self-imposed total immersion program in the Beaver Indian language and customs. They loaded onto a sleigh their blankets, a few cooking dishes, a cross-cut saw and an axe, water buckets, a basin, their Mass supplies and their books. Father Jungbluth stocked up on pipe tobacco for the Indians.

The Sisters of Providence in Fort Vermilion gave them milk frozen in cans, meat formed into frozen patties, and a sack of "smashed" potatoes, already cooked. Once at Eleské, the priests kept their supplies stored outside, suspended from nails in big "pillow bags." The potatoes froze like a sack of stones, requiring a sharp axe to cleave a serving from the bulk.

Although Father Jungbluth and Father Mariman thought they were prepared for anything, there was one thing they had failed to consider: neither of them knew how to cook.

In Europe people didn't use much lard and the miserly portion the priests spooned into the pan hardly covered the bottom. When smoke fumed up, in were tossed the frozen potatoes. The outsides would burn black and stick for life to the bottom of the pan, while the centres would still contain ice crystals. An Indian taught them to use a generous portion of lard ("A week's supply!" exclaimed Father Mariman), allow it to heat slowly, then add the potatoes and put on the lid. "You cook lots of lard," their Cree instructor said, sitting back to fill his pipe with the priests' tobacco. "You make it very hot. Then your potatoes melt. Ready in no time."

Potatoes were not the only culinary obstacle for the two priests. When they were out of bread and could not go to the Mission because they had no way to travel, they received a visit from the young son of a Cree Indian family who were camping beside the church.

"I would like to make bannock," Father Mariman said to the boy, "but I don't know how."

The boy instructed him: "You take a cup of flour. You put it in the basin, so you can mix everything. Now take a spoon level with baking powder, half a teaspoon of salt, you put it like that and mix it well together with your hand, or a spoon, or with shaking it. Then you put in maybe half a cup of water. Then like that you make your batch. Mix it all up. Now it's ready to put on the stove, or you can put it in a frying pan, or in anything. That's it."

Father Mariman tested the recipe. He filled the stove up with wood. When the wood was all burned, he filled it up again. When he took his bannock out of the little oven he couldn't pry it out of the pan; it felt like a brick. He assumed that the bannock was supposed to be hard — after all, this was a land where everything was hard.

Paul Ollivier from the Boyer River Reserve came by to visit. The son of Albert Ollivier, he had been brought up in the mission residential school, and was a welcome visitor to the priests.

"Come in, Paul," Father Mariman called. "Taste the first bannock I made in my life."

Paul spun a block of firewood over to the table and sat down. He picked up a chunk of the dry grey-looking bannock and tested it with his teeth. His face turned red. "Father," he mumbled, "you have made a stone. How long did it stay in the oven?"

"Oh, an hour or more. Two loads of wood."

Paul started to laugh. "Fill up the firebox with wood one time; that will be the length of time it needs to cook. When the fire is down, the bannock is ready. Also, your stove is a poor one," he added.

Their new diet of greasy food affected Father Mariman, who developed a severe case of diarrhea. Father Jungbluth had to borrow Chief Narcisse Fournier's team and sleigh to take the poor Father to Fort Vermilion. Father Jungbluth covered him up warmly with hay and blankets, then sat on him to keep him from freezing in the sub-zero temperatures.

Father Mariman's illness necessitated several stops on the way in to town. Holding back the stamping team while Father Mariman suffered through his painful duties on the packed trail behind the sleigh, Father Jungbluth paused to wonder why such ignoble problems had never been mentioned in *Aux Glace Polaires*. Perhaps someday he would write about his experiences; he vowed that the young missionaries who read them would get the whole truth about life in the Ice Missions.

During that first Eleské winter, the young priests had more problems than adjusting to a new diet. Their living quarters upstairs in the church were really only a bare attic. Located directly on the floorboards without benefit of a mattress or even hay, their beds caught the worst drafts that whipped between the roof and the walls of the unfinished building. When Father Habay had constructed the church, he had not foreseen that it would ever be used for a residence. No attempt had been made to insulate it, and although the Fathers stuffed the gaps with rags and pieces of cardboard, the wind blew them out again.

When the single-pane windows were coated with a thick layer of ice, the Fathers simply peered through the frost-split wooden wallboards to see what was happening outside. At nighttime the house snapped in the corners, the boards bursting like rifle shots.

Father Jungbluth's meagre mattress lay on one side of the attic under the eaves; Father Mariman's on the other. The ceiling dipped down so low they had to crawl on hands and knees into their beds. Although Father Jungbluth wore three pairs of socks at a time inside his mukluks, his feet remained cold; he had to dress warmer in bed than out of it.

In the mornings there were usually patinas of ice around their heads, like wreaths, caused by their breath freezing on the blankets and boards directly above their faces. One morning on waking, Father Jungbluth had to laugh: Father Mariman's beard had frozen right onto his blanket.

On February 24, 1936, the temperature dropped to 54 degrees below zero. "I can't understand why Father Habay let us stay in such a poor place," said Father Jungbluth.

"Remember, we asked to come out here," said Father Mariman complacently.

"Il se glorifie dans sa misère," Father Jungbluth muttered.

A typical day for the priests began at five o'clock in the morning, under a black sky. One priest arose, stiff and lethargic from a cold comfortless sleep, and shuffled out to the kitchen area to light the coal-oil lamp on the big table and to stoke up the fire. Then the other got up. All the while the "Great Silence of the Night" was observed; huddled around the stove, waiting for the pail of snow to melt so they could make breakfast and wash, they said their morning prayers and made their daily meditation. The morning prayers lasted nearly half an hour. Then, after warming up the chalice and cruets, and taking the wine from beneath the blankets of one bed — the only place where it would not freeze overnight — each in turn would offer the Holy Mass (at that time they could not concelebrate). After Mass came the little Thanksgiving for the Holy Communion, which lasted about 20 minutes. Then breakfast.

Each took a week's turn cooking, washing dishes, and cleaning the house (which meant running a stiff broom over the plank floor). After the household tasks came the reading of the Latin breviary. The Indians did not usually get up very early, especially in the winter, so these rituals were performed long before the camp was awake.

The outside chores consisted mainly of cutting wood. The Indians had brought over a load of wood on a sleigh, and it was left to the priests to cut it with the crosscut saw to a length that would fit into the gas-barrel stove downstairs in the church. They only needed to split the wood for the little cookstove upstairs.

After this the priests might go visiting, taking along their notebooks. They preferred the Indians come to them, as they could then spread out all their papers and books. Sometimes two or three would come at once and help each other teach the priests Beaver.

One time Father Jungbluth invited an Indian in for a cup of tea, but instead of having the man come upstairs, he decided to bring the teapot down. But the teapot was empty. Another Indian man, sitting alone upstairs for a few minutes, had drunk it all. A new pot was made, and the lessons begun. Father Jungbluth recalled how he had brought over one little teabag from the old country. His mother had given it to him in case he took sick. One teabag. Over here they drank it by the pound. In the old country, tea was used as medicine — black tea or elephant tea, tea that is not commonly seen in Canada — but here it was drunk from the time one got up in the morning until one fell into bed at night.

They also learned of the Indian history and beliefs. They found the graveyard at Eleské particularly interesting. It looked, said Father Mariman, like a bunch of dog houses. When he came upon an old man building a house over the grave of his daughter, Father Mariman asked him about it.

"We cannot pay for stones," the bereaved man told him, "and we want to keep our graves dry. So we build a little house over them so the water may not come in, so the bodies won't decay so fast in the coffins. It's respect for them."

"I don't like it," Father Jungbluth said to Father Mariman. He interpreted it as superstition, a position he later allowed to mellow as he became more familiar with the Indians' philosophies. The Indians also put tobacco inside the little houses, or the gun of the man who died, and some of his clothes, or his boots. He saw that they believed in their own form of after-life. But he said nothing to the Indians. To anger them and perhaps alienate them at such an early stage would be disastrous.

They witnessed the Indians perform their Tea Dance in the dance ring right outside the church. They danced, slightly hunched, feet shuffling quickly back and forth in the dust.

"It's to honor the upcoming sun, in the spring," they were told. "When you look at the cookstove," the Indian man went on, "you can see above the iron a kind of dancing, the waves of the heat. Every spring when the earth gets warm, if you lay on the ground and look, you will see the same heat waves dancing. The Indian dance is like that. The sun makes life, so we dance for it."

"Like the pagans in Rome, from whence comes the word 'Sunday,'" Father Jungbluth said in an aside to Father Mariman.

"Yes, and also the reason why Christmas is celebrated on the 25th of December, to honor the day when the sun begins to come brighter and brighter at the solstice," Father Mariman replied, nodding his head.

As the winter wore on, opportunity for learning improved in Eleské. They would approach a person who knew some English or French and say,

"How do you say in your language, in Beaver, 'It is cold this morning?'" The man would say it slowly, and the Fathers would repeat the phrase 10 or 12 times and then write it down phonetically. The Indian men had no formal school training and could not understand the priests' request for conjugations; the grammar base for Beaver was quite different from any other language the priests had studied. None of the women spoke English, so they had little contact with them at first.

The progress was very, very slow. "I think they only come here to fill up their pipes, or to roll a cigarette," Father Jungbluth would sigh.

One day Father Jungbluth visited with old, blind Sijoli, hoping this patient old man could teach him more quickly than the younger volunteers.

Father Jungbluth with one of his parishioners at Eleské

"Good day, Sijoli, how are you?" Father Jungbluth said, in Beaver, as he entered Sijoli's hut. He then sat down quickly and awaited an acknowledgement of his presence. Seated on an old box, Sijoli smoked his pipe and stared into nothingness.

Although he could neither read nor write, Father Jungbluth chose him as one of his professors. Sijoli pointed out to his students that neither reading nor writing are of any help in killing a duck or a moose, and after experiencing the long relentless winter of Eleské, Father Jungbluth had to agree.

He looked around for a wooden block of some kind to sit on, and pulled it up close to his teacher (Sijoli was also hard of hearing). Sijoli lit his pipe again, slowly, took a deep pull, and the introduction was complete. The lesson began. On the very first word, Sijoli stopped him.

"Fetch the *tth* from the bottom of your stomach," he growled. "Drag it to the left side of your mouth — and snap it hard!"

Ten times . . . twenty times . . . Father Jungbluth made attempts at the evasive *tth*. Soon he was soaked although it was cold in the hut. Suddenly he felt a sting. An insect had migrated from the scalp of Sijoli in search of younger blood. No use trying to search out the intruder. Gritting his teeth, Father Jungbluth gave a grunt as the insect made another bite and *voila!* the evasive *tth* came out perfectly. Sijoli complimented him, and the lesson continued.

Father Jungbluth with old Sijoli learning the "tth" sound.

After about an hour the professor stopped. *"Despot!"* he said, and stretched his hand toward what Father Jungbluth had taken to be an old half-burnt root. After he had cleaned it, as one would a beet, he shoved it into his mouth and cut the protruding part with a huge knife. His jaws were at work instantly. Father Jungbluth quickly assumed that the burnt root was actually a piece of dried meat.

"Udjon! Udjon! It's good. It's good." Sijoli sighed, his mouth full. He lay his hand upon Father Jungbluth's stomach. *"Dinpot! Dinpot!* You are hungry too?"

Father Jungbluth murmured assent, noting the new word. "At this rate," he thought, "I shall know at least 365 words at the end of the year."

The priests' principal professor at Eleské, the pure-blood Beaver who neither of them would care to meet alone in the dark, was Albert Ollivier, the man recommended by both Father Quemeuner and Father Habay. Called Isidool by the Indians, Ollivier was a rough looking man with a reputation to match. The five years in jail were for rape. According to the other Indians, Ollivier's father was the wildest Beaver Indian in Fort Vermilion. One day the Ollivier père came down the bush trail he had followed for years and there in front of him, blocking his path, was a fence. He jumped from his wagon, grabbed an axe and chopped the wires right off the posts. Everyone was scared of him, and his son carried the same threat.

The priests sought Albert Ollivier's help because of his unique expertise in English, in Beaver and in Cree. He was talkative, happy to show off his knowledge, whereas the other Indians were quiet. Inevitably, Albert Ollivier also took advantage of their trust, and made the priests the subjects of his jokes. Instead of the word "sin" he taught them the word "urine", differentiated only by a mistaught accent. It somewhat changed the effect of the sermon.

The R.C.M.P. made regular trips out to Eleské and Albert Ollivier was the first one they checked on. One day the police, after entering Ollivier's house with an interpreter, Bourassa, got an immediate whiff of home brew. A woman, washing clothes in a washtub sitting on a stand, silently ignored the police. After conducting a search of the interior of the shack, the police constable went outside to see if he could sniff out the still. Bourassa, lingering inside the house, looked over at the woman. Assuming the Metis interpreter would never side with a white officer, she gave him a wink and pointed beneath the wash stand. Bourassa ran outside and called the constable. There beneath a trap door underneath the floor was the ripening brew.

The priests were without a professor for 60 days.

Nevertheless, Father Jungbluth and Father Mariman made progress. The Indians liked to come to the church since they had moved out to Eleské, and the two Fathers spared no energy in making their visits worthwhile, rewarding the Indians' regained interest in the church.

One of their more elaborate Sunday services at Eleské took place on a cold miserable day in mid-winter. About nine o'clock in the morning the storm that had been howling throughout the night seemed to abate. The priests had been anxiously watching the sky, praying the weather would clear so the Beaver Indians, most of whom had come from a great distance, would be able to assist at Mass. When the Fathers had made their rounds the day before, they had informed the Indians that at sunrise they would all be in the House of God.

About ten o'clock they sighted the first dog sleds speeding toward the chapel. Then came Chief Narcisse Fournier and his family with his team and sleigh. Next came old blind Sijoli, wearing three pairs of pants; it was very cold and one pair covered over the holes of the others. Lastly came old Suzanne, huddled up in the blankets from her bed. By half-past eleven all of Eleské had arrived, about 50 people. They gathered to visit around the gas-barrel stove, exposing by turns every section of their bodies to the heat.

The Fathers listened to confessions, and added a few more logs to the stove. Then, at the given signal, all dropped down onto their heels (their unique method of kneeling). The doors that had hidden the altar opened and the congregation exhaled their breath in a prolonged *aaaaah!* of admiration. The tabernacle, painted and installed last evening, was a masterpiece to people who never before had seen marble or precious woods. The ornamental flowers adorning the altar were, to them, exotic and marvelous.

None like those grew in Eleské. But it was the image of the Virgin Immaculate enshrined in the chapel for the first time that attracted their eyes — a real oil painting by the brush of the eminent artist, Father Mariman.

Father Mariman struck up the Asperges, while Father Jungbluth played the accompaniment on a diminutive organ donated by a benefactor from France. After the gospel (evangile), the celebrants turned around and re-read, in Beaver, the message of the archangel Gabriel to the humble Virgin of Nazareth. With heads erect and mouths open, the Indians received the divine message. Even old Sijoli had given up seeking the parasites in his hair and turned toward them his dead eyes.

Father Jungbluth began his short sermon. Hardly had he pronounced the first words when he heard his professors murmur: "*Anhan. Udjon!* Yes, yes, that's it!" Thus encouraged that he was using proper Beaver Indian words with adequate pronounciation, he continued, bolstered by the same exclamations that punctuated the whole sermon. A baby shouted for its dinner, but nobody seemed to notice. Outside the chapel the dogs began quarrelling; a young man stood up quickly, jumped over the heads of the people behind him, and, before he reached the door, he let out a yell so loud that the dogs crept under the steps. The Fathers, somewhat upset by the performance, hesitated in their sermon, stumbling momentarily in their deliverance of the unfamiliar words, but the congregation seemed not to be disturbed at all.

After the Holy Mass they started a catechism class for the children, but the adults too decided to join in. It was warm in the chapel, and they found the pictures interesting.

Around seven o'clock in the evening, when the Beaver Indians returned for the recitation of the rosary, another surprise awaited them. Father Mariman had repaired the old statuettes of the Virgin of Lourdes, had sculpted Bernadette in a piece of birchwood, and also had constructed a grotto. But that wasn't all: he had managed to procure, from the depths of his trunk, a little light projector. That night, for the first time, the Indians of Eleské saw projected images — one on Lourdes, one on the catechism, and thirdly a comic film. Then, as the finale, the priests played for their enthusiastic congregation a record of *Solemnes*, the *Salve Regina*, which was listened to with great piety.

At ten o'clock in the evening the women slung their babies onto their backs, knotted them securely, and the men picked up their warm hats and left, without saying a word. The two tired priests checked the stove, turned off the gas lamps, and trudged upstairs. Their dry throats, sore from pronouncing the gutturals of the Beaver language, were soothed by cups of hot cocoa.

And so ended a Sunday at Eleské.

9

Coming Attractions

$\mathcal{F}$ather Jungbluth and Father Mariman worked hard to improve the structure of the church. Father Mariman replaced the board-and-stump benches with long planed benches that hinged to the wall, enabling them to be flipped up and secured to the wall by latches so the church could be used as a hall. They installed a sanctuary one step above the main floor, which could be closed off by two broad doors. When the church was used to show slides, the doors were closed; when they opened, religious services resumed. They built shutters on the outside window casings that could be closed to make the church dark inside for showing the slides.

Father Mariman had brought a number of filmstrip slide presentations from Belgium about religion, catechism, the creation of the world and Bible stories, as well as general-interest fare.

Father Mariman describes the shows:

> One of the films they liked was about Eskimos. It was in color, painted by a young lady from Brussels. Some were funny — some of the Eskimos had bones in their lips — the Beaver Indians liked to laugh at all kinds of things they had never seen before.
>
> We had two films on the Negroes of the Belgian Congo. Our Indians liked to laugh at the Negroes — some had their teeth filed into little points — and they were interested to see the snakes and other animals of that country. There was one picture of a big snake that had swallowed a goat. He choked with it, but you could see the belly of the snake all swelled up.
>
> Another favorite film was about a greedy elephant. The Beaver Indians had never seen an elephant, and they called it, in Beaver, "the big animal with the long nose." The elephant was drinking water. He drank and drank and at the end he sucked himself up. You could see his snout going up, he swallowed his own snout, and at the end he'd swallowed himself until all that was left was the tail. The Indians liked to laugh at that, and Father Jungbluth was good for commenting on it.

The slide shows were a successful drawing card. On a small cast-iron flywheel was a bicycle generator used to produce the electricity, with a little rubber ring around for cranking. They had a small projector mounted on an iron bar; this was set up about 2.5 metres from the wall, on which was hung a white blanket for a screen. The reflected pictures were about one metre square.

Father Mariman continues:

> The Indians liked to turn the emery stone, and the faster they turned it the brighter the light came. Sometimes they flipped it around and around at amazing speeds until PFFT! the light would burn out. Luckily I had quite a few reserves, but we told them, "Don't turn too fast!" But they liked to see it go brighter, and show that they were stronger than the others, that they could turn it faster.

Of course, enjoyment and laughter were not the sole purpose of the shows.

"That is the start," one priest would announce, when the congregation was captivated by the novel entertainment, "and now we are going to pray."

"Say with me!" Father Jungbluth would encourage them, as he carefully enunciated the Our Father in Beaver Indian language. When the religious lessons were over, when the priests could sense that the congregation had had enough and was getting restless, they would cry, "Don't go home yet. We have another film, a comical one." So they all would stay then for the second show.

Father Mariman describes the shows:

> We had pictures on catechism and also funny things. Father Jungbluth liked always to narrate the funny films. There was one about a zoological garden in Antwerp, Belgium. It started with visiting the monkeys. Oh, the Indians laughed! They called them "animals with a man-face." I remember there was a picture that showed a monkey mother with two or three babies around her, and she was busy trying to catch the flies out of her hair. Father Jungbluth would say to the Indians, "See, just like you do! She's lousy!" and those Indians, they were not mad. They'd laugh. Sometimes he'd take the cap from one Indian's head and put it on his own. Then he'd grab it off and scratch in his head, pretending he'd found something, and nibble on it. Oh, they laughed with him!
>
> They were very good-character Indians; they had a fairly good sense of humor. The joke didn't have to be very elaborate, just a mimic of their actions or something like that.
>
> They came every day to look at that little picture show. The whole population, from the first to the last, were there every day, in the beginning. And Father Jungbluth always liked to make them laugh with the few words he knew in their language. But every day we learned more and more.
>
> When he was gone I repeated them sometimes, and they always laughed, but then came the big moving pictures and mine

meant nothing to them anymore. But at that time, when we first came, they had never seen a film.

Another device used to teach religion to the Indians was an illustrated catechism designed by Father Lacombe. It was made of paper glued onto a piece of cloth, and could be rolled like a scroll for easy transportation. It showed the Indians choosing between two paths, Good and Evil, and was illustrated with biblical scenes.

Father Jungbluth liked to amuse the people of Eleské by taking their photographs. He brought the films from 'outside' and developed them himself using three wash basins. With no electricity to provide steady light, it was pretty tough. First he'd put blankets up at all the windows (or simply wait until nightfall), then put the film into a basin containing developing solution; as the pictures formed, he put them into the next basin that contained fixer; then he'd shake them, put them into usually three solutions of clean water, and dry them by laying them on the bed.

Father Jungbluth's ingenuity and dexterity gave him another means of access to the community. His special creation, an alarm-clock pocket watch, was a source of interest to the Indians. It hung on the wall of the church above the stairway leading up to their quarters, and rang out every quarter-hour. He had devised the ringing system when he was a student in France: hanging from the little pocket watch was a weight made from a pointed World War One-vintage 35mm shell. Hoping to impress the wisest of the Indians with his creative abilities, Father Jungbluth showed off his workmanship to Alexis Elias, the closest neighbor to the church and a very well-respected man whom the Indians called Inlaye.

Alexis Elias leaned closer to peer intently at the mechanism. He said nothing while he studied it. "All this works with the weight of the shell?" he finally asked.

"Yes," Father Jungbluth nodded, waiting to be congratulated for his ingenuity. But Alexis Elias did not look at all interested in the watch, or even the ringing system. He took the shell in his hand and reverently rolled it around.

"If we could use that to shoot a moose, it surely would be well-killed!"

When the news traveled around Eleské that Father Jungbluth could fix watches, the Indians produced their old broken timepieces. The Chief, Narcisse Fournier, brought in an old pocket watch.

Father Jungbluth turned the watch over in his hand. It was a heavy thing, old and shining from rubbing around inside a pocket. The seams in the metal were crusted with dirt.

"How much did you pay for this watch?" Father Jungbluth asked.

"One dollar."

"Oh . . . then I know how to repair it." He dropped the watch onto the floor.

The Chief stood still and quiet, looking without expression at his watch, then at Father Jungbluth. The Chief bent down and picked up his watch. It was ticking. He grunted and walked away. Father Jungbluth's reputation as a watchmaker had been established.

(Father Jungbluth explains: "Had it been a precious watch, I wouldn't have let it drop. But those cheap watches have rough gears and the little backs do not close, or the place where they wind them up is not airtight, and sometimes dust gets between the gears and stops them. When I let it drop to the floor, the speck of dust fell out.")

Repairing watches aside, triumphs at the mission seemed few. Father Jungbluth read that some tribes had a chief of prayer and a chief for ringing the bells, a chief for this and a chief for that, all organized. But that system could hardly be followed in Eleské.

"I am often the best and the worst singer in the congregation," he wrote home, "because I am the only one uttering a sound."

When Father Jungbluth and Father Mariman started to say the Mass at Eleské, the Indians crept up to peer into the chalice. A youngster shyly pulled on Father Jungbluth's chasuble. They were simply curious. One young boy lay upon the floor to see if priests had legs under the long dresses. Children lined up for the Communion. It was difficult to smile and continue while gently wresting away a sticky hand that tugged at one's embroidered silken stole.

There were some laws of the Universal Church that Father Jungbluth and Father Mariman had no hope of ever instilling into their Indian congregation. One was the rule against eating meat on Fridays, or on the Ember Days before Christmas and Easter. They observed the rules themselves at first, but slowly, when conditions made the rules seem completely impractical, they used their own judgement and hoped that the Good Lord would agree with their decision. What could one do, as a guest in an Indian's home, when all that was offered was meat? There were no salads, no steamed vegetables, no rice or macaroni or potatoes. Perhaps some dried berries, pounded into pemmican, might be offered as a treat, but canning was impossible as the jars would freeze. Indians were not gardeners. They were hunters and berry-pickers, and their hospitality was a delicate and prized offering. To offend them was easy enough with a misplaced accent, or a "possibility" given that they took as a "promise."

Although the Indians might regularly attend Mass, they still put their faith in dreams. When somebody had died they often saw apparitions and would run quickly to the priests' house and ask them to come with "lots of Holy Water" to bless the house and thereby rid them of the visitations. "Such visions are occurring because you are still thinking about that person," the priest might say. But they blessed the house nonetheless. Never would they accuse the person of wild imaginings when they reported knocking on the walls or at the doors. After a while the knockings would cease, but the power of the Holy Water would be remembered.

The Beaver Indians also believed in teleportation; they would tell the Fathers when they had seen a vision of where a moose was standing, waiting to be killed. The priests noticed that some of these visions occurred after the man had had a few drinks. "Well," said Father Jungbluth once, when he was sure his audience would take it well, "if you had taken another drink perhaps you would have seen three moose!"

On the other hand, they were particular in their beliefs. "What do you think of these totem poles?" a Beaver Indian once asked the Fathers, after coming back from a stay in hospital in Vancouver. "That's all those Indians down there talk about. Crazy stuff."

The drinking parties at Eleské bothered the young priests; they stayed discreetly in their own house, falling into fitful sleeps to the hypnotic steady rhythm of tom-toms. Just the sight of their liquor made the Fathers sick. The Indians made it sometimes from the bark of trees, or if they could get hold of some potatoes they made it from that. It was often fermented, something like wine, rather than distilled. It looked like dirty dishwater, with bits of debris floating in it. When the Indians drank it they had big circles around their mouths, the foam and all. They didn't often drink in front of the priests; the Indians remained polite and respectful and if their visit was expected, there would be no evidence of moonshine in the house. But they chewed tobacco, and they spit, and it made them unattractive. The women did it too. Even in church. And as yet the Fathers did not know the Indians well enough to tell them they must stop.

Typical home in Eleské

The Indians did not like to see the priests angry. They would stare with big eyes at a raised voice, a face reddened in wrath, a banging of hard-heeled boots on the floor as one or other of the Fathers retreated, stomping, slamming a door. "Usually when there is anger, reason departs," commented one old Indian man mildly, his words floating out amidst the curling smoke of his ever-present pipe. And the offending Father was shamed, and vowed silently that it would not happen again. He would be patient, kind, bending.

The rite of Confession also had to be adjusted to the situation. Patiently the priests would explain to their parishioners the purpose of the Confession, but it was not the Indian way to tell — especially to a white man — about the sins of his soul, or about those of his neighbor. Haltingly some came, but the occasion usually turned into a visit. He might start off with the story of his life, and the priest would impatiently interrupt: "Just tell me, tell me, what you want forgiven. What are you sorry for?"

"Nothing. I didn't do nothing. We were fighting. It was her."

"Just tell me," the priest would say in a low voice, "how have you offended God? I don't want to hear what the other one did."

"It wasn't my fault."

"You are the accusor of yourself in the confessional, my friend. There must be something, even something small, that you are sorry for, that you come to ask forgiveness, to gain the purpose of doing better. You must have the contrition . . ." Hopeless. Start again. "What have you done that you wish you hadn't done?"

"Went to town."

"Alright. What did you do in town?"

"Nothing."

"Then what was the problem?"

"Didn't come home."

"Now we're getting somewhere. Do you promise not to do this again?"

"Yeah. She's no good no more, my woman. I don't go home until she's good and hungry."

Father Jungbluth had to accept that there existed a territory he could never penetrate, and it sometimes frustrated him.

"My Indians are very colorful," he wrote in a letter to Alsace that winter, "but it's not everyone who can point it out. One can write about them, in verses just like those of Robert Service, but to another fellow they are just strangers, that's all."

Church at Eleské

*"A photograph of Fathers Jungbluth and Mariman taken the
winter of 1936-37 shows two fuzzy creatures . . ."*

10
Rhontsedudiél!

A photograph of Father Jungbluth and Father Mariman taken the winter of 1936-37 shows two fuzzy creatures: Father Jungbluth is wearing the fur coat he brought from France and Father Mariman is wrapped securely in the great fur coat of the Red Fox.

"My fur coat was second-hand when I got it," Father Jungbluth says. "When it started to tear, I tried to fix it up but it was too old; when I held it up to the light I could see it was vented, like, full of moth-holes. The folds just came apart."

Adds Father Mariman: "I sent my sister a picture of myself taken that winter, wearing my big fur coat, and she wrote back saying, 'What's the matter with you?' I had gained so much weight! I had not been used to eating rolled oats in the morning — we never ate that in the old country — and here we used sugar and milk on them besides. And my cheeks were all puffed out from eating all that lard that the Sisters sent.

"I used to sleep in that fur coat. They also gave me a rabbit skin blanket from that Father Petour, with rabbit fur inside and a tarp on the outside. But, we were young, we did not find it exceptional. 'Well, we came to the North!' we said, and we thought it was normal."

The two priests were all the while preparing for their separation. During the summer of 1936 Father Jungbluth had been sent on a "reconnaissance trip," as it was understood that a priest would soon be needed to attend to the Beaver and Cree Indians in the Fort St. John, British Columbia, area.

In January, 1937, a telegram from Bishop Guy ordered Father Jungbluth to Grouard to begin learning the Cree Indian language. Father Habay was planning to make a trip out to France to visit his mother, so the two priests arranged to travel together to Grouard. The same crowd of people who had gathered along the riverbank to supervise their arrival in Fort Vermilion — the priests, the Sisters, the school children, the Indians who were in town for the day — now watched them leave.

The horses pranced impatiently, their harness bells jingling sharply in the cold air. Father Jungbluth stood for a moment beside the cutter, looking back at the sombre faces, all in a row, of those who had come to watch their departure.

Catching the eye of Father Mariman, he gave him a wink and, with a wild whoop that any Indian would have been proud of, he threw his cap high into the air. Leaping, he caught it as it spiralled downward. Then with a flourish he clamped it upon his head and jumped into the sleigh. His last view, as they left the ice-enshrouded town, was of the laughing faces of those dear people he was leaving behind.

Accompanying Father Habay and Father Jungbluth was a Metis named Beauchamp, a helper engaged by the mission. Their destination was Peace River Crossing, approximately 400 kilometres up the river. The snow was deep covering the river ice, but the trail was fairly well-marked and the weather held for the first two days.

On their second day out they came upon a trapper with a frozen foot. The priests stopped the cutter and took him in. He needed medical attention, but an extra passenger slows one down, makes it hard on the horses, depletes the food supply. The trail became worse. The third day out a storm hit. Father Habay, who had traveled the area many times, was not distressed. "There is a cabin up ahead where we can find shelter for the night. It shouldn't be too far."

The horses were tired. One man and then another had to go ahead of the horses and break trail; all but the trapper with the frozen foot walked behind. One horse stumbled, then fell, laying on the trail with its sides heaving. Bloody foam bubbled from the other horse's nose. They had to stop.

They were surrounded by meadow, the nearest brush half a kilometre away. They unhitched the horses and upset the sleigh onto its side for a windbreak, then dug a hole down into the snow and piled hay from the bottom of the sleigh to make a sleeping burrow for the night. Beauchamp volunteered to wade out through the hip-high snow to gather wood for a

Preparing to make camp.

campfire. He returned nearly an hour later, exhausted, with an armful of twigs. If they kept their coals low, it would do to cook their supper and their breakfast.

As night darkened the landscape each man bundled up, closing up his coat, pulling down his hat flaps, wrapping himself as securely as possible in his share of the buffalo robe. Rolled into compact furry balls, they resembled a den of coyotes. Never in his life had Father Jungbluth felt so exhausted. Sleep came drifting over him — welcome, relieving sleep. A sharp kick in the ribs shattered his dreams.

"Fire! Fire!" Father Habay was jumping about, waving his arms, his black silhouette surrounded by dancing fireworks. "The hay's on fire!"

In the black night all that could be seen were tiny dancing flecks of light that reeled in mad circles. Coals from their fire had landed on bits of the hay. This in turn had ignited Father Habay's one token of comfort, his feather pillow. In his wild attempt to beat it out, the casing had ripped and the dancing feathers bounced everywhere, some sparking like winter fireflies, others floating bits of fluff that blinded the men to the source of the flames.

When they eventually beat it out, Father Jungbluth discovered that his fur coat, the one brought "already vented" from France, was now even more so.

Fathers Jungbluth and Habay and Mr. Beauchamp en route from
Fort Vermilion to Peace River Crossing.

Now fully awake, they broke camp. The horses seemed to have recovered, and the storm had abated to a steady windless snowfall. They continued on, but the experience put a damper on their spirits for the rest of the trip.

"I knew, I knew the horses were too tired," Father Habay kept muttering to himself. "I knew we should not try to make that cabin. But a fellow never learns." He was in his 70s then, a man well respected in the North. In his lifetime he had pulled himself out of many a misadventure. It was sobering to the young Father Jungbluth to hear this old man lament, "A fellow never learns." There was so much to be learned about the North.

They arrived without further mishap at Peace River Crossing, and Father Jungbluth traveled on to Grouard.

The *Academie du Cris* at the Grouard Mission was headed by Father Fahler, an expert in the Cree language. Father Jungbluth was looking forward to his stay there. But an even finer discovery awaited: his friend from the seminary in Burthécourt, Father Alfred Bruckert, was also among the five students studying under Father Fahler.

Father Jungbluth settled quickly into his new environment. The surroundings were pleasant, and he was learning Cree with considerably more ease than he had the complex Beaver. English was another matter. Sister Jean LaBissoniere was one of Father Jungbluth's teachers at the Grouard Mission:

> My clearest memory of him as he sat in the back of my classroom with his great friend, Father Alfred Bruckert, was a tense look on Father Jungbluth's face as he tried desperately to understand what I was saying. Then he would cup his left ear with his hand, trying to entice my voice into his hearing area. I knew what his difficulty was, so I would slow down and enunciate as clearly as I could. The smile of relief as those clear blue eyes expressed their gratitude for my slowing down was rewarding.
>
> Father Jungbluth was our Mr. Fix-It. I appreciated his dexterity in repairing my clock, and in keeping my classroom piano and the church organ in tune. He was always so gracious, one never felt as though one was imposing on him.

"It perhaps sounds like a contradiction, having a hard time hearing in the classroom, then tuning pianos," Father Jungbluth says with a smile. "Maybe it is, a bit. Therefore I was likely not the best piano tuner."

On June 22, 1937, Father Jungbluth received his Obedience Orders for Fort St. John, British Columbia. He would now have his own territory, although still working within the Vicariate of Grouard under the supervision of Bishop Guy.

His new mission territory still ran along the Peace River, although nearly 800 kilometres upstream from the mission of Fort Vermilion. The area

Father Jungbluth was expected to cover, on horseback or on foot, had a circumference of some 2,400 kilometres.

He was to travel over graded gravel roads, bulldozed dirt roads, and rutted trails. He had to ford or ferry across bridgeless rivers. His territory included the Indian and Metis settlements of Rio Grande, Big Slough, Wapiti, Horse Lake and Kelly Lake, Jackfish Lake, Moberly Lake, Commotion Creek, through Hudson's Hope to the Halfway Reserve and out to the ever-changing hunting and trapping camps in the bush. In the 480-kilometre trip from Fort Nelson to Fort St. John, he would be visiting the Indians around the Prophet River and calling in the camps around the North Pine or Blueberry reserves. He was also to say Mass in farmhouses, stores or halls — any place large enough to hold a gathering — in the farming communities of Montney, North Pine, Rose Prairie, Cecil Lake, Baldonnel, or at the remote residence of any Catholic family who could not be served by the parish priest. He would need a horse.

The animal he chose was a beautiful long-legged sorrel mare. He bought her from the Cassidys, who lived north of the river at Sunrise, and he sent the bill for $30 to the Vicariate. She was about four or five years old, gentle but spirited, and on those long legs she just ran like the wind. He named her Katie.

Father Jungbluth also needed a guide. "Jumbie," (his real name was Jean-Pierre) was about 30 years of age and had lived in the Fort St. John area all his life. He knew everyone, he knew all the trails, and he could assure the new priest a welcome wherever they went. All such services carry a price-tag, however, and Jumbie's was this: he must look presentable. He would need a completely new outfit: shoes, slacks, new coat and hat, everything. And some food of course, but not much. Jumbie could hunt for game as they went. No cash was requested. The necessary purchases were made: Jumbie's new outfit (which he showed off to everyone immediately), and a few emergency rations for the trip such as chocolate bars, some canned food and some dried meat, (which got all mashed together by exposure to heat and water and by the grinding of the baggage).

Father Jungbluth selected the barest necessities for his Mass supplies. He had been provided with a spare Mass kit especially packed for traveling. In it were a thin altar stone containing a blessed relic, three linens for the top of the portable altar, altar vestments, an alb, a small missal, two candles, cruets and a chalice. In a small canteen he carried the Mass wine. It was an awkwardly packed assortment contained in a square black case that was obviously not intended for transportation on a horse. Later he would design a more practical kit.

Jumbie silently helped him adjust the box-like valise along the sides of the pommel where it was sure to bang against his knees. Already there were two duffel bags along each side and on the back behind the saddle lay a sleeping bag and a piece of canvas for a lean-to. Each man carried a change of clothes. Jumbie transported their few rations and a rifle.

It took 14 days to make the 480-kilometre trip from Fort St. John to Fort Nelson. Father Jungbluth was not yet used to spending all day in the saddle, nor was he familiar with Katie. She was a fast horse, ever eager, and highly spirited. Jumbie thought she might be the fastest horse in the country. She quickly became a conversation piece at every Indian camp.

Jumbie spoke some English and Father spoke some Beaver, so although they could make themselves understood to one another, communication was difficult. The Indians they called on were polite, but uninterested. The aboriginal people of his new mission territory were mainly the Beaver and Cree, with a band of Saulteaux Indians sharing with the Cree the East End Reserve of Moberly Lake, and a band of Sekannais Indians living north around the Prophet River.

Very quickly, Father Jungbluth second-guessed his wisdom in choosing a guide who knew every Indian in the country. "I thought he could introduce me to the Indians," Father Jungbluth recalls, "but that was the trouble — he did not introduce me enough. When we came into a camp, he could speak the language, he was known by these Indians and some of them he hadn't seen for a long time. So they got into conversations and they talked and talked, they smoked a pipe together, and they let me stand in the corner."

Jumbie's culinary arts also left much to be desired. They took game as they went, shooting whatever happened to cross their trail. One night it was porcupine. Not knowing much about the preparation of porcupine, Father Jungbluth left Jumbie to take care of the cooking, then watched in horror as Jumbie simply threw it into the fire — quills, guts and all. Jumbie dragged it back out at regular intervals with a big stick to see if it was cooked, as Father watched his supper turn black. The smell of burning celluloid — like a comb set afire — wafted through the air. He presumed it was the quills.

Jumbie finally decided it was properly done and dragged it back through the ashes to lay at his feet. He slashed the underside with his knife and tossed the sizzling organs into the bush. For dessert they had a mashed bar of chocolate that had been soaked in river water from their last fording.

They stayed nearly two weeks at a camp near Prophet River called Klua (Fish) Lake, where Father Jungbluth found a more responsive audience. He had brought along his camera and a tripod, and his photography sessions always attracted a crowd.

The Beaver Indians at Prophet River, some 110 kilometres southeast of Fort Nelson, recall the first visit of the "Little Beaver Father:"

> We did not know what a priest was," John Chipesia, who was a young boy at the time, later reported to Father Mariman. "We thought he was an ordinary guy and we wanted to find out if he was strong. We tried to throw him down, to wrestle him. And

Father Jungbluth shouted, "Do not do that! I am a priest! I am not like an ordinary man."

"So we quieted down and listened to him. We sat under the shade of the lean-tos and teepees. We had no houses because we never stayed more than a few weeks in any place; we followed the moose."

When Father Jungbluth and Jumbie arrived at a camp, Father would ask to talk to the chief. The chiefs were mostly oldtimers who remembered when Bishop Joussard used to come some years before. "*Rhontsedudiél!*" they would cry aloud to the camp. It took Father Jungbluth a minute to translate the word to mean, "people in general, come outside with the idea that you could go back again soon."

When the Indians had gathered, Father Jungbluth tried to learn their names, their marital status, their previous religious training, and then tried to convince them that he brought a message.

Father Jungbluth recalls those first journeys among the Indians of his mission:

In those days we baptized practically anybody, not like now where you have to have preparation. We just lined them up and it was quite a job because we didn't know their names at all. The women had no names. They were just called something like "Little Jack-rabbit" or "Charlie Bigfoot's Woman" or just "That Fellow's Girl." And when you asked the name of the father of the child — oh! what a mix-up! Well, I tried my best to get the name and so on, and some of them did stick to the names I gave them. But a few years later when I'd see a child I thought I hadn't seen before, and I'd ask, "*Joo-ah, long-any?* Was he baptized?" (baptized means "big process by water" in Beaver), those Indians would turn to me and were they mad!

"What's the matter with you?" they'd say. "You gave him his name. You should know it!" I didn't baptize many adults at that time. I didn't know them. I didn't know if they were married, if they were shacked up, or if they were living with their sister. I didn't know anything. You can't just baptize them that way. I had to have time to instruct them.

First I had to find out if they were living correctly, if they were living with just one woman. Also I had to teach them catechism. I had my picture of the two ways, the chart designed by Father Lacombe, showing the poor Indian traveling the wrong way, and the other showing the happy Indian who accepts God. If they were interested and seemed to grasp something from that, if they were in good disposition and wanted to be baptized, well, then I baptized them. I took their names and put them in a book and then later on they got married, some of them.

The first trips were rough. Father Jungbluth didn't know the bush, and the Indians didn't know him.

"When he came, we didn't know what preaching was," John Chipesia later told Father Mariman. "All this talk about God and so on. Many of those people listening to him were smoking during the sermon, and chewing. Father tried to teach them that it was not polite to do that when he was teaching us about God. But we liked him."

In a very short time, Katie proved to be an excellent bush horse, manageable and trustworthy. Father Jungbluth eagerly made plans to travel the entire circumference of his territory before snow came.

"This is a fine country," he wrote to his friends in Alsace. "When I asked for the Polar Missions, I never believed it would be this moderate. Sure, the country is as yet undeveloped, it's still in a natural state, but its riches are there for whoever makes the effort to seek them."

Father giving Mass in tent using Father Lacombe's chart.

Father Jungbluth with Metis at Grouard.

11

Bush-Bailiff

*W*hen Father Jungbluth made his reconnaissance trip through the territory in the summer of 1936, he had briefly acted as interpreter at the Treaty Payment in Moberly Lake. Before he could sound out his protests to Dr. Brown, the Indian Agent, he had been appropriated as interpreter of Beaver, of which he knew little; of Cree, of which he knew nothing; and English, a language with which he was only slightly familiar.

The Beaver Indians in Moberly Lake had had less contact to the "outside" than those at Fort Vermilion or Eleské, and this made the language even more difficult to interpret. "I made a terrible job of interpreting that day," Father Jungbluth says in retrospect. "How could I speak Beaver when I was not even a year with the Beaver Indians? I did my best, but I made lots of mistakes, I'm sure." He still cringes whenever he thinks of it.

When he returned a year later to Fort St. John, Mr. Galibois was the new Indian Agent. As Mr. Galibois' territory approximated that of Father Jungbluth's, it was intimated that everyone would benefit — Indians included — if there was cooperation between the government and the church in registering the Indians, recording their ancestry, and establishing their locations. The government was also interested in establishing who was, and who was not, eligible under Treaty 8 for benefits.

The Indians could choose to consider themselves white, and renounce their Indian privileges; for compensation they would be given a piece of land, some money, some machinery and trade goods, and from then on they were to make their own living.

"Usually," says Father Jungbluth, "when a status Indian chose to be considered white, it was a big mistake, for then and there they renounced their birthright."

Father Jungbluth found himself witness to one such case concerning Philip LaGlace. He recalls the situation:

> It happened about 1938. In the summer, the Indian Agent and a retinue of helpers — quite often a Mountie — went into the different Indian camps, usually on the reserve, to pay the Treaty. Each person who was considered a status Indian and belonged to a tribe received five dollars. He was also given blankets, ammunition, flour, enough material for a teepee, things like that, all kinds of equipment. They got this once a year.
>
> Now Philip LaGlace was originally from the Horse Lake Reserve, but he had moved to Moberly Lake and married and

settled there. Still registered as a Horse Lake resident, he attended the Treaty Payment there. That year the Inspector from Ottawa was in Horse Lake to sort out who was actually eligible for Treaty and who was not; although some of the residents' ancestors had once renounced their Indian rights, the grandchildren still stood in line for Treaty.

The first question asked of Philip LaGlace, through an interpreter, was, "What's your name?" and there came all the trouble.

"Philip," he had answered.

"What's your last name?"

"Well, they call me LaGlace and they call me Onyande, and sometimes they call me Philip Davis . . ."

"Who is your father?"

"Eh?" Philip held himself up proudly. "My father! He's a white man."

"Oh."

"Yeah."

"Oh, that's good . . ."

"Yeah."

"So, you are a white man?" the inspector smiled. "Me too."

"Yeah, me too," Philip said. "Me too, white man."

"Alright, Mister Philip, please step outside. I am finished with you."

So poor Philip had nothing coming and he had quite a family by that time.

He came to Father Jungbluth for help, and Father took up his case. He first contacted a lawyer from Grande Prairie who was very interested in the Indians and the way they were treated, he wrote letters to the Indian Affairs Department, he took around petitions. The case was finally won, after five years, in Philip LaGlace's favor; he proudly handed Father Jungbluth five dollars for his efforts — but he never did come to church. That case was something Father Jungbluth was very proud of.

Father Jungbluth comments:

These names are very confusing. An Indian child may be born and raised at, let's say, Horse Lake. Perhaps a white man had come to the reserve and slept with a woman there, and that woman gives birth to a boy. It's a one-time encounter, and the child never sees his father. Perhaps his grandparents raised him and he takes their name, or his mother marries and he takes on her husband's name. Or sometimes they just hear a name and like the sound of it. But that's what we, the clergy and the Indian Affairs Department, had to work with.

Often I hear people talking against the Indian Department and perhaps what they say is true. But how could they have been better? They couldn't play Santa Claus all the time. They couldn't give them everything for nothing.

The clergy was also brought in to interpret for the British Columbia Provincial Police. "There were always disputes over traplines," Father Jungbluth says, "between the whites and the Indians, between Indian and Indian, and also white with white, one trespassing on the other. The lines were delineated on a rough map drawn by the trapline inspector, a kind of game warden. The problems concerning traplines were at their height in the 1920s and 1930s, when the government tried to regulate trapping on a straight-across set of rules for Indians and whites alike. Excerpts from old police records indicate the confusion.

Because of the high value of furs, the traders, instead of waiting for the Indians to come in to see them, traveled themselves practically to the traps, into the Indian camps, trying to beat one another out of the furs.

Father Jungbluth relates:

My first winter in Fort St. John, the trader, Mr. Sylvester (not his real name) offered to let me ride with him out to the Indians so long as I would be the cook and help out a bit. He was, of course, trying to get to the Indians ahead of his competitor, Mr. Bond (not his real name) from Montney, and they always watched each other to see who would get there first and try to beat each other on the trail.

We left on a sleigh, heavily loaded with trading supplies — flour, ammunition, tent material, beads for the women to sew on the moccasins — anything the Indians might use. I just brought along my sleeping bag and my little Mass kit.

Along the trail we saw sleigh tracks, meaning that the other trader was already ahead of us. Sylvester somehow figured, though, that Bond would not make it all the way to the Indians that day, as judging from the tracks he looked overtired and would likely camp for the night. So in order that we could travel all night, Sylvester unloaded half of our goods and urged the horses on with the whip so we would be to the Indians by daybreak. We camped at Squaw Creek, north of Montney, with Johnny Beatton, the son of old Frank Beatton, and Sylvester started his store right away. The Indians thought it odd that Sylvester was there and not the other trader whom they had expected, and they wondered where he could be.

"I have not come across him at all," Sylvester said, calm as could be, "and I am sure he will not come anymore, so you can sell me all the furs you have."

"How come you have so little here to trade?" the Indians asked.

"You'd just better take what I have here," Sylvester said, "for you'll have to wait a long time before the other trader shows up."

So the Indians traded their many furs for a lump sum of goods, and when Bond arrived two or three hours later, all the furs had gone, as well as Sylvester.

The actions of Sylvester and Bond once involved Father Jungbluth with the law courts:

One time Bond, it seems, accused Sylvester of having swindled the Indians, or selling some furs which he had no right to get, out of season or something, and the hearing was to be held in Fort St. John. Sylvester, because I was travelling with him at the time, wanted me to be in court as a witness. I laughed through the whole thing.

The judge couldn't understand any of the gibberish they gave to him. There were also some Indians there — both Bond and Sylvester had brought their customers and friends to vouch for them — and they didn't understand anything that was going on. The police were there, trying to sort it out. It was quite a crowded court.

Sylvester didn't talk always the very best English, and the judge had to lean forward and listen intently to what he was saying. All he could make out was something about "scraping the floor with a cup." Now the judge had no idea what they were talking about.

"Scrape the floor?" he said. "Scrape the floor?"

He didn't know there was a trap door in the floor of the trading store and underneath was some home brew. Bond was accusing Sylvester of dealing the Indians out of their furs by pushing aside the trap door and "scraping the floor." I was supposed to be a witness for Sylvester. I could only say that I hadn't seen that. That's all I said. I hadn't seen the drinking and I hadn't heard that he made moonshine. But all those traders offered drink to the Indians. Always. Homemade or otherwise. It was common knowledge.

It depends on the attitude you took, if the Indians fared badly at the hands of the fur traders or not. They didn't give them much money, but you must also remember that during the summer when there was no trapping all these Indians were supported by the trader. They'd come in to Fort St. John and they wanted bacon, flour, tea, and all that was entered in the books, "on jawbone" it was called. And they had to pay it back with their furs. So they didn't give them much in the winter. They were kept fairly dependent.

Also, the Indian Department used to treat the Indians like children. When I came here in 1937 an Indian couldn't sell a horse

Preparing to leave the Beaver Indian camp
north of Fort St. John on his trusty steed, Katie.

to a white man without the consent of the Indian Department. That rule was supposed to protect the Indian, but then they went too far.

I still don't know what is really best for them.

The Indians' nomadic habits made it nearly impossible to impose the same rules and restrictions as must be followed by the white population. Even their marriages called for separate government regulations.

When Father Jungbluth visited with the Beavers north of Fort St. John he did not have enough time to give them the necessary instruction for marriage. In his opinion, many of them were already married. If no priest were available and two fairly young people wanted to marry, the boy would talk with the chief or with the parents of the girl, saying simply, "I would like to live with her." The parents may not have approved, but they were the witnesses anyway, and so everyone accepted that she would live with him for life. If the man and woman were not close relations and both were free and adult so they could make the commitment for life, the Church would recognize the marriage.

A notice in a 1945 edition of *La Voix*, the official publication of the Vicariate of Grouard, reads:

On this occasion it is good to tell you that the Indians and Metis are not obliged to have a marriage licence; also the bans do not have to be published three times, nor must the bans be published on two consecutive Sundays before the marriage. The regulations ask only that one publication be made and this one can be made immediately before the ceremony of the marriage, and on any day of the week. If the Indians prefer to have their licenses for marriage, they can be procured from anyone who is authorized to give licenses of marriage (government agent or Indian agent) and by paying only $2 instead of the regular $6.

Father Jungbluth would often conduct a little ceremony when he came through, but there were no licenses or registrations. At the beginning, he made out no papers at all. "When I married them, I usually made up the ceremony depending on where it was and how much the participants understood," Father Jungbluth says. The marriage rites were kept as simple as possible, based on good intent rather than on intricate detailed promises. He would explain the exchange of vows, emphasizing that the promises were made for life, otherwise it was not a marriage; then he would have them hold hands and say, "I take you," and "Yeah, I take you now, for life," both of them saying that.

Father Jungbluth described one of the more sophisticated Moberly Lake weddings in a letter to *Immaculata* magazine:

On the appointed day, a little late of course, arrived the bride with her helpers. She asked for the use of my room behind the church to fix herself up. After half an hour she emerged, to my surprise, in a beautiful wedding dress. But she had no bouquet, so she asked to borrow some of the artificial flowers from the altar. To say "no" to a woman is a difficult thing. She got her flowers.

But where was the groom? In another hour of waiting, no groom. The church was by then filled. I inquired of the congregation if someone had seen the groom.

"Yes," I was told by an unexcited youngster. "He went into the bush with his team to get some wood."

"Well, does he think we are going to wait till night?" I sent a young fellow with a fast horse after him. After another hour both came back with full speed, riding double.

And there stood the groom, clad in torn "Cowboy King" trousers and an old moosehide jacket that had all the colors except the original one. The poor guy had made a mistake in dates. He thought the wedding was tomorrow. Again I gave my room so he could wash up. Soon he appeared in quite decent trousers and a new windbreaker. He had changed outfits with a friend of his. From then on, the ceremony proceeded in a more conventional manner.

But just within a week of the wedding, I heard a rumor: it seems that the day after the wedding, the bride sent the wedding dress back to Eaton's, explaining that it did not fit.

Father Jungbluth did not see too many cases of polygamy, but sometimes a man would "change wives", although they only kept one at a time. Divorce was a subject that hardly ever came up with the Indians, but it did once, at the Halfway Reserve:

When I was visiting up at the Halfway, Antoine Hunter, the brother of Thomas Hunter who was the chief, called me aside. "Father," he said "I want to divorce my wife."

"Why would you want to do that?" I asked.

"She's no good anymore. She's no good for anything."

I looked down at the ground, thinking. This must be handled with care. I would not be back for a month or so. "Let me see your woman," I said finally. "I will talk to her and perhaps find out the trouble."

Antoine Hunter led me to a teepee located some 50 yards [46 m] from the river. I lifted the tent flap and crawled inside. In a dark corner lay a bundle of rags. As my eyes adjusted to the light, I made out a pair of black eyes, glowing in the dark like a rat's. There lay the source of Antoine's unhappiness. I greeted her in Beaver. She didn't reply, just blinked her eyes and looked away. Her skin, dark and wrinkled like a long-dried apple, showed her age as much greater than that of Antoine, but this often happened: an older woman in the position of guardian might indeed marry a younger man, to ensure support for her old age.

I spoke to her quietly in Beaver, getting for my efforts a few uninterested grunts. The near toothless tobacco-stained mouth worked constantly at her wad; at times a dribble of juice glistened in the corners of her mouth and seeped into the wrinkles of her face. A little dark tongue flicked out periodically, gathering it up. I sat a while, then gave her a quiet blessing, and crept out.

Antoine was waiting for me down at the river, smoking a cigarette, watching the smoke waft up on the lazy summer air.

"Well?" he said, as I walked toward him. "Well?"

I mounted my horse, the creak of the saddle leather the only sound to break the silence.

"You're right," I told him. My eyes met those of Antoine Hunter and a look passed between us. "But see that she has enough to eat." I added.

"Thank you, Father," he said.

I turned my horse and headed down the trail to Hudson's Hope, 40 miles [64 km] to the south.

As Katie resumed her slow trot, I had time to reminisce about my training in the seminary, especially about the clear-cut principles and solutions of the old professors of moral theology, and then the somewhat flippant answer I had given to Antoine Hunter. Would Antoine have understood a sermon on the love and devotion he ought to have for his decrepit wife? Not a chance. But such were the situations I found in my work.

Both church and government have been criticized for administrative decisions that have had social and economic impacts on native people. Perhaps evoking the voices of the past to remember the sometimes complex legal and moral universe that existed in Father Jungbluth's far-flung mission will bring their intentions into focus. As Father Jungbluth says, "The answers have never been perfected."

12

A Night in the Hut of the Medicine Man

During one of his trips to the Indian camps with the trader Sylvester, Father Jungbluth met Charlie Yahe, one of the Pine River Indians. They talked at the trading post and, finding Charlie intelligent and intriguing, the young priest said he would very much like to talk with him again. With a slight smile, Charlie Yahe invited Father Jungbluth to his place by the Halfway, near Holdup. Father Jungbluth said he would be there in a day or two, traveling with the loan of some dogs and a sled.

It was almost midnight when at last he spotted a light in the distance. He had been traveling all day, and was so tired that his snowshoes dragged like leaden weights. His dogs were also played out; one or the other from time to time would lay down in the snow as if about to die, and only the whip would bring him back to his feet. During the day a chinook wind had sprung up suddenly. The snow had become sticky and wet, adhering to the snowshoes and sled runners. Toward evening the winds calmed down and the cold returned, causing Father Jungbluth's pant legs, wet during the day, to freeze stiff. They now crackled as he walked.

The noise of furious barking greeted him, but over the howling and yelping of the dogs he heard another sound, a strange wailing that rose over a slow, steady drum beat. He pulled into the camp, but nobody came outside to greet him, no one looked out from the hut.

Charlie Yahe's small trapper's shack was just high enough so one could stand. In accordance with the Beaver custom, Father Jungbluth went to enter without knocking, but this time it was different; he stopped in front of the door, not knowing what to do. From inside throbbed the eerie beat of tom-toms and the rising wails of scarcely human voices. Fear caused him to lose any idea of custom, and he knocked loudly.

The tom-toms stopped abruptly, the wailing ceased, even the lights went out. Slowly he pushed open the homemade door of canvas stretched over a frame, and slid inside. In a voice that sounded strange even to himself, he cried, "*Denerraodetietchne!* The Man of Prayer!" and struck a match. Reflected in its glow was a row of dark faces, glowing and glistening with sweat, eyes either closed or open and lit with a light of frenzy. No one moved. A shiver ran from the priest's head down to his toes.

"*Denerraodetietchne!*" he repeated, and, softly, "The Little Beaver," the nickname the Beaver Indians had given him. The brown faces seemed to relax; some broke into smiles; his courage flowed back, and he too allowed his body to relax, his face to offer a smile. The bitch-light, made from a wick dipped in a dish of moose-grease, was again lit, and in its sputtering light he could see extended hands. He shook everyone's hand, even those of the wives who sat quietly in the back corners. The women shook hands like small timid children and looked down at the spruce-bough covered floor. After the greetings he squatted by the fire to warm up. His pant legs lost their stiffness, the little icicles that had adorned his nose and eyebrows disappeared.

His hunger was taken care of by a good piece of dried meat and hot tea, served in a tin can. Their welcome and their good food rejuvenated his spirits, but the apprehension still lingered. The celebrations had been broken off sharply by his arrival; the Indians looked worried and tense, and he still could not relax completely. They did not ask, as was the custom, how many signs of foxes he had seen on the trail, or at what distance the wolves were howling, or if he had seen any moose. They knew his thoughts: while his teeth worked to bring the dried meat to the swallowing point, he wondered whether Charlie Yahe, the one with the menacing eyes, was a sorcerer, a medicine man. Those eyes looked right through him and, while he knew that all the Indians there, with the exception of perhaps two men, had been baptized, he also knew they sometimes fell back into superstition, particularly belief in sorcery.

All of a sudden one Indian spoke: "Man of Prayer, when are we going to pray?" and Father Jungbluth stood up immediately.

"Yes, yes, pray! Right away," he said quickly. "Yes, pray, that is exactly what we must do." In his luggage he searched for the Father Lacombe picture catechism and carefully hung it upon the wall of rough logs. He lit two candles and, at the given signal, everyone fell on his heels.

They began with a general repetition of the Sign of the Cross, followed by the "Our Father" and the "Hail Mary." Word by word they labored, until eventually they reached the "Amen." More than one then took a deep breath, as if they had been under a strenuous task. Another hymn to the Blessed Virgin, in Beaver, but in the note of the "Ave Maria Stella," and at last the picture catechism was unfolded.

All drew close to get a better view; even the women crept out of their corners to view the Blessed Trinity, the Flood, Bethlehem. On the dark and gloomy way, leading to Hell, demons rushed against the bad Indians and hurled them into the Big Fire. "*Indaudetla* . . . it's too bad," breathed the audience. On the other side was the beautiful lighted way that led to Heaven; white angels accompanied the good Indians to see little Jesus.

The catechism lasted more than an hour, and Father Jungbluth's eyes were literally numb with fatigue; another short hymn, and more of "Our Father" and "Hail Mary" and "*Kwakula* . . . that's enough."

Sleep. Sleep. There in the corner his blanket was already spread. Even though the Indians had spit tobacco juice randomly all over the place, and a heap of stinking rags lay quite close to his head, he hardly noticed. He had but one craving: to sleep. A short "Prayer of the Evening," a "good-night," and he crawled inside his bedroll, spread upon spruce boughs over the frozen dirt floor. Sleeping bodies were strewn all over the floor, bedrolls and blankets spread wherever there was available space.

Father Jungbluth was just floating into sleep when he felt his shoulder being shaken by Charlie Yahe. He installed himself beside Father Jungbluth on the floor, and leaned on one elbow. "Man of Prayer," he whispered hoarsely, his face not far from Father Jungbluth's, "your prayer is good, but for whites. Mine is better."

Cautiously: "What prayers?"

"You heard them when you came in."

"You mean those dances and tom-toms and singing? That can please only the Devil!" But he said this with a chuckle in his voice, realizing the delicacy of the subject.

"No!" Charlie responded. His voice became sharp, like a pointed knife. "It's the real prayers of the Indian. It's just like we are calling the Great Spirits. When I sing like that and dance until I can dance no more and fall from exhaustion, then I get visions. I can see, for example, where to find a moose, or which plants to use to cure a certain illness."

Father Jungbluth kept quiet and listened carefully. Obviously, Charlie Yahe believed what he said.

Charlie Yahe argued his point for a while, and said, in Beaver, "Man of Prayer, don't worry. You are my guest. I know that you mean well for us. Sleep in peace."

But Father Jungbluth did not sleep so well anymore. In his mind he still heard the howling, the tom-toms, the frenzied dance of Yahe beside him, whose breath now came in peaceful, even rhythms. He could still see him as he leapt and jerked and fell, his eyes shining, his vision piercing through bodies and walls, seeing things that no one else could see.

Father Jungbluth slowly drifted off . . . to feel the Medicine Man stroking his arm, his hair . . . he was taking his hair! He uttered a scream as his hands flew up to defend his hair, a scream that was equalled by the shriek of the dog whose fur he had grasped in his two clenched fists. Whimpering from his attack, the dog scuttled over to find a more welcome warm place than against Father Jungbluth's head. He rolled over in his sleeping bag and tried once again to sleep.

Near morning, daylight filtered in through the floursack-covered window, illuminating his sleeping companions. A noise. He opened one eye and saw the Medicine Man crawling on hands and knees around the sleeping bodies. Yahe rummaged in a pile of clothing in one corner and withdrew a knife, his hunting knife. Sitting back on his heels he ran his thumb over the blade, testing its sharpness, then, putting the knife between his teeth, he quietly and cautiously crawled toward Father Jungbluth. Father couldn't bear to look; he closed his eyes and ceased breathing. "I am lost," he thought. His beating heart reverberated throughout the room. He stiffened, then cautiously opened one eye.

The Medicine Man knelt in front of the stove (which was a pit dug into the floor in the centre of the hut) and began shaving woodchips to start the fire.

After the Holy Mass they had breakfast, served like all other meals, on the floor, on a flour bag that was once white. The tea was strong and the meat he was given was the best dried meat in the camp. He began to stand up to get salt from his bag; immediately he was slammed down again by an Indian sitting at his side.

"You don't stand up!" the man whispered fiercely, still holding his arm. "You go like this." And he showed Father Jungbluth that he must crawl on hands and knees. Father Jungbluth hesitated. He did not understand, but somehow thought it best to do as he was told so, like a baby, he crawled over to his bag to reach the salt. On his return, his advisor pointed to the Medicine Man.

"He dreamed once that he was a moose. A moose cannot eat when he is interrupted, when he must put his head up to look. That's how he is. When he is eating, nobody has the right to stand up or walk about."

During the four days Father Jungbluth stayed at the camp, Charlie Yahe's wife, Bella, mumbled and muttered at the back of the hut, turning away and talking with her face toward the wall. It seemed to Father Jungbluth that she talked against him, that he shouldn't be there. She offered no tea, forcing the other women to take the part of the hostess; she would neither shake his hand nor smile. Her darting eyes stayed aimed at the floor whenever he addressed her. Father Jungbluth was troubled by her attitude.

Charlie Yahe's intelligence intrigued him. After his experience with Yahe, Father Jungbluth became more tolerant of Indian dances and strange rituals; he ignored their reverence to their amulets, the bones and pieces of bones that they kept in some kind of a medicine bag. Rarely did he call them superstitions anymore, but believed that often they were their way of praying to the Great Spirit. But he continued energetically to make Christians out of them nevertheless, citing the command of his master, Jesus: "Go, teach my name to all nations." The difference between the Indians' "Great Spirit" and the Christians' "Holy Spirit" was, he reasoned, that the Indians' spirits asked them often to do things that did not make sense. The Indians said their prayers gave them knowledge of where to find the deer or moose, or herbs for sickness. That might be beneficial, but they shouldn't claim it was spirits.

THE ICE MISSIONS

13

The Circuit Rider

*B*y the spring of 1938, Father Jungbluth had ventured, with Katie, across the Peace River ferry at Taylor Flats and cross-country to Moberly Lake.

"I had been traveling from Fort St. John enroute to East Pine, but part way there my horse played out. Somebody told me there was a German couple living at Sunset Prairie where I could stop over. It took me hours to get there — possibly because the road was so bad or because my horse was so tired, but when I arrived, my gosh, that fellow bawled me out!

"'That was too rough on her!' he said. 'You know the horse isn't like you. It can't stand quite as much!' And on and on he went. They took the horse in, fed her and stabled her down, and they also took care of me because I was tired too."

Those first years of traveling were hard on the man, but they were equally hard on the horse. "A dedicated missionary is one thing," people said, "but the horse hasn't taken the vows."

Mrs. Agnes Scheck of Fort St. John remembers feeling sorry for Katie. "Father Jungbluth couldn't carry the feed too, and it's quite a trek from here to Hudson's Hope or to Moberly or to the Halfway. It was too much for the horse sometimes . . . but it was too much for the man too. When he'd go on these trips he'd have to eat with the Indians, sleep with them, everything. But he was always happy. That's what he dedicated himself to. But that poor horse suffered a lot."

Father Jungbluth had his first big row with Father Schwebius, the parish priest in Fort St. John, over Katie. His companion argued that he drove the horse too hard; it was cruelty to animals, and he was going to report him to the Humane Society. Father Jungbluth, struggling with English, understood him to mean the "Human Society," and he laughed.

"Humane!" Father Schwebius thundered. "Humane! Not human!" He stalked out of the room, and Father Jungbluth could hear him stamping around in the church on the other side of their living quarters.

It was not the end of their arguments over Katie. In the spring, Father Jungbluth noticed that Katie seemed sluggish. He mentioned it to Father Schwebius. "No wonder," was his response. "You abuse her. She's not able to take such long trips in her condition."

"Condition? What do you mean, in her condition?"

"She's going to have a foal."

"A foal? Not possible! I use that horse all the time."

Father Schwebius put down his breviary and sat back, his hands folded in front of him. "Quite possible," he said. "When you were away, I took her to a stallion."

It was Father Jungbluth who now stormed out of the room, angry beyond words. A foal! Katie was his horse! He used her all the time. A foal would be a nuisance. Impossible!

The two priests hardly spoke for the next two days. It turned out that Katie was not in foal, but Father Jungbluth was still rankled by Father Schwebius' interference.

"I must admit that I sometimes used the horse too much," he says now. "Sometimes she was lame in the morning because I had got her too tired. That was the trouble with that horse anyway. She was a tall horse and her front feet were kind of weak, tender-footed. But I had her shod regularly, all four feet. I spent quite a bit of money on that horse, for in the summer the horseshoes are different from in the winter, when they have cleats for the ice.

"She was never really sick. I never had to leave her at home. If she was lame in the morning, I took off half the day, sometimes the whole day, so she could recover. I don't know why she would become lame. I just wanted to arrive where I wanted to go, so perhaps drove a little too long. At other times if I got there and there was nobody home, I would decide to go a few more miles to the next neighbor, and that was a little too hard on the horse."

Perhaps the horse and rider had, in fact, some similarities of disposition.

"She was a horse you had to hold back all the time; the minute I'd let the reins go, she'd start to run. The farmers said, 'If you let her go like that, she'll kill herself. In a couple of years she'll be finished.' But I liked the way she could run.

"I was quite surprised when Father Schwebius said I was too rough. I knew I was rough, but gosh, I had a hard life too. Why shouldn't my horse?"

Father Jungbluth never used a guide after his first experience with Jumbie. "When the trails branched off, I might follow the wrong trail for a half-mile [.8 km] or so, then come back to the fork and take the other trail for a ways before I made my decision," he recalls. "Sometimes I was wrong, but I learned then where the main trails were.

"I didn't take much food along. I was too tired to eat much. I practically never took a rifle. A rifle is just a big nuisance. The danger from wild game, bears or wolves, is so little. Sometimes in the night I saw — or thought I saw — the eyes of a wolf peering through the bush like two coals, and I heard them howl, but that's all."

Father Jungbluth bought a packhorse soon after moving to Fort St. John, thinking it would be of help to Katie, but the packhorse kept wandering off into the bush and Katie ended up taking most of the load, hauling the packhorse along. He tried putting the packhorse in front, but it was too slow. He sold the packhorse and reduced his gear. Instead of taking a tent he used a tarp to make a lean-to for the night, pegging the tarp down with two sticks at an angle according to the wind and rain.

In the spring of 1938, Father Jungbluth bought a motorcycle, a 250cc Frances Barnett. (It was called a 249cc on the registration papers in order to escape the higher tax imposed on 250ccs and up.) The English bike was judged light enough to traverse the snow and mud of the main trails. It was the first motorcycle in the country, and caused quite a sensation. He wrote about it to his readers across the sea:

> At last I have a motorcycle — a handsome gift from His Excellency, Bishop Langlois, OMI — for my work with the Indian and breed missions scattered around Fort St. John. Henceforth I shall be able to "fly" to the rescue of souls!
>
> The weather being ideal and the roads in good shape, I start on my round of summer visits, first to my mission in Moberly Lake 120 miles [192 km] away. Father Schwebius, still skeptical of the value of this new two-wheeled machine in such rough country, warns me to go slowly. The motor roars and the fresh wind whips against my face as, like a bullet, I pass the Hudson's Bay Company post where the trader looks at me like I once looked up at airplanes: with envy.

His distant readers were treated to a detailed portrait of a strange new figure on the northern landscape:

> My little bike is quite heavily loaded. On one side of the back wheel is my portable chapel and on the other side rides a suitcase containing my breviary, my sick-bag, a provision of rosaries and books of prayer in Cree and Beaver. Over the front wheel I have managed to place a larger suitcase containing my black cassock, my Oblate Cross, a change of clothing . . . and some provisions for the mouth. Finally, on top of everything lays my rolled sleeping bag and a little tent. The one-cylinder motor doesn't seem to protest as I balance myself comfortably on the large seat supported by two long springs, and I speed along at 40 miles per hour [64 km/h].
>
> In less than an hour I arrive at the Peace River ferry at Taylor Flats. By horse it took me a day. My little machine is taken onto the ferry and during the 10-minute ride across the river the ferryman examines the bike with great curiosity, exclaiming, "What a beautiful horse you have here, Father!" I reply, "Yes, and he doesn't eat very much. Not a gallon of gas for 100 miles."

Arriving at the other side of the river, we begin the long steep three-mile [5 km] incline, with lots of turns which call for wary driving. My bike is marvelous and shows me that it can climb with no stress or heating of the motor, and when we reach the top the motor resumes its usual quiet purr. I feel happy, content, free, and I begin singing loudly against the wind a Beaver hymn to the melody of "Ave Maris Stella," "Netta Nithron Marie."

With flashing speed I travel through the forests that before seemed interminable, past a stand of spruce trees where last winter I camped overnight during a blizzard. I whiz past a creek where my horse once took off and arrived at the ferry a day before me.

"My little bike is quite heavily loaded with my portable chapel, my rolled sleeping bag and a little tent . . ."

But the motorcycle was undeniably before its time. Father Jungbluth continues his vivid report with a growing consciousness of the machine's limitations:

Thus far the roads of packed dirt were good, though dusty, but now I approach the end of civilization. The road narrows and becomes rough, and then come long stretches of soft sand. My speed is reduced to 20 miles per hour [32 km/h], then 10. Finally I am crawling like a turtle as I weave past rocks and deadfall trees on a road that still demands to be constructed. The little machine lurches under its too-heavy load and threatens to fall over. My wrists stiffen as my hands grip tightly onto the handlebars and shake like with a fever. I manage somehow to hold on with the help of thrusting a foot once in a while to bring back my balance, but the motor is good and responds well to my manipulations. Finally I approach the East Pine River, but from the worst side for the wheels to attempt a descent. If Father Schwebius could see my descent he would be tranquilized, because I advance so slowly that I give the impression of hardly moving at all.

There is no bridge and no ferry to cross the river, just a basket suspended from a cable that reaches from one side of the river to the other. It wouldn't be impossible to attach the motorcycle underneath the basket and bring it over, but the old basket seems so dilapidated that it's enough that I risk my own life without also risking my machine. What would it serve to take it over? The other side has only a forest trail going through swamp where often even horses have a hard time getting through. So I hide my bike in an abandoned barn and look at it with a tender farewell. Then I get into the basket, taking with me only the most important parts of my luggage.

I stay the night with the Maddens, a good Irish family, and after breakfast one of the young boys harnesses for me a big heavy workhorse that, in the eyes of a motorcyclist, is the image of slowness. It is on this heavy thing that I must do the last 35 miles [56 km] to Moberly Lake. While I am attaching my chapel, my bedroll and the rest of my paraphernalia to the sides and back of the saddle, I ask myself if my motorbike hasn't already spoiled me, if I wouldn't feel the trip by horse too hard.

While the heavy horse takes his time, I meditate on the important news that I heard at the Maddens concerning the vital future of my mission at Moberly Lake. Apparently there is oil at this side of the river; the area has just been photographed from airplanes; it has been surveyed from one side to the other, and the government has decided to drill at Commotion Creek and probably also at Moberly Lake. A ferry is going to be constructed at East Pine and good roads will be built through the forests.

"You will soon be able to go to Moberly Lake on your motorcycle," Mr. Madden had said. At first Father Jungbluth liked this news. He wouldn't lose time and patience on the old horse such as the one he rode now. He would be able to leave Fort St. John in the morning and arrive at Moberly Lake at night, whereas before it took him a week. Then dark thoughts clouded his optimism:

But now I think about what the old missionaries often told me and what experience has already shown me: that contact with the whites too often spoils the Indians and ruins the fervor of the mission. The Beavers and Crees in Moberly Lake don't yet have the taste of modern amusements. They are ignorant but at the same time simple and poor, and I hope that there will never be big roads going through Moberly Lake. I hope that no car, no motorbike, ever comes to this side of the river. To bad that I should still have to do these 35 miles [56 km] on the laziest horse in the world! Certainly my motorbike is an excellent method of locomotion, fast and economical. But happy is the missionary of Indians who still has to go by horse.

Father Jungbluth sat back, pen in hand, and looked over what he had written. It seemed to indicate a turning point, a swift surge into a technical age. He thought of Katie, out in the corral, unaware of her impending obsolescence. He thought of the time last spring when he attempted to cross the Moberly River. Katie had refused to cross, even at his incessant urging. He had gone along the bank and tried her again at a place that looked like an easy approach, but again she refused. She didn't like the look of the ice and there was no way he could convince her to cross. She balked, reared, turned in tight circles, but she would not put a foot onto the ice. Finally he rode her back to the old crossing, brought his bags up in front and behind on the saddle, put up his feet and they waded across.

A side-car on skis provided extra capacity for supplies.

"That horse has more intelligence than you!" the Indians told him later when they heard him chastise Katie for her stubbornness. "If you would have gone where you wanted to, you would have drowned. There's a big hole there."

Still he continued to make full use of the motorcycle, covering his territory quickly, if not cleanly. People around Fort St. John recall seeing Father Jungbluth stuck in the heavy gumbo that massed the unpaved and largely ungravelled roads. One day, enroute from Kelly Lake to East Pine, he was pushing his clogged bike along the road when he was passed by a two-wheel cart pulled by two strong horses. The cart was filled to overflowing with girls. It seemed girls were hanging onto the sides, perched precariously on the back, girls everywhere. "Hello, Father!" they called as the horses pulled out and around him. He waved back, astonished. It turned out to be the Wright family from Goodfare on their way to the sports day at North Pine.

Father Jungbluth was quickly becoming known in the North, not only by his parishioners but also as a frequent subject of discussion among his fellow priests. Father J. Gerard Redmond, CSSR, a Redemptorist who met him when he was stationed in the Peace River country from 1937 to 1939, remembers Father Jungbluth on his motorcycle, "traveling not in a cloud of dust but in an overcoat of mud on the way to Grouard."

> There was a celebration at Grouard that day, in 1938. Vicariate priests from all over were congregating at the residential school where the festivities were taking place. I invited Father Jungbluth to travel from Grande Prairie with me by automobile, but he wished to bring his motorcycle to Grouard as he would be staying there for a while. So he set out on his bike.
>
> The trouble was that it had rained all night. The roads at that time were of dirt, not hard-top, not even gravel. Now and then one came to stretches of fearsome gumbo. It was very difficult to stay on the road with a car; it was impossible on a motorcycle.
>
> This was our strategy: Father Jungbluth went ahead on his motorcycle. I followed in the car. Whenever the gumbo plugged up his wheels, choking off his motor or causing him to slide into the rain-filled ditch, I would pass him. He would clutch onto a rope and be towed by the car through the muddy ruts. About every half-mile [.8 km] he would lose his balance and be towed through the mud for about 20 yards [18 m] before I could stop the car. Motorcycle and man were caked and blanketed with mud long before we reached Grouard, and thus Father Jungbluth made his entrance into the Bishop's residence.

The Indians enjoyed Father Jungbluth's new mode of travel. It was the first motorcycle they had seen. When the Indians heard the noise they ran out to the road to watch his arrival.

"I was just a young girl when he first came here," recalls Mary Gladu of Kelly Lake. "He was always full of fun. Everybody laughed. He was young and handsome. He had light brown hair, reddish-brown, you know. He'd have been in his early 30s then. First he brought the saddle horse, then the horse and buggy, and then later the motorcycle. You never knew what he was going to come in.

"He used to give rides to the older people. He'd go fast and turn around really quick, and oh! give them a scare! And they would laugh. He thought that was funny, making the old people scared. Celestin Gladu would get so scared, but every time Father came he wanted another ride. Father would take pictures and then come back and show us the pictures.

"He still jokes a lot with us, he's still funny. We really love him. He's a real nice person." Then, softly, "We're really going to miss him, in case he goes before us, eh?"

Taken in front of the cathedral at Grouard.

14
"Every Country has its Troublemakers"

After living for almost two years in Fort St. John with Father Schwebius, Father Jungbluth felt great admiration for his companion. The older priest had courage and daring. He was also, undeniably, outspoken. Father Jungbluth would often urge him to be less vocal in his opinions but to no avail. Father Schwebius was not a man to mince words.

He was also a terrible driver and his car often needed repairs. "You know what this country needs?" he would rage when presented with the bill. "It needs a Hitler!" That he was referring to "price-fixing", in protest over the ever-increasing costs for repairs, was often unclear to those who heard his remarks.

Father Jungbluth did not tell his supporters back home of the problems the war was creating for them, and especially for Father Schwebius. Although Father Schwebius had been a Canadian citizen for many years, and had come into the country around 1902, he was German at heart and loved his homeland. It enraged him to hear the Germans, one and all, being called down. Sometimes when he preached on Sunday he would bring up the subject.

"Every country has its troublemakers," he would cry to his congregation, who looked uneasily from one to the other. "In Germany, they had Bismark! In Italy, they have Mussolini!" He would pause a moment. "And in England . . ." he would thunder to the lowered heads of his parishioners, "in England, they have Churchill!"

Talk of war permeated every household. Germans were despised; even those with German names were looked upon with suspicion.

"I've been accused of being a Fifth Columnist," Father Schwebius whispered to Father Jungbluth one evening as they sat eating their evening meal in the hospital kitchen. His voice was unsteady. His hand shook as it supported his fork.

Finally the Fifth Columnist allegations reached the ears of the Bishop, who dispatched a telegram requesting Father Schwebius' presence before him immediately. "Leave right away," the message urged, "leave everything behind before you find yourself in a concentration camp."

But Father Schwebius was not one to let himself go without defence. Before leaving he visited all his friends. "See what I got from the Bishop?" he said, waving the telegram. "He wants me to come. If you want to keep me, write a letter right now to the Bishop telling him these allegations are untrue."

"Father Schwebius had many good qualities," Father Jungbluth says, recalling the situation. "He had a certain eloquence, he was very active, he was a good man even though his quickness of tongue often got him into trouble."

The letters were duly sent. The Bishop made inquiries on his own and decreed the accusations unfounded, so Father Schwebius won that round and returned. But in July when the priests were sent on their retreat, the Bishop issued Father Schwebius his obedience orders for another mission. Although many letters had been sent to the Bishop on Father Schwebius' behalf, it is possible that a similar number were sent from the parish asking that he be removed. He was moved to Berwyn, near Fairview, not too far away, and Father Otterbach was moved in to Fort St. John to take his place. By moving in another German, the Bishop perhaps felt it would take the barb out of Father Schwebius' transfer.

Father Jungbluth got along quite well with Father Otterbach, a young fellow who somewhat lacked the impetuosity of the older priest. Father Otterbach was a bit more refined, and Father Jungbluth, now a seasoned Northerner, used to laugh at him sometimes. Father Schwebius, for example, would go everywhere in his car. When the road was bad and people were getting stuck between Dawson Creek and Fort St. John, Father Schwebius could hardly control the urge to try it. Father Otterbach was the complete opposite: he would first ask how the road was and when he heard that someone had become stuck he went home. Father Jungbluth was like Father Schwebius in that regard: "Did one person get through?" he would ask, and then go. "Did one person get stuck?" Father Otterbach would ask, and then turn back.

The new priest arrived at a time when Father Jungbluth had decided to embark on his first major building project: a church at Moberly Lake. His trips there had convinced him that Moberly Lake would someday attract more people. He began saving money for the needed materials, and drumming up interest for volunteer labor and supplies. And this is where he ran into his first big blow-up with the new Father.

Father Otterbach enjoyed administration. He had the qualifications to handle money, and he informed Father Jungbluth that it should be his job to administer the funds that came into and went out of the parish. Father Jungbluth objected. The parish was Father Otterbach's, but the missions were his, and he could handle the money slated for them.

When the Provincial Superior came for a visit, he was quietly informed by Father Otterbach that "things were not quite right." Father Birch called the two priests in together and gave them a lesson on how the Rule of the Oblates should be honored, and how a Vow of Poverty meant obtaining permissions. Father Jungbluth sat and sulked.

("I handled my own money and I wasn't going to tell Father Otterbach how much I had and where it was spent. And I was right!" Father Jungbluth relates. "I bought a motorcycle and all these things, but always with permission of the Bishop. I didn't bother with the Provincial too. The Bishop was my boss. I was saving to build the church at Moberly Lake and I was also looking after my horse and my motorcycle and it kept me pretty poor, so I didn't think much of the talk he was giving us, really. And that's what grated the Provincial. He felt I should turn in all the money, then ask for it back. I didn't want to do that because Father Otterbach had no idea what the costs were for things at Moberly Lake. He might have refused me this or that, thinking it was too expensive. Besides, I was getting my own money from benefactors overseas. I wrote my benefactors, I sent them stories, I solicited money from them for my missions. It was mine to spend on my missions.")

Father Birch turned suddenly on Father Jungbluth. "I want to bring to your attention that I feel the Vow of Poverty is not being observed in this House!" he thundered. "No accounts have been submitted. My instructions have not been observed." Dead silence. Father Jungbluth vaguely remembered receiving a letter directed to everybody stating there was to be an accounting submitted for all funds. In those days, the hierarchy was strict, and Father Birch was the most austere of all.

"And what about accounts for the Masses?" Father Birch continued, leaning forward in his chair. "Which is supposed to be for the House!"

When he made reference to the one or two dollar donations received for saying special Masses, Father Jungbluth knew he had him in mind, very much. So he spoke up: "Father," he said, "it's not quite right, what you're saying here."

The man exploded. He jumped out of his chair. "When I am in the chair, I am in the chair!" cried Father Birch. "Nobody has the right to interrupt me. One more word from you and I will close my book, get up, depart, and disciplinary action will follow!"

Father Jungbluth cowered — Father Birch was a big man — but he wasn't exactly frightened; he just didn't say anything more. Father Birch carried on. Then toward the end, when Father Jungbluth thought he might be winding down, Father Birch said abruptly, "That money you receive from overseas, from your so-called benefactors, where does it go?"

Father Jungbluth just looked at him. "To my missions," he replied in a quiet voice, "To my work, which is the intent of the donors."

"It's all supposed to go to the House. To the Superior."

Father Jungbluth said nothing.

"Furthermore," Father Birch continued, "didn't I give instructions that the Masses usually celebrated in the House, the money you receive for saying special Masses, goes to buy food for the House and to help pay our expenses? Did you do that?"

"Yes."

This time Father Birch went into a true rage. "I can show you in black and white [his favorite expression] that this is not so!" And he brought out the book of the Masses. Every time a Mass was said, the date and the amount of the offering was inscribed in the book. Sure enough, Father Jungbluth saw columns under his name marked "pro me," (for myself, for my missions). From time to time one was marked, "pro domo" (for the House). Entries marking bi-monthly Masses prayed for the eternal rest of the Fathers who had died in the congregation were likewise marked "pro me" under Father Jungbluth's name.

"How do you explain that now?" asked Father Birch.

Father Jungbluth laughed to himself. He knew he should have given his explanation immediately, but since Father Birch had bawled him out right from the beginning, he hadn't felt in the mood to respond. But the time had come to give him something. "Yes, I wanted to give all my money from these Masses to the House," he said, "but then Father Otterbach gave me instructions that this money was to be used to pay my gas and repairs and all my mission expenses. The first time I gave my monthly account to Father Otterbach he looked at it — do you remember, Father? — and he said, 'So much? From now on say your own Masses and pay your own damned bills!' He told me that, so that was the instruction from the House itself."

There was utter silence in the room.

"And furthermore," Father Jungbluth continued, "since Father Otterbach told me to pay my own expenses I didn't hand in the money, but I gave him a financial statement at the end of each month. Is that not so?"

Father Birch looked at Father Jungbluth, then over at Father Otterbach. Father Birch coughed and walked over to the window. His voice seemed strangely hollow as it bounced from the windowpane back to his audience of two: "Father Otterbach," he said stiffly, "that is quite different from what you told me."

Father Jungbluth looked sideways at Father Otterbach. He looked back and smiled weakly.

They had been friends, and it was Father Jungbluth's opinion that Father Otterbach could have been more frank. They had talked everything over together, their work, the cost of their operations, everything, but it cooled off a bit after that incident.

At the end of each month, Father Jungbluth handed in an account, and that was it. Slowly the two priests regained their former trust and again became friends.

"You know," Father Jungbluth says reflectively, "Birch apologized to me afterward. Not in a very formal way, but he let me know he was distressed over the incident. But somehow I felt he never really liked me after that. I came to suspect it even more after I moved to Moberly Lake and he seemed to forget about me completely for two years. I had to live off the Indians, and the fish I managed to catch from the lake.

"But that's another story."

15

When God Made Time . . .

*B*uilding a church at Moberly Lake was now Father Jungbluth's immediate objective. The location in the Rocky Mountain foothills was prime: a lake 19 kilometres long, over three kilometres wide, rich with jackfish and lake trout. The lake had been named after Henry Moberly, a Hudson's Bay Company fur trader who resided there from 1865 to 1868. Some time later, after the Riel Rebellion in 1885, a band of Saulteaux Indians from Saskatchewan found their way to the area, guided by a vision of a lake lying east and west, guarded to the west by twin mountain peaks. When they arrived at Moberly Lake their vision came to life, and there they stayed.

Treaties established two separate reserves: one at the east end for some 300 Saulteaux and Cree Indians, and one at the west end for 100 Beaver Indians. An increasing number of white people chose Moberly Lake as well. The surrounding land was arable, and the fur trade and big game still provided a good living.

Father Jungbluth liked the people of Moberly Lake, and it seemed they liked him in return. He thought of old Matilde, an Indian woman who had sent a message to him in Fort St. John. She was dying, she said, and wanted to make her confession. He set out immediately on horseback to make the three-day trip. It was autumn and a cold misty rain had been falling for the better part of a week. He arrived in Moberly Lake with his clothing heavy with rain, his body chilled, both man and horse exhausted, and immediately turned his horse down the trail to old Matilde's cabin.

His knock was answered by a youngster, a grandchild or perhaps a great-grandchild of Matilde. The interior of the cabin was dark and the air close. Through the gloom he could barely see the old lady lying on a bed in a far corner. He greeted her in Beaver.

"No priest," she mumbled. "No more sick." She had recovered and now had no need for confession or to take communion.

Father Jungbluth sat down on a chair beside her cot. "Well then," he said, "I have come for nothing. But it is a three-day trip back to Fort St. John and I am not leaving until I'm good and ready. My horse and I both need a rest. We will stay here with you."

Matilde's old eyes blinked rapidly.

"Yes, I will stay right here," Father Jungbluth continued brightly, looking about the room as if to secure a place to lay his bedroll, "and I will eat your meat and drink your tea until you have nothing anymore." The two looked at each other. "I will eat you poor," he added.

The next morning after Matilde made her confession and took Holy Communion, Father Jungbluth set out for Fort St. John. It came as no surprise to receive a message two weeks later that Matilde had passed on.

It was not easy to gain respect. No one was sitting waiting for a priest. He had to prove first that he was a man, competent and rugged enough to withstand the severe climate as well as the natures of the people who populated it. Only then might they listen to his message. He had excelled at theology and felt a total commitment to teaching the gospel. But first, it seemed, he must sell himself.

"When was the last time you met someone like me?" he would ask when he met a new group of Indians. Or, "I just came from Moberly Lake. Do you know William Calliou? He is a good friend of mine." In response to their nod, "I stayed at his place and I bring you his greetings." Then he might produce presents, brightly colored holy pictures, medals, rosaries.

"How many people are in the camp? It would be good to have a meeting. You can point out to me who is sympathetic." Sometimes there was silence and he had to say, "Well, it is a nice day," shake hands and go on to another camp. He relied on the Indians' natural hospitality. Although they seldom put anyone out the door, it was important not to offend. He gave the canonical rule against eating meat on Fridays a wilderness interpretation: if there was a choice, he would not eat meat. He accepted meat if it was the only thing offered. If his hosts were Catholic and should know better, he might venture to say, "Well, you know it's Friday . . ."

At times he found himself in a Protestant home and often got the feeling that his hosts were sitting back thinking, "Now let's see what he is going to do." In such cases he chose his words carefully: "It's Friday, you know, and I should not eat any meat. But, I see you have cooked just meat and there's nothing else. I don't want you to go to any trouble of frying me some eggs or anything like that. Therefore, I eat what is on the table."

At times he had to abstain from eating meat if they appeared scandalized as he reached for the platter, and he would hurriedly pass it on. In any case, a short explanation was usually offered. Some priests might just have eaten a potato or vegetables, but he didn't do that. "I didn't want to fall down on the trail," he says, laughing, "but, I didn't feel I had to pontificate exactly. I valued the hospitality I was offered, anywhere."

Winning the respect of the Indians was one thing; convincing other whites of his virtues and purpose was another.

Harry Garbitt was an important man in Moberly Lake. He had left his home in Aberdeen, Scotland, at 16 and had shown up in the Peace country around 1895. He worked as a fur buyer, trapper, and in his later years as mail hauler and trading-post operator. He spoke fluent Saulteaux and Cree, and was married to an Indian woman, Martha Desjarlais. Her father, William, had signed the treaty for the East End Reserve. Father Jungbluth had met Harry and his wife briefly on his reconnaissance trip through Moberly Lake in 1936. Now that he was a frequent visitor to the area and no longer a stranger to whom hospitality is offered as a matter of course, he got the feeling that Harry Garbitt was not too impressed with him.

Harry was not in favor of the attempts of strangers to improve the Indians: "Education is no good for an Indian!" he would say, shifting the big stogie from one side of his mouth to the other. "The more Indians are around whites, the worse they become — lying, stealing, wanting something for nothing."

Father Jungbluth once visited Harry at dinnertime along with Margaret "Ma" Murray, the great lady who along with her husband George ran the weekly newspaper, *The Alaska Highway News*, out of Fort St. John. She was a good friend of Harry and Martha Garbitt, and would make a trip out to Moberly Lake as often as possible to "cover the news."

Ma was greeted with enthusiasm, but Father Jungbluth with bare civility. Harry took another plate from the cupboard and set it on the table. Pulling up a chair he said, "C'mon, Ma, have a bite here with us."

"I didn't know if he was being directly unkind, or if he just figured priests didn't have to eat," Father Jungbluth says, remembering the situation, "but it left me quite embarrassed."

Father Jungbluth sat in a chair, somewhat near the table but not at it. He looked around the room. In a corner stood Harry's radio, one of those high wooden-cabinet affairs with a dial pointing out Tokyo, San Francisco, practically anywhere in the world. "May I look at your radio?" Father Jungbluth inquired.

"Go ahead and look at it all you want," Harry replied. "That's all you can do with it. It doesn't work."

Father Jungbluth examined its inner works. A tube was in the wrong place and some wires were loose or missing. "I might be able to fix it for you," he offered.

In a few minutes the house was filled with static, then faint voices, then a full-bloomed burst of song. Harry walked over to the cupboard and took down another plate.

From that time on, Harry Garbitt and Father Jungbluth were the best of friends. Although Harry remained a *mécréant* (an unbeliever), their friendship lasted many years until Harry's death and opened many doors for the young priest, for Harry was respected by Indians and whites alike.

William Calliou was another such man, considered the patriarch of Moberly Lake. A non-status Indian, he had received some education and religious instruction at Lac Ste. Anne in Alberta. William donated two acres of lakeshore land to be used for the church and graveyard, the latter to be on the hill rising up from the lake, the church down below near the shore.

The first grave in the new cemetery was that of William Calliou's wife. She died shortly after Father Jungbluth's first visit to Moberly Lake and was buried by the Indians in Father Jungbluth's absence. He blessed the grave upon his return.

There was no difficulty in recruiting a willing crew for church-building in Moberly Lake. William MacDonald from Lac Ste. Anne was the superintendent. An excellent carpenter himself, he showed the volunteers how to make saddle corners. The logs were hauled across the ice from the far side of the lake where the timbers grew to large diameters, and all were donated. The windows and nails and other necessary pieces of hardware were obtained partly from the Bishop and largely from the Church Extension Society of Toronto. Their gift of $500 bought nearly everything they needed. Few nails were used, and the shingles (or shakes) were made by Maurice Paquette. He soaked the pine logs, 40 centimetres long and split into square blocks, in a big tub of hot water overnight, which softened them for cutting. He then placed the soaked logs on a low table, set the guide, and used a big black gelding horse named Jake to pull the rough 3.5-metre diameter wheel (or horse-froe). As the horse made his rounds, the blade fell methodically, splitting the shakes.

"Oh, that Maurice Paquette is smart," thought Father Jungbluth as he watched the precision-cut shakes fall into a pile. Maurice kept some hay in the manger so the horse could grab some during pauses while the men cleared away the pile of split shakes. For rafters they used straight poles, still in place to this day. Only the shakes have had to be replaced.

The road to Moberly Lake from Fort St. John posed a major problem for transporting materials. Twisted string-lines of bush road would ripple into a series of sharp little hills that could barely be scaled. The track would then fall into deep descents where drags were needed to slow down the charging wagons. In places the road dipped into sloughs, muskeg and gumbo. Wheels stuck fast, causing even a good team to bog down helplessly.

"There was no difficulty in recruiting a willing crew for church-building in Moberly Lake."

Always on the look-out for a bargain, Father Jungbluth persuaded the Bowes and Herron Garage in Fort St. John to save all their used oil for a preservative for the logs and shingles of the new church. As the wagon brought in a load of precious windows and the oil from Fort St. John, an accident occurred on one of the sharper hills. The image will never leave Father Jungbluth's mind of the horses screaming with fear, sliding backward down the greased hillside as the wagon jack-knifed and tumbled over the bank. There was sudden silence, broken only by the snorting horses as they tried to gain their feet and rid themselves of the burden still hitched to their traces. The upturned wagon lay with its four wheels spinning in air. Father Jungbluth scrambled around in the mud, trying to quiet the horses and right the wagon. When the horses were under control and the wagon set upright, he surveyed the damage.

Dirty motor oil spurted from split ten-gallon pails, soaking through his food supplies, staining his portable chapel, bedroll and clothing. But what about the windows? He anxiously shook the crates. No slivers of tinkling glass fell from the slits. All the windows had survived. But the odor of the dirty used motor oil stayed for weeks.

"Is your church at Moberly Lake now finished?" Bishop Ubald Langlois inquired of Father Jungbluth. They had met at the yearly retreat in Grouard. "Will you invite me to bless it?"

Father Jungbluth could hardly sleep that night from worrying about the Bishop's safe transport. Even in the best dry season a traveler was continually ambushed by rocks, ruts, deadfall trees and brush that reached out to tangle the wheels and slap the riders. And if it were raining, could the Bishop make the trip on a horse? The next morning he summarized the difficulties.

"That's alright," the Bishop replied nonchalantly, "I'm sure I've seen worse."

The plan was for Father Jungbluth to meet the Bishop in Dawson Creek in three weeks time and escort him to Moberly Lake. On the appointed day one of the Dawson Creek priests drove them as far as a car could go, to the East Pine River. There they crossed by means of the overhead baskets strung on cables, first crossing the East Pine, then making a one kilometre portage, and crossing the Murray River by the same method. The Murray had flooded its banks in March, killing eight people and many animals. Now the crossing was made without incident. On the other side, they looked in vain for the Indian man who was to take them over the last, most treacherous 56 kilometres from the East Pine to Moberly Lake. The man had instructions to be there at ten o'clock in the morning. He finally showed up with two horses and a wagon at four o'clock in the afternoon, too late to go all the way to Moberly Lake.

"You were supposed to be here at ten o'clock!" Father Jungbluth cried. "You promised me. I was waiting for you."

The Indian man looked down at his boots, then into the eyes of the enraged priest. "I promised that I will be here if I can make it . . . but I couldn't make it."

"What happened?"

"I couldn't find the horses."

"Why did you let the horses go? Why didn't you keep them in overnight?"

"The grass is green. I was just going to let them loose a little bit. But I couldn't find them in the morning."

There was nothing to do but travel as far as Jackfish Lake and camp overnight with Peter Calliou, a son of William, then continue on to Moberly Lake in the morning.

The road beyond Jackfish Lake was too bad to take the wagon so Calliou gave them horses. The Bishop seemed comfortable so Father Jungbluth relaxed and enjoyed the scenery, trying to see it through the Bishop's eyes. The rippling leaves of poplar trees were a bright June green. Birds called from tree to tree. Even the wind sighed melodiously as it dried up the rutted mud that served as the road into Moberly. In the bush the roads took a long time to dry, kept cool by the shade of tall poplars, tamaracks and evergreens crowding in from both sides. The road steepened over the rise of the mountain. Reaching the crest, they slid down the trail over deadfall that had succumbed to the heavy snow load and bitter wind.

They arrived finally at the Moberly Lake church. Father Jungbluth showed the Bishop the small living quarters behind the altar where he would be sleeping. It smelled of new logs and old oil.

That night the mosquitos attacked, pushing in through spaces between unchinked logs. The Bishop fought them bravely. He flailed his arms, yelled and thrashed again. Later, in the dark of night, perhaps on the recommendation of the mosquitos, came one or two mice which nibbled his ears. He said they did. Maybe so and maybe not, for Father Jungbluth slept through it all in a tent pitched beside the church.

"Sometimes a mouse would make a dash and run right over my face," the Bishop said, "right while I rested in the bed I thought looked so secure, high above the floor. Have you experienced that?"

"Well, yes, although I didn't think much of it," Father Jungbluth admitted. "Sometimes I feel a little something around my head and if I grab quickly I have a mouse in my hand. Squeak! I just fling it outside."

(Later on Father Jungbluth learned to sleep under a "mosquito bag", a square tent on four posts that fit over the bed. After the material was securely tucked in under the blankets, the hunt began for the mosquitos trapped inside. If he was careful to catch every one, flushing them out from all corners, he was assured of a few hours' comfort.)

Father Jungbluth relaxed and enjoyed the scenery, trying
to see it through the Bishop's eyes. Church of St. Theresa, Moberly Lake, B.C.

In the summer of 1939, Father Jungbluth was called to conduct his first funeral at Moberly Lake. The deceased was his friend and benefactor, William Calliou. There were no legal formalities, no doctor, no death certificate, no records. Harry Garbitt and Father Jungbluth looked after the arrangements; the family dressed the body.

After the funeral, Calliou's numerous sons brought to the church a big box, almost as large as a coffin, and asked Father Jungbluth if they could leave it in the church for a year. It seemed that William Calliou's possessions were in the box and the sons wished to wait 12 months before they were divided. This way, they said, there would be no misunderstandings, no dispute. A year later they opened the box together and divided up a nice hunting knife, boots, a gun and other possessions. There was no friction.

The Indians made their own coffins, always with a double "outer" box. Sometimes Father Jungbluth made the coffin, and kept boards handy for that purpose. The family of the departed would line the coffin with pieces of cloth or a sheet and put in a few religious articles — a crucifix, prayer beads, a medal. The outer box was intended to protect the inner coffin from the elements. The ground was hard and often a corner of the cumbersome outer box got stuck. Father Jungbluth's sense of decorum was often disturbed by one of the pallbearers jumping on top to joggle the coffin back and forth until it could be lowered by ropes to its final resting place. Women and children of the bereaved family wailed without restraint throughout the proceedings.

The Indian agent, Mr. Galibois, objected to the informal recordless burial system and in one case demanded that the body be exhumed. Father Jungbluth reported to the family that the agent wanted the body dug up. "Let him come here," said the family spokesman, "we'll just see what he does!" But he never came.

From then on, Harry Garbitt and Father Jungbluth began to make out death certificates, but it was a long one- or two-day trip to Pouce Coupe to register the death and secure a burial permit from the government agent. Sometimes when road conditions were extremely poor, Harry would say, "Oh, we can do all that later. We'll bury him right now." The certificate would be made up when the agent or the doctor came, often much later.

Now that the church was built, with living quarters in the back, Father Jungbluth endeavored to get to Moberly Lake as often as possible. It seemed exceptionally important to be at Moberly for Christmas in 1939, the first Christmas in the new church. He left Fort St. John a good week early, traveling with Katie and a sleigh. The weather was bitterly cold and the snow deep. He had been advised to go later when the cold snap ended, but was determined to be on time.

Katie pulled the sleigh very slowly and with great effort through the deep snow, with Father Jungbluth following. He had been on the trail nearly a week and he was still 56 kilometres from his destination. With Christmas just two days away, he began to fret. He had once been asked why few used dogsleds for traveling in this area. He fervently wished he was following a team of barking dogs now, rather than this panting plunging horse. In Fort St. John a good dogsled cost as much as a horse, and he would need at least four dogs.

The trail narrowed and shrubs closed in to the point of obliterating the track. It became apparent they would never make it in time. Remembering the instructions of various northern teachers, he unharnessed the horse, parked the sleigh under a tree, and hung the harness high up in the branches away from hungry animals. He then drew a blanket over the horse, climbed on her back and proceeded down the trail.

The weather seemed to have warmed a bit and he was quite sure of the way. Soon he would arrive at Jackfish Lake where he could spend the night with Peter Calliou. A warm bear hide would give comfort and warmth to his tired bones! He could now see the cabin but there seemed to be no smoke coming from it. Probably Calliou was already at Moberly Lake, waiting for him.

"There is a certain communism in the Indian way of life," Father Jungbluth mused, "but it follows the Christian way. Everyone has the right to set foot into an empty cabin and spend the night, to take things to eat if there is anything. It is not considered theft." He dismounted and opened the door.

There was enough wood inside to start a good fire under the kettle. With no barn, the poor horse would have to remain outside. He gave Katie all the blankets he could spare and spread them over her back. A quick look into the faithful eyes, and he turned and shut the door.

The next day, the day before Christmas, dawned extremely cold, with an icy north wind blowing. Half an hour down the trail the sky showed signs of an approaching storm. It became colder. The wind whipped at his face and through his clothes. Katie was already covered with ice and snow from the warm fumes from her breath that froze immediately. Icicles hung from her nostrils.

Father Jungbluth hunched forward, trying to hide his face in his furs. He could no longer see. His eyelids were encrusted with ice-curds. He rubbed his face constantly to prevent freezing, but had less and less feeling in his hands and feet. He slid stiffly off the horse and stumbled in front, breaking trail, holding onto the bridle. He felt like a drunkard as he lurched from side to side. His legs could barely move; it was all he could do to just drag them through snow that whipped in behind his footsteps as if he had never passed.

He was well aware of his condition and realized he must stop and light a fire before he got frostbite. Only two more hours would see him in Moberly Lake, but the important thing was not to freeze to death. Fumbling, he collected dry spruce twigs from the undersides of trees and piled them into a brushy cone. Lighting the fire was a problem; he could no longer hold a match, although he tried again and again to make that single bold strike. In vain. He remounted the horse, his last hope to hurry before both of them froze to white statues on the trail.

The horse trembled and snorted as she sunk with each step deep into the snow, shifting from the right side to the left; finally she fell onto her knees. It was then that the advice of an old missionary came back: "If you can no longer keep a match in your frozen fingers, hold the matchbox in your hands, pull a match out with your teeth, hold it firmly and rub it onto the matchbox until it lights." He had added, "And never give up. Otherwise, you are lost."

He returned to his little pile of spruce branches. He knelt, opened the matchbox and brought out a match with his tongue, keeping it tight in his lips. Then, holding it between his teeth, he shook his head from side to side. It sparked, then sent up a tiny flame. Before he burned his nose he dropped the match onto the pile of twigs, calling upon all the saints in Heaven to guide its spark into a flame.

It worked. He was saved. Even the horse seemed delighted with the warmth of the fire, for she came in slowly, approaching with head and nose.

"No Indian would leave a campfire in this cold weather," he thought. "It must be all of 50 below zero."

He stayed by the fire the rest of the day, venturing away only to gather more wood. It was Christmas Day. What would the Indians be thinking?

Christmas Eve and a new church and no priest had come to celebrate Midnight Mass. Such neglect.

He arrived in Moberly Lake the next day, Boxing Day, to find the Indians anxious but not in the least disturbed about the delay.

"That paleface of a man," one said. "He is much too heedless. In such cold nobody ever should stray from the warmth of a fire. It could mean death."

Father Jungbluth was disturbed. He only wanted to be there in time to celebrate Christmas with them. He told them so, with a bit of a pout, and they laughed. One added, so wisely that he cringed from the tender rebuke, "Man of Prayer, can't one celebrate Christmas one or two days later in such a case? When God made time, He made plenty of it. Why should you ever be in a hurry?"

He turned to hide his red face, and looked out the frost-encircled window of the little church to see Sam, one of the Indian men, leading the ice-covered horse to its well-deserved rest in Calliou's stable.

16
The Alaska Highway

On a cold Sunday afternoon during Advent in 1942, an event occurred in Fort St. John that was to become a legend.

The High Mass, conducted by Father Otterbach in the St. John the Apostle Church in Fort St. John, had been completed. The farmers had hitched up their teams, relit the small stoves in their cabooses, and with a jingling of bells and a trail of pungent woodsmoke, headed for home. Father Otterbach felt chilled as he entered the sacristy at the back of the church. He stocked up the gas-barrel stove with green wood and wearily curled up beneath the heavy quilt he had won at a bazaar. The next service was not until seven o'clock in the evening, the Benediction of the Blessed Sacrament in the hospital chapel.

He had barely drifted into that agreeable numbness which precedes a good sleep when a loud knock sounded at the door. He burrowed deeper into the quilt. The knock persisted. Eventually his conscience dictated he should get up and see who was there. He threw back the quilt and sat on the side of the bed, rubbing his eyes. The knock grew louder.

"Hold your horses, I'm coming!" Still yawning, he stumbled to the door in his bare feet. A stocky officer stood outside.

"Good evening, Father," he said. "I hope I'm not disturbing you. My name is Spellman."

Father Otterbach stood staring, suddenly unaware of the blast of wind that ruffled his shirt and whipped around his bare feet. "Not Cardinal Spellman?" Father Otterbach said softly. "Cardinal Spellman from New York?"

"You bet your life! Now may I come inside before I freeze to death?" Then, noticing the bared feet of the priest he said, "O quam pulchri . . . how beautiful the feet of those who spread the gospel."

While Father Otterbach hurriedly buttoned his shirt and pulled on his socks, Cardinal Spellman explained that he was on his way to Alaska to celebrate Christmas with the American troops stationed there. His plane was being serviced on the airstrip just outside Fort St. John and he decided to see if he could find a priest to give the Midnight Mass to "the boys who were punching the road from Dawson Creek to Alaska."

Father Otterbach assured the Cardinal that he had a companion called Jungbluth who visited the soldiers' camps, but right now he was with the Beaver Indians at Hold Up — or was it Squaw Creek? Yes, Jungbluth had already made arrangements to celebrate the Midnight Mass at the camp.

"Fine, Father, fine. I was just checking." The Cardinal, warming his back by the gas-barrel stove, looked around at the small unpainted room shared by the two priests. "Is this your year-round palace?"

"No, no, this isn't all. Father Jungbluth lives upstairs."

Cardinal Spellman's eyes followed the stovepipe up through a hole to a dark frosted attic. "Up there?" he said incredulously.

"It's good enough," Father Otterbach said with a shrug. "He says it's better than his last place."

The Cardinal was still for a moment. "Well," he said in a quiet voice, "if you fellows don't get to Heaven, there's not much chance for me." Then, as quickly as he had appeared, he left, roaring off in his waiting jeep.

The forces of war were pulling settlers away from the North to foreign fronts, even as the American government was bringing in truckloads of southern army personnel to build a defence road from Dawson Creek, British Columbia, 2,400 kilometres northwest to Fairbanks, Alaska.

"It's a race against time!" the news broadcasters said. "The Japanese are in the Aleutian Islands. North America is being threatened by invasion."

Supplies and equipment trucked through Fort St. John, continued north over the old Nelson Trail to Fort Nelson, and on to the Liard River. Local packtrains were hired to transport supplies further. The highway changed the economy, the customs and the geography of Father Jungbluth's old Indian territories. It was also to create an abrupt diversion to his missions.

Father Jungbluth on his 250cc motorcycle on the muddy roads of the newly constructed Alaska Highway (at Charlie Lake). Sign says "Fairbanks, 1,459 miles."

He wrote on Sunday, May 11, 1943, to *La Voix,* the official publication of his diocese in Grouard:

The 341st Regiment of the American soldiers arrived in Fort St. John. With the absence of Father Beaucage, who is in Fort Nelson, it is me who has been asked to assure the religious services at Charlie Lake where 1,200 men reside in two camps.

On Sunday, May 10, 1942, I celebrated the Mass in open air in the military camp. About 130 soldiers, plus the people of Charlie Lake, attended this Mass and 23 soldiers received the Holy Communion.

The other evening I went to visit them and I had a lot of fun. An evening with the soldiers is equal to 10 days of holidays, they are so comic. I had supper with them, then I played the harmonium in an improvised orchestra, and they were singing, "Holy, Holy" and the "Ave Maria" with great inspiration. I gave a ride on my motorcycle to the blackest of the bunch, and they tell me that he became white with fear.

Father Jungbluth's first Mass was offered at 7:00 a.m., 112 kilometres from Fort St. John; the second at 10:30 a.m., 130 kilometres from Fort St. John; and the third at 2:00 p.m., 147 kilometres from home. The soldiers in the more remote camps who attended the second and third Masses had not seen a priest for two months.

On August 22, 1942, Father Jungbluth received his official orders from the Military Ordinariate of the United States of America:

Dear Sir:

We have appointed the bearer of this letter, the Reverend E. Jungbluth, OMI, of Fort Saint John, British Columbia, as an Auxiliary Chaplain to serve the Catholic personnel under your command in the absence of a Catholic Chaplain.

We commend him to your good offices and we trust that he may be given such access to the military areas as may be necessary for the performance of his spiritual duties.

Respectfully submitted, John F. O'Hara, CSC

This appointment to Auxiliary Chaplain was to last as long as there were American soldiers in the area.

The extra duties allowed Father Jungbluth to apply for a privilege unique to the Catholic Church at that time: he was the first to get permission — in the North, anyway — to have a cup of coffee between Masses, and to say Mass after noon. These special privileges, granted to service the army, were

While Auxiliary Military Chaplain, 143rd Regiment,
U.S. Army, during the construction of the Alaska Highway.

bestowed by the religious authority of the army in New York, the Head Catholic Chaplain of the American Army (and Cardinal Spellman's co-adjutant), Bishop O'Hara.

Father Jungbluth explains:

> The permission came because of the amount of traveling involved from camp to camp. Even at that time we were not allowed to eat or even have a drink of water between midnight Saturday night and noon, after the last Mass, on Sunday. We weren't supposed to even have a drop of water. Some even claimed that you should not wash your teeth on Sunday morning because you might swallow water; that was exaggerated, definitely, but, it was our way too, the Church's way, to show respect for the Blessed Sacrament, for the real presence.

Every month Father Jungbluth reported to New York how it had helped to have a cup of coffee, and how many he had.

> They were strict! They didn't want any abuses to come into the Church. And we observed that. I remember sometimes I would get up at three o'clock in the morning to feed the horse before I had to go 30 miles [48 km] on horseback to say the Mass around Rose Prairie. We tried to eat as late as possible. Just before midnight, Father Otterbach and I would go to the hospital where we

were eating and prepare a good, good lunch, real solid . . . and then we were looking at the clock. When it was just five minutes to midnight we'd hurry, just shovel it in, and then when we saw the hand on midnight or heard the gong, we wouldn't take anymore. Just left the rest on the plate.

Shortly after the visit by Cardinal Spellman, Father Jungbluth gave a special Midnight Mass in the principal camp half-way to Fort Nelson. The roads were well-frozen by Christmas Eve, and the big command car sent to bring Father Jungbluth to the camps had no need to use the squealing radio to call for help to haul them out of drifted ditches.

The recreation hall had been transformed into a chapel: pin-up pictures had been removed or covered over with spruce boughs. A table, supported by four tall milk cans, served as an altar. The Protestant chaplain had donated a collapsible organ. By midnight the hall was full of soldiers.

The four-voice choir, trained hurriedly by Father Jungbluth, began with *Adestes Fideles*, but soon were joined by the men sitting on rows of benches. Father Jungbluth pumped furiously on the asthmatic little organ which wheezed along in a "faltering tremolo." The voices became louder, overpowering the choir and the organ, until the rafters overhead shivered in sympathy. Father Jungbluth played on, his mind whirling.

"What a puny protest voices make against the magnitude of the war that rages against them," he mused. The men sang abnormally loud in an attempt to drown out the wind, the cold, and their own icy fears. The gas lamps that hung along the outside walls shone without mercy on tear-stained faces, and the singing often halted or broke completely as voices caught and throats tightened.

The officers, standing quiet and humbled in their roles as altar boys, later told Father Jungbluth that never in their lives had they prayed so hard for peace as during that night, in a shabby wind-shaken hut, somewhere along the great road to Alaska.

As the winter of 1942 gave way to the bedraggled northern spring, Fort St. John became unusually forlorn. The rich contractors were pulling out, their machines now reduced to tired, mud-spattered wrecks. The big camps, equipped with running water and modern sewer systems, were now standing empty. Only the little maintenance camps containing perhaps a dozen people, scattered every 80 kilometres up the highway, were left to maintain the muddy road that had been slashed past their doors.

Local people watched in utter disbelief as the army destroyed thousands of dollars worth of machinery, appliances, surplus clothing and food that were no longer needed. These things could be neither sold nor given away as they had been brought into Canada under a special duty-free agreement solely for constructing the highway. It was cheaper (and more beneficial for American manufacturers) to destroy the goods rather than ship them back. Cast-iron stoves, refrigerators and washing machines were bulldozed into useless junk; blankets, bales of sheets, and mattresses were saturated with gasoline and set ablaze; carcasses of beef were left hanging to rot; canned and boxed food by the case was bulldozed and covered by hundreds of metres of dirt and gravel. Rather than watch it all be destroyed, the people took to thievery. Waste was unforgivable in the North.

Father Jungbluth was one of the first to plunder the waste piles of the army he had served. His partner in crime was none other than Ma Murray. In Father Jungbluth's Model A — a recent acquisition — they drove out to the disposal site where Father was told that boxes of new clothes had been dumped, and were soon to be buried. They had to wait until dark, as it was a crime to tamper with the army's business.

Sneaking up over the ridge that bordered the dump pit, Father Jungbluth extended his heavy-line fishing rod and carefully reeled in a pair of rubber boots, still tied together so the sizes wouldn't separate. The next cast yielded a bale of boots. He laughed silently at the thought of cartoons of fishermen reeling in old boots and throwing them back in disgust. Up came a bale of mackinaw jackets, and another, and a third, until they had piled behind them a good variety of sizes. He and Ma were exclaiming with delight over their surprise booty when headlights suddenly arrowed across the ridge. The army was coming back! There was time only to cache their loot on the floor of the car under a tarp, and slowly roll past the convoy moving in to complete the burning job. Father Jungbluth and Ma Murray gave them a wave and continued on, looking neither right nor left, but hardly able to contain themselves.

Father Jungbluth's poorest Indians had dry feet and warm backs for a long time to come.

"I know that I speak the sentiments of the Archbishop Spellman and the Military Ordinariate when I say that we are extremely grateful for the splendid work the Fathers did for our men . . ." wrote the Most Reverend Walter J. Fitzgerald, the Bishop from Juneau, Alaska.

Father Jungbluth's involvement with the building of the Alaska Highway had ended.

17

Wilde and Lawless

𝓕ather Jungbluth's first 10 years in Canada would have fulfilled an anthropologist's dream: he had come to know ancient ways of life. He had stayed in the poor log shacks of native people, sharing their meat and sleeping on their floors; he had prayed under hide-and-pole teepees; he had traveled on horseback, with wagon and sleigh, or on foot over wilderness more awesome and unending than could ever be imagined by Karl May. But he felt in his bones that changes were coming, from isolation to an invasion of the industrial world.

By the mid 1940s, horses were becoming obsolete as transport; only the Indians still depended on them. Father Jungbluth took advantage of the new highway and bought a Ford with $200 from the sale of his motorcycle to an American chaplain. The Church supplied the extra $50 needed for its purchase. He named the car "Eileen" for the way it tilted precariously on the sharp, ungraded turns.

Not all mission priests were so progressive. Father Habay, ever cautious, wrote the young Father immediately about the dangers of such a modern device. But Father Jungbluth's subtle reply won the reluctant old missionary to his point of view:

> Your recommendations concerning the dangers of the modern locomotion possibilities are welcome. But don't you think, my Father, that if our Saviour could live now He would travel by auto? Maybe not in a new and luxurious car, and surely not at dangerous speeds! And if our Holy Founder would give today His recommendations concerning the trips of His missionaries, He would formulate them probably differently . . . infusing them with the same spirit of poverty, but dealing realistically with the actual distances now involved . . .

Father Mariman's negative advice was based on practicality: "If you have a car, the Indians will come steadily to you asking for rides. That's what happened here in the mission at Fort Vermilion since they got a car: "Oh Father, the baby's sick. Oh Father, I want you to bring me to my brother. Can you take me to my trapline? With my canoe on your pickup? I have to go to the store in High Level.

"Very often these requests are without reason. Sometimes they use the excuse to go into town to buy booze. The Brother often caught them. And if you do not take them, they will say, "I'm never going to come to church! You never want to do anything for me!" And so, I will never have a car. They all like me. They come to church. And they give me rides."

During Father Jungbluth's association with the American army, he had always kept foremost the welfare of his prime mission — the Indians. Through his extra duties as Auxiliary Chaplain, the Indians of the Peace River country drank coffee and smoked cigarettes (the latter through Father's ability to make purchases in the P.X.), while the rest of the world could only crave such luxuries.

One day Father Jungbluth and Father Otterbach arrived at their quarters behind the church to find full coffee cans stashed under the porch, in the shed, under the foundations of the church, wherever there was a little hole. Father Otterbach became extremely nervous. Where had they come from? Perhaps they were being set up. There must be some trick.

Discreet inquiries revealed that one of the army contractors had decided to make a contribution. He had loaded a pick-up, covered the haul with a tarp, then stashed the cans as well as he could.

"What if anyone should have seen him do it?" Father Otterbach said nervously. "We are sure to get into trouble."

"Let's make a compromise," Father Jungbluth said. "Some we will keep for ourselves — not much — and the rest we will donate to our parishioners."

Father Otterbach did not like it. "If I start handing this stuff out to my white parishioners, there will be trouble. There is a great likelihood of the news getting back to the police," he said.

"Well, then," Father Jungbluth conceded, "I am sure I shall have no such worries with my Indians. I'll give it all to them when I visit their camps."

When the army moved on, and such contributions were a thing of the past, the Indians were greatly disappointed. They could not understand why Father Jungbluth could no longer bring them things. But, for the present, they were delighted with superb gifts from the departing army. Father Jungbluth described the latest enticement in a letter to Father Habay:

Hello Father,

It has been a long time since I wrote you but I'm still good and alive and my Ford is too. I would like to give the Sunday of tomorrow to the people of Kelly Lake, but the winds of today have blocked the roads and so it will be Horse Lake that profits. Thanks to my Ford, I have all my equipment with me: two harmoniums, a projector with two catechism films, and even a projector for animated 8mm films. This last apparatus is a gift of the 341st Regiment of Engineers. Even though it was built for only 110-120 volts, I have managed to fix a little 6-volt motor and my Ford gives it the necessary electricity for the motor and also for the lights. It means that I don't have any problems to assemble my "world" and they say the Rosary quite voluntarily when the harmonium plays at every decade.

I don't have to say how, with all this equipment, I am welcome in my different missions. And the ones who were more recalcitrant before now ask to assist in the devotions. We start with a *cantique* in Cree, accompanied with the portable harmonium. Then I show a movie from Lumen, or an article of the "Credo" for example, with the appropriate explications. Then perhaps another movie on the missions of the Chinese, followed by the recitation of the Rosary with hymns. At each decade a picture illustrates the Mystery, or else I project on the screen a beautiful picture of the Holy Virgin. Finally comes the animated movies, scenes of the Alaska Highway with trucks stuck in the snow, scenes of Moberly Lake with the old Indians, others of Fort St. John and the Sisters at the hospital, or the Fathers saying Mass at the chapel. Then all of a sudden the spectators recognize themselves on the screen and you can imagine the success! Everything finishes with the evening prayer and an exhortation to receive the sacraments the next morning.

"In those days," Father Jungbluth explains, "the Horse Lake Indians went to town only to find beer or liquor, although they had their own stills. They didn't go to bingos or to movies or to any other entertainment. A little projector like that with a film, especially when I took movies of them or of their friends in the other reserves — well, that was quite an attraction. It brought them there, and they got some religion too — that night and also the next morning. I would stay overnight there with one of the families, or in my car, but mostly inside."

The roads to the Indians were still rough, but Father Jungbluth wrestled seasonally through mudholes or half metre snowdrifts, winching Eileen over the bog, her wheels massed solid with mud or ice. One time, while putting on the chains to get up a bad hill, something "clicked" inside his knee and the following morning he was too crippled to say Mass. He refused to stay in hospital and "be condemned by inaction." Instead, he insisted he could still get around in the car and, by the use of a cane, take little steps. He wrote to Father Habay:

The doctors of the army said to me that there is a piece of cartilage detached. One said the best thing to do was operate, but the other says not. I am in favor of the latter diagnosis. The first doctor said there is a big danger that the joints will be stiff afterwards if they operate. I prefer to give nature a chance, helping with some liniment and heat treatments.

Traveling by car over the newly constructed roads allowed Father Jungbluth to visit remote winter camps that would have been inaccessible just a few years before. His letters, sent with regularity to his friends, to *La Voix* in Grouard, Alberta, and to *Immaculata* in France now bore postmarks from all parts of his territory. He wrote early in 1944:

> Who knows Calliou Lake among the readers of *La Voix*? This winter without much snow permitted me to visit this camp where I've never been before, located about 80 miles [128 km] from Rio Grande, to the south of the Monkman Pass. Another place visited for the first time was Big Slough, 45 miles [72 km] from Rio Grande, where there are four families. . . .

Big Slough was the end of the trail. Here were mostly trappers' cabins, sometimes just crude holes dug into the hillsides where the trapper might spend a night every 10 days or so as he made his rounds. Even the better cabins were small and squat, with doors constructed of boards pieced together and held on by moosehide hinges. Inside might be an orange crate for a table, a gas-barrel stove and a little bunk bed made of boards nailed to the wall and covered with hay for a mattress. The small square window would be covered with a waxed flour sack.

Big Slough was a patch of prairie, a terrible place, all bush. It was here, in this almost-inaccessible area, that Father Jungbluth discovered much about the Indians' philosophy.

"What brought you here to this godforsaken country anyhow?" he asked a resident Indian, after fighting 32 kilometres of bad to nonexistent trails. "There are no roads. Just bush and mosquitos and black flies. There is absolutely nothing here!"

"Bad for you . . . but good for us," was the calm reply. "Trapping is good, better than where the land is open. And no taxes." The man's dark eyes followed the gaze of the priest across the empty bush-covered expanse. He shrugged and smiled, almost apologetically. "Towns have never been too good for Indians."

The residents of Big Slough, Rio Grande and Kelly (Calliou) Lake were non-status Indians, commonly called breeds. They had to buy their land, make their own way in the world, "just like a white man."

Dalphus Belcourt, a handsome fun-loving man who grew up in Big Slough, recalls that "it was all bush around there. Good trapping. We trapped — well, not mice — mainly lynx, coyotes, lots of foxes; not so many marten, although they're coming down from the mountains now, but there used to be lots of foxes and they went at a good price. There used to be wolves but the game warden put out poison for them and the poison also killed off all the foxes. It cleaned out the country — wolves, foxes, coyotes, everything."

Dalphus Belcourt breaks his storytelling to allow his wife to set out tea and cakes, served on Royal Albert china.

"At first we lived in log houses with plank floors. In the summer, people worked out on farms and we trapped in the winter. Years ago there was no work — and no welfare. Nothing. Some men got work with farmers and all they would get was butter and eggs or something, maybe the odd dollar but not very often. We ate moosemeat and rabbits, but you couldn't keep the meat in the summertime, just make dried meat and that's what we lived on. Nobody had gardens, just meat and berries.

"Before the white man came, people would make their dried meat and just leave it in the bush. White men came and they stole anything. I'll tell you a good one. I didn't see it, just heard it. It's a story of the coming of the white men:

"It used to be that the Indian never stole. He didn't know how. Anyway, if a person stole he'd get caught right away, so nobody stole. White men came and made half-breeds. Gotta be a white man to make half-breeds. The half-breeds are getting smarter, they steal anything. So one day an Indian trapper came through and he set a trap to catch a fox. When the fox was caught he took it and skinned it right there, leaving the skin in the tree, and reset the trap. Next time a half-breed came there, and finds another fox in the trap. He skins the fox and takes the other skin too. Getting crooked. Next time a white man comes by, and there's another fox in the trap. The white man takes the fox, and the trap, too. That's what I heard.

"When you're not a treaty Indian," continues Belcourt, "you have to find your own place, follow the same rules as the white man. But somehow whenever we run into trouble with hunting or trapping regulations, the subject of 'drunken Indian' comes up. They worry about giving the Indian something for nothing.

Rio Grande

"Drinking was never a problem in Big Slough. There were hardly any people. But at Horse Lake and Kelly Lake there was drinking, just about anything: lemon or orange extracts."

Belcourt speaks with certainty and sadness:

"The women never used to drink; that's different now too. The women sometimes drink more than the men. All over. And the women get meaner when they drink than men . . . all of them, white or Indian. You can't beat the white people in anything!"

In the summer, in order to find as many people as possible in one place and cut many kilometres from his circuit, Father Jungbluth followed the rodeos and treaty-payment days, circling around from Horse Lake to Rio Grande, Bonanza, Doe River, and back to the big, highly professional rodeo run by promoters Tommy Wilde and Jack Lawless.

A parade and various festivities accompanied the big, highly professional rodeo run by promoters Tommy Wilde and Jack Lawless in the 1940s. Main Street, Fort St. John, B.C.

Father Jungbluth would arrive at the rodeo site outside Fort St. John one or two days early, and greet the Indians as they set up their camps. In the morning he would begin with an open-air Mass where everyone sung out hymns "with voices loud and off-key." Then he would perform baptisms, give a little bit of instruction, ask were certain couples married and, if not, was there a chance to get them married? (Only the arrangements would be made. Father Jungbluth would determine where the various bands were going after the rodeo and later would perform the service at their camps.)

In the evenings he showed his movies, and would invite the assembled Indians to attend Mass again in the morning. But once the rodeo started, he couldn't keep their attention. He sat back and enjoyed the show. The Indians competed not only in the regular bareback bronc riding, bull riding and steer wrestling events, but also in skillful exhibitions of Roman riding. Here the performer rode at full gallop with his right foot on the back of one horse and his left foot on another. Alexis Gauthier and Angus Davis of Moberly lake usually won prizes in that event. In the evening, there would be a barbecue organized by Wilde and Lawless.

Father Jungbluth sometimes participated in extraordinary events himself. Ernie Carrier from Fort St. John, then the local undertaker, performed motorcycle stunt rides, making spectacular jumps through fire on his big Indian motorcycle. He and Father Jungbluth would, for fun, organize a race in the evenings.

Father's second motorcycle, a 350cc Panther, was not a practical bike for the country. It couldn't be shifted into high gear until 80 km/h, an astounding speed for the condition of the northern roads. Although the Indian was a more powerful motorcycle, it was hampered in the take-off by handlebar gears that momentarily slowed it. Father Jungbluth's bike, with the foot shift, surged ahead, causing dust clouds that took an hour to settle. Ernie Carrier usually won on the distance, but it was a spectacular show. Local people would gather rapidly to watch two men — one a priest and the other an undertaker — scream down the flat dusty road outside Fort St. John on an Indian and a Panther, as daring as any riders from the Wilde and Lawless rodeo.

Father Jungbluth's motorcycles gave way to the Model A Ford; the Model A to a new 1946 Mercury half-ton truck. He could now haul almost anything, including, sometimes, Katie. Occasionally he tied her on behind and traveled slowly, but she didn't like a harness and the traffic frightened her. Perhaps she had once been scared by a car, for she shied whenever they whizzed past. Father Jungbluth installed stock racks, and brought planks along to load her on and off. He could travel at regular speeds where the roads were good, then park the truck in the bush and ride Katie the last 32 kilometres to Moberly Lake, or into a remote bush camp.

Katie could also help haul the truck out of a mudhole. Father Jungbluth would get the horse out of the back, hitch her harness to the frame with a single-tree, and hook up her rigging. He would get in and start the motor, holding onto the horse's lines through the side door, then put the truck into low and engage the gears as slowly as possible, letting the horse pull slightly. It didn't always work smoothly. The danger of the operation became apparent when the truck would jump suddenly out of the mudhole and bump the horse or drive over the singletree.

He eventually invented a better method: he fit a hook into the hole on the wheel and welded a second hook onto the frame above the spring. He then would fasten an 46-centimetre chain onto these two hooks to prevent the car from lifting up while the wheel stayed stuck in the mud. When the wheel lifted up with the body, Father Jungbluth would pile boards or branches under it. He also carried a jack-all that he could hook around a stump. Thirdly, he could use the one-metre planks he carried for loading Katie. To further outfit the truck for his mission trips, he built a caboose on the back.

Now, as he pulled into the farms and camps, the attention that was once directed at his horse was switched to his truck and his inventions, especially the chain. He would often be asked to demonstrate his invention, pulling the wheel a metre off the ground and building up the "hole" with branches.

The time had come for Katie to be sold. She was still in good shape, about 14 years old, and he got the same price he had paid for her. Katie went to an outfitter who made his living taking rich Americans on hunting trips. She was back on familiar bush trails, while Father Jungbluth now traveled fast and unimpeded over roads that penetrated every corner of a once wild and lawless territory.

Father contemplating a difficult stream crossing.

18

Life in Moberly Lake

*I*n the summer of 1947, Father Jungbluth received a shock. The Bishop sent him, unannounced, a letter of Obedience. He was to move forthwith to Fort St. James.

In 1944 Pope Pius XII had divided the territory into two Vicariates. In 1945 Bishop Anthony Jordan, OMI, took charge of the Vicariate of Prince Rupert, encompassing the Yukon Territory and the most northerly part of British Columbia (including Fort St. John and Dawson Creek). This resulted in Father Jungbluth being no longer allied with Bishop Langlois and the Vicariate of Grouard, but rather with this 216,000 square kilometre Vicariate of Prince Rupert that stretched west from the Alberta boundary to the Pacific Ocean, and north to the land of the Eskimos.

Located some 240 kilometres west and north of Prince George, British Columbia, Fort St. James might have been on the other side of the world. At the time there was no mountain pass connecting the Peace area with Prince George; one had to travel to Edmonton, Alberta, and back west through Jasper and McBride by train to Prince George and then on to Fort St. James. The Indians there were Carrier; Father Jungbluth knew nothing about them. The move would represent a final farewell to the area he had come to know so well.

The people of Fort St. John threw a party for him in the Anglican Hall. His friends had prepared a skit starring Ma Murray, who whooped out crying, "White man's sun! You fix 'em!" She was dressed in Indian costume and waving an alarm clock in her hand.

Stories were told about Father Jungbluth's legendary watch-fixing: one about the American soldier who possessed a masterpiece that told time, date and season. It was broken and he couldn't find a watchmaker in all the country who could fix it. One day a local cafe proprietor heard about his problem and said, "There is a priest here who seems to have a genius for such things. You should let him examine it."

The soldier immediately took it to Father Jungbluth who put on his magnifying eyepiece, then slowly and meticulously took the watch apart. "I see you are missing a piece here," he told the soldier. "Whoever repaired it last forgot to put it all back."

"What can I do? Is the watch ruined?"

"No, no, I can make a piece."

The soldier looked on in amazement as the little priest went to work examining, measuring, until he had figured out what the missing piece must look like. He then manufactured it from a tiny piece of spring-wire.

Cecil Pickell, a local Fort St. John resident, had a beautiful watch bought in Italy, but wore it as an everyday accessory on the farm, while hammering, driving posts, working horses, whatever had to be done. The watch seemed intended for more delicate surroundings and kept breaking down. The third time Cec took the watch to Father Jungbluth to have it repaired, Father refused to give it back. "This watch and you are not meant for each other!" he declared. "It is not a watch to be worn while you drive in fence posts." And so Father Jungbluth kept it and, so the story goes, sold it to somebody else.

A collection was taken at the farewell party, and Father Jungbluth was presented with a purse containing $165. The Fort St. John newspaper headline read: "He'll Repair Your Radio, Your Watch . . . Your Soul."

Father Jungbluth's trunks were shipped ahead to Fort St. James. His new truck would stay with the mission as, in keeping with the Vow of Poverty, a missionary owns nothing. He bade his friends good-bye and boarded the shuddering swaying old NAR (Northern Alberta Railways) train in Dawson Creek. But, just before arriving in Edmonton, he heard his name being called. There was a wire from the Bishop: "Go back where you came from."

What had happened?

It turned out that they could find nobody else to take his place in Fort St. John. It was a difficult territory; no one wanted it. Few were able, as he was, to speak both Beaver and Cree Indian. He was back, almost before he had left.

"Hey, Father, I thought we got you the hell out of town!" said one parishioner with a wide grin, as he ran across the street to shake his hand.

"Didn't we make a collection to get rid of you?" another called to him as he drove down the street in his pick-up. Father laughed and waved.

With more people moving into the North, the Vicariate soon saw the need to send another priest to Fort St. John and divide the mission territory in two. One man would reside in Fort St. John and look after the missions on the north side of the Peace River — Blueberry, Doig, Halfway and up to Fort Nelson. The other would travel to missions on the south side, and reside at Moberly Lake.

Father Jungbluth received his third Obedience Order from the Provincial Superior in Ottawa, written in Latin, assigning him to Moberly Lake. Along with the official order was a more personal letter, written in English:

October 11, 1947
My Dear Father Jungbluth:
    Enclosed please find your letters of Obedience for Moberly Lake. You know how to interpret the *quamprimum* it contains. It

is perfectly agreeable to the Bishop and to me for you to wait until after the Mission at Fort St. John before moving to Moberly Lake.

It is a great honor to be chosen to be the first permanent pastor of Moberly Lake, and I am sure you will measure up to such a responsibility. So much depends on good foundations in a figurative sense as well as in the material. I beg of you to be a good Oblate, a man of the Rule, combining the interior life with the active ministry, docile and motivated in all things by a spirit of perfect obedience. Living as such, God will be pleased and so will your Bishop and your Provincial. And you will be happy too.

Work intensively in the territory that the Bishop has given you. I realize that your first winter there will demand self-sacrifice but I know that you are capable of it for you are a zealous priest. You can rest assured that we will do our utmost to give you a companion next year. Cooperate with the Bishop and he will be good to you. If I can help you, do not be afraid to write to me.

Tout a vous en J.C. & M.I.
Joseph R. Birch, OMI Provincial

P.S. *Union de prieres!*

Father Jungbluth read it again. His smile broadened. He then got up and carefully filed the letter in his record box. Such piety! Such flowery phrases! He laughed aloud. "Self-sacrifice," "zealous," — these were words a seminarist thrived on, but not a seasoned northern Oblate.

He had no way of knowing just how much self-sacrifice would be required that first winter, or the next one either, for both the Bishop and the Provincial seemed to thenceforth erase him from their minds. And he never, ever, received a companion.

Shortly after Father Jungbluth moved to Moberly Lake, Bishop Jordan paid him a visit at the little church. Father Jungbluth was proud of his church. The oiled logs blended beautifully with the sylvan surroundings. It was new and clean. It had been built by the love and labor of the people it was to serve. Bishop Jordan did not share his sentiments.

One evening Father Jungbluth sat on the front steps of the church, watching the Bishop as he strolled along the stony beach, mumbling and muttering into the wind. In a moment of quiet from the wind and the waves, the Bishop's words carried clear and evocative, back to the stricken little priest: "What in Heaven's name induces men to live in this godforsaken country?" muttered the Bishop, banging the rocks with his stick, "Nothing but bush! Bush and mosquitos!"

"I would like to buy more land here," Father Jungbluth had said to the Bishop earlier in the day, as the two walked along that same beach. The Bishop had raised one eyebrow. "Not only for the fact that we've discovered from Alwin Holland's survey that the church extends six inches [15 cm] onto the next lot," Father Jungbluth continued hurriedly, "but things are changing. People want to come to the lake and build their cabins. I see these people coming and I get scared they'll build their cottages right at the church, and I'll have no more privacy . . . all those bathing suits running around . . ."

Here the Bishop gave a slight cough. Father Jungbluth continued quickly to make his point: "Also, the road I use up past the graveyard to get to the main road is on someone else's land. Every time I use it I'm trespassing."

The Bishop hurled to the ground the walking stick he had been using to keep his balance on the rough beach. "More land will just raise our taxes! What is the matter with you? You should have planned more carefully. The land here is useless, who would want to settle out here?"

In the end, very reluctantly, the Bishop gave permission to acquire two more acres adjoining the church on the west, which belonged to Sam Calliou, the son of William.

Father Jungbluth at first experienced few hardships living in Moberly Lake. He moved out in the fall, and the Indians brought him moosemeat, grease for cooking, a warm pair of mukluks. He had a little money set aside for essentials. At Christmas, Father Otterbach sent out parcels from former parishioners in Fort St. John containing cookies, cakes and candies. The treats kept him well-supplied for a month or more, even after giving much of it to the children at the Christmas party. He also received an unexpected bonus: Father Birch sent $20 tucked in with his formal Christmas letter. Did this mean that he was now forgiven for the altercation in Fort St. John? Was it a personal gift, or a standard church donation sent to all missionaries? Whatever the case, it was gratefully received. At the time, Father Jungbluth had no foreknowledge of how far he would have to stretch that precious bill.

It was impossible to even think of living off collections — there weren't any. At times he might find eight cents in the plate, at other times nothing at all. It wasn't that the Indians were stingy. Money was a rare commodity and the church collection plate was not first on their list of priorities. Before winter was over, Father Jungbluth realized he must seek work. He repaired watches and radios in return for a dollar or two from the Indians' family allowance cheques, or from their fur sales.

He did not accept furs in trade. Only a licenced fur buyer was able to accept pelts, and there was so much competition that spies were planted throughout the trading areas. A fur buyer was required to see the trapping licence and record the number every time he bought furs. "Buyer beware" was the motto when dealing with furs, and Father Jungbluth would take almost anything but pelts for his services: watches, moosemeat, old radios.

Over the winter he devised a new system to bring in cash. With the engine and a few other used parts from the old Model A, he constructed a little buzz-saw. (At the time, chainsaws did not exist). He built his saw on a stand, and it was just light enough for the back of the pick-up. The 76-centimetre

*Bishop Anthony Jordan, OMI, and Father Jungbluth in front
of the church in Moberly Lake.*

sawing blade impressed the Indians; one by one they hired him to come and cut their wood.

"Now, don't call unless you have at least 10 cords for me to cut," he admonished.

"Oh, I've got lots of wood," was the reply, "lots of wood. Come and cut it now."

He would arrive and there would be only enough for 10 or 15 minutes work. The buzz-saw went through the wood faster than the Indians had ever imagined.

He bought a big game rifle, a 30.30. But the more he thought about it, the less practical it seemed. Supposing he shot an animal. He'd have to come back, get a horse, tie it to a skidder, go back in the bush and try to load the carcass. Then there was the job of cutting it. He was not interested in hunting either as a sport or as a means of support, if he could possibly help it. His problem was finally resolved. The gun was stolen.

He bought a .22 and killed a few partridges, but he couldn't seem to keep a gun. The Indians would come around: "Oh, I see that you have a gun there. May I borrow it? I just saw a deer." And they would take the gun and forget to bring it back, or bring it back in poor condition. He took to hiding his .22, the third one he had to buy, under the bed.

In the end, the main thing he used a gun for was shooting packrats in the church. He would hear them at night, scampering and scratching around. Armed with his gun and a flashlight, he would quietly open the door joining his quarters with the church and flash the beam onto the log rafters. When he found the glittering eyes, he'd shine the light on them for a moment. It seemed to mesmerize them. Then, carefully setting the flashlight down on the organ, he would take aim and fire until he heard the squeak and plop of the falling body. The French army had taught him to be an excellent marksman.

A .22 bullet doesn't penetrate very deeply into a log, just three to five centimetres, and it makes such a small hole that the wood closes up behind. Although the church was pocked with .22 bullets, the holes could hardly be seen.

He had more luck with fishing than hunting. Moberly Lake contained many whitefish and it wasn't difficult to make good catches of fish 20, 25, or 30 centimetres long. One could also catch ling cod, a snaky-looking bony fish that could swallow a small fish whole.

The best fish were caught at Cameron Lake, about 16 kilometres to the north, but Moberly was handier, although the fish in Moberly Lake were possibly unhealthy. They had spots. Some claimed they were from worms, others said they were fat deposits. One resident, old Mr. Benson, sent them out to be analyzed and the report came back, "unharmful to man or animal," so they ignored the "beauty spots." It was sickening, though, to open up a fish and see it infested with dozens of white lumps. The Indians didn't seem to mind, but Father Jungbluth, at times, could hardly bring himself to eat them. But there was not much else.

In the summer he fished with a line for jackfish, in his little wooden boat. In October he'd catch big trout, which, on occasion, would weigh in at 5 to 7 kilograms. But it was in the winter that the serious fishing was done. The fish could be kept frozen for months in a cache, a big wooden box on the shady side behind the church. If a warm chinook wind blew in, he would hurry out back, dig a big hole in a snowbank, put his fish in there and cover them up, keeping them frozen through the sudden increase in temperature.

One time, when a Chinook lasted two days with no sign of dying down, he quickly loaded his fish into his pick-up and drove in to Fort St. John. Pulling into the Bowes and Herron Garage, he yelled, "Come and get it!" The garage owner came out and chose his fish, then the mechanics and other employees, until everyone had a few free fish. It was one way he could return the favor for repairs or parts they gave him so cheaply.

Father Jungbluth and two Indian men did their fishing in the bay directly in front of the church. Two nights of gill-netting resulted in a whole truckload of fish.

At Moberly Lake a standard northern method was used for winter fish-netting. A big hole was chopped in the ice, about a yard in diameter. Further over, another hole was chopped the same way. The tricky part was to run a rope (on which a net could be strung) down one hole, through the water and up through the second hole. They used a plank about 3.5 metres

Father sporting one of his prize catches.

long (so it would keep the direction) and 20 to 25 centimetres across. Exactly in the centre, they cut a slot. In this slot they installed a simple spring mechanism with sharp metal prongs extending above the upper surface of the board. A light rope was attached to this propelling device.

After pushing the plank through the hole into the water and aiming it at the other hole, they then pulled on the rope. The prongs caught on the ice and propelled the plank along. A spring brought the prongs back into place. As they pulled on the rope again and again, the plank would surge forward beneath the ice in the direction of the second hole. If they had aimed well, the edge of the plank would catch on the second hole, but that didn't always happen. It might veer to one side or the other, sometimes completely off target. In that case they had to take a shovel and an axe, and scrape off the snow at the point where they could hear the prong scratching along under the ice. One man would lay on the ice, peering down until he had located the plank (usually painted bright red or orange so it could be easily spotted). When he saw it, they made another hole.

Now, with the rope going down through one hole and back up through the second, the plank was pulled out, the net attached to one end of the rope and then pulled through under the ice, thus stringing out the net. The fish caught their gills in the net, and they were in business.

To retrieve the net full of fish, the entire rope-line of netting could be pulled through the hole, the fish removed and then the net reset for next time.

With the Indians supplying moosemeat, deer meat and bear fat, plus his own catch of fish, Father Jungbluth managed to just get by. He made it through the first year. But for the second winter he knew he had somehow to raise money to buy supplies and gas for his truck.

One evening he drove over to the Hudson's Bay post to visit the factor and his family. The man's parents were up from the south, and Father Jungbluth had been asked to bring his movie projector and show his animated films.

The projector was operated from two 6-volt batteries wired together to produce 12-volt power. The 12 volts were too strong for the projector motor — causing the film to go too fast — so he used a little rheostat from a car heater on the projector to reduce the power and slow the film at the proper speed. He had two circuits: one for the 12-volt electric lightbulb on the projector, which received the full 12-volts, then the voltage altered by the rheostat going directly to the projector motor.

"I would give anything to have films like these," said the factor's father after the show. "They're treasures. Absolute treasures. All those pictures of the old Indian ways — baptisms, weddings, funerals. No one has such pictures as these. They're priceless."

Father Jungbluth was silent for a moment. He turned to the man. "They're for sale," he said in a quiet voice.

"For sale? But why would you want to sell them?"

Father Jungbluth made an impatient gesture with his hands. "Oh, I'm tired of them now. The Indians don't want to look at them any more. When they've seen them once, they want to see something new."

"How much do you want for them? The films and the projector?"

Father Jungbluth was silent again. "You have to do this," he said to himself, "it's the only thing."

"I'll make you a deal for the whole works," he said finally. "The 8mm movie camera — which was a gift to me from the army — the projector and all the films. I want to keep only one or two, a wedding in Moberly Lake, a funeral in Kelly Lake, just something so if I ever go back to France on a holiday I can take them along."

His mind was busy calculating: how much money did he have in his strongbox? Well, not much, not enough to see him through another month. What is the least it would cost him to exist, even with the wild meat and fish, and any other donations? How much gas would he need for his truck? Could he get by another year on the old set of tires? He figured a sum, then deducted a few dollars to make the deal go over. The factor's parents paid him immediately, in cash. It was more money than he had held in his hand since leaving Fort St. John. It would see him through the season.

In all this time he heard little from the Church except for the regular newsletters and periodicals. No one asked if he needed help. And he was too proud to ask.

It wasn't that the Church deliberately ignored him. He eventually felt it was likely that Father Birch, the Provincial in Ottawa, thought Father Jordan, the Bishop in Prince Rupert, was looking after him, and the Bishop thought the Provincial was. In any event, the situation Father Jungbluth found himself in was "a little bit unusual."

He found little comfort in the fact that Father Mariman seemed to be doing well in his territory.

"I think they took special care of Father Mariman because he is so helpless," Father Jungbluth said later, recalling those years. "For me, they didn't bother. I'm more liberal in interpreting things; they knew I wouldn't let myself starve altogether. And I didn't exactly starve. I just had nothing in surplus. The Indians would remember how I lived."

In May of 1945, Father Mariman began his ministry as director of the pilgrimage at Eleské. He wrote to *La Voix*:

> Since the 5th of August, with the help of a Beaver Indian man, I have assembled around 20 piles of stones to construct a grotto for the Saint Virgin. Then came the official permission and a feast of the dear Saint Virgin and the benediction of the statue on September 17th, the solemn feast of Our Lady of the Seven Sorrows, by Rev. Fr. Henri Routhier. So, the year of grace, 1945,

In front of Moberly Lake Church

brought the execution of my desires. Providence has favored us on all sides: first, the federal government gave to the Indian reserve wells which give water in sufficient quantities for the use of the pilgrims to the grotto; on top of this, we acquired a little electric centre, a windmill with the capacity of 18 volts.

The report went on to describe the pilgrimage to Our Lady of Lourdes at Eleské (which was to become an annual affair), held for the first time on September 8, 1947:

The day of September 7th was indeed a very busy one for Father Mariman. He was sacristan, catechist, predicator, confessor and cook, all at the same time.

And he preached in three languages.

Father Jungbluth, alone in his little shack behind the church in Moberly Lake, read the report from beginning to end. Then, with a great sigh, he put the paper down on the table and walked over to his stove. Picking up a fork, he began to laboriously pull off the skin and fillet the bones from his sodden boiled whitefish.

19
Health and Welfare

*I*n the summer of 1945, Father Jungbluth appealed for Sisters to teach summer catechism classes. The Mother Superior of the Sisters of Providence sent out Sisters Gilles-Marcel and Marie Marcelle. *La Voix* printed their report:

> We got into the unique but reliable vehicle of Father Jungbluth for the trip of 120 miles [192 km] toward the mission of Moberly Lake. After 30 fast but comfortable miles [48 km] on the Alaska Highway, we turned off onto a side road that led through the trees. We were then shaken about for the next eight hours, surrounded by suffocating clouds of dust and 1,000 blackflies.
>
> We stopped finally on a nice, long, new bridge constructed at the mouth of Moberly Lake. These few minutes gave us time to admire this magnificent lake with water like crystal that seemed to reach as far as the impressive Rocky Mountains. This spectacle so absorbed us that we forgot our fatigue of the trip.
>
> A little farther on we saw the first Indian cabin and we stopped to visit them. The children were all grubby and examined us with as much fear as surprise, because it was the first time that Sisters had come to them. Some candies distributed quickly gained their hearts and even those of the parents. After another couple stops of this kind, we could see in a clearing the steeple of the nice little church made of oiled logs which shone in the evening sun. Great was our astonishment to find in the woods this beautiful little chapel so well finished on the outside as well as on the inside, even to the nice floor. We also found well-arranged and comfortable beds. Then Father said, "watch out you don't go through the floor! And take care that the mice don't chew your noses off during the night."

But the night went by without the visit of those four-legged creatures, so feared by the two Catechist Sisters.

> Our first work consisted of visiting the people, each family of the two reserves. What misery in those hovels! What poverty. And also, if I allow myself to say so, what dirtiness. But all over we were welcomed like the messengers of the Good Lord, with great reverence and cordiality.

On Sunday we were surprised to see so many people: Beaver, Cree, Saulteaux, Metis and whites, attending the Holy Mass. Some of the most remote came the night before. It was nice to see their campfires around the church, illuminating the shadows of the evening. The spectacle was more than picturesque.

Father Jungbluth was delighted with the Sisters' visit. "They were very enthusiastic. Even in those long habits they could move pretty fast."

Through their eyes, Father Jungbluth saw again the beauty — but also the wretchedness — of his parishioners' condition. With the influx of white settlers, the Indians were being subjected to legal as well as social changes.

The soldiers were returning from the war, and they needed land. The Department of Veterans Affairs found some land suitable for cultivation and within easy traveling distance of Fort St. John. There was only one problem. It was Indian land, the Montney Reserve, located just a few kilometres north of Fort St. John, in Father Jungbluth's former territory.

The Department of Indian Affairs outlined an arrangement whereby the Indians would relinquish to the Department of Veterans Affairs the Montney Reserve in exchange for land at three separate reserves at the Blueberry, Doig and Halfway Rivers. It was reasoned the more remote areas would suit the Indians' lifestyle; they were nomadic and used the Montney Reserve mainly for their summer camp, after trapping season and before the early fall hunt. In winter they used it to pasture out their horses while they went out onto their traplines. They were obviously not interested in farming it, and the soldiers were.

"The Indians didn't know what it was all about," Father Jungbluth says. "Nobody did. I didn't know where those other reserves were, exactly, how good they were, how agreeable the move would be to the Indians. I couldn't say much. It all sounded fairly good. And it was for the returned soldiers. How could I say much against it?

"The agent was a good talker. 'Instead of one piece of land, you will get three pieces, three reserves,' he said. And so they were persuaded to put their Xs on a piece of paper by which they relinquished the reserve at Montney to the Department of Veterans Affairs."

In July of 1949, the Fort St. John Indian Reserve was opened to V.L.A. settlers. When the Indians returned the next year they found the place all surveyed and fenced off. They didn't understand what they had done.

"I don't remember being at the meeting . . . and I am absolutely sure that I was not a witness to it, that I did not sign anything," Father Jungbluth says. But, some 35 years later, the issue has resurfaced. Compensation for this lost land is being sought by the Indians who can now read and write English. And Father Jungbluth's signature has apparently been spotted on at least one document. He was informed, by a caller whose name he didn't quite catch, that he did at least witness a signature dealing with this land trade.

"I wrote for the Indians occasionally," he says, "and once in court they asked me if I had signed a certain paper and I said, 'never.' Then the police came over and showed me, on the folded-over edge of the paper, my signature. Then I remembered. The paper listed a complaint by an Indian against the Indian agent, saying he had not received some goods that were supposed to have been sent to him. The Indian dictated what he wanted to say, in Beaver, and I wrote it out in English. He put his X and I signed underneath, as witness to his signature. I was just the interpreter. It could be the same in this land case, just witnessing a paper. But I had no part of the deal that cheated the Indians out of their rich reserve at Montney. Never."

The Indian populations of the Peace area suffered heavily from diseases; the worldwide flu epidemic of 1918-1919 had nearly wiped them out. Tuberculosis was a recurrent devastation. Smallpox and diphtheria — the disease that Father Jungbluth had suffered in his childhood — were only now being checked with vaccines.

While he was living in Fort St. John, Father Jungbluth had become close friends with Dr. George Cormack. He was a handsome young medical man who had previously worked with the Indians in MacLeod Lake north of Prince George before coming to Fort St. John in 1945. Dr. Cormack lived in a little house across the road from the rectory and took all his meals at the hospital, where he and Father Jungbluth met. He was greatly interested in working with the Indians; he was concerned about their remoteness from medical help, and also about their poverty and ignorance of hygiene. He wanted to visit the reserves and camps, and asked Father Jungbluth to go with him. The priest would act as interpreter while he conducted his medical surveys.

They had made their first trip together in early September, 1945, leaving Fort St. John at 7:00 a.m. on horseback. On that trip, Dr. Cormack was quite pleased with the condition of the Halfway Indians. Though they lived in tents during the summer and in little poplar-pole cabins in the winter, they were in pretty good shape. The Indians had been subjected to ever-increasing contact with outsiders since the construction of the Alaska Highway, but as yet it was a difficult road from the Halfway Reserve out to Mile 132 of the Alaska Highway. Isolated residents of the Halfway were in better health than the Moberly Lake Indians who had much more contact with outsiders.

Dr. Cormack's prime concern at the Halfway River settlement was to immunize the Indians against tuberculosis, smallpox and diphtheria, and to check them for venereal diseases and other ills brought by encroaching civilization. The problem was to get them all in one place long enough to do a thorough job. Although he did his best to get them all immunized, diphtheria did break out again in 1948, causing some deaths.

After Father Jungbluth moved to Moberly Lake in 1947, Dr. Cormack made numerous trips to the area. One morning, Father Jungbluth was chopping wood outside the church when he spied a large dark object moving toward him over the lake ice. "What can it be," he wondered. Then, as it neared, "No, it can't be. No, I don't believe it!"

Dr. Cormack's big green Hudson car was skimming across the ice, appearing on the horizon like a green space ship racing over a barren lunar surface. He stopped the car on the snow-covered beach in front of the church and got out. "Hello, Father, have you got the coffee on?"

"Come in, come in!" Father Jungbluth laughed. "It will take just a minute to melt some ice." He turned and trudged up to the church, shaking his head. He couldn't believe Moberly Lake being so accessible. Dr. Cormack had come over the Jackfish Lake hill in one of the first winter car trips to Moberly Lake. Then, following sleigh tracks, he had driven over the ice to the church door.

Dr. Cormack wanted to visit the more remote Indians and Metis on the west side of the lake. Father Jungbluth started up his truck and, with Dr. Cormack following in the Hudson, they headed across the ice. It was dark by the time they set out on the return trip. They could not see the shore, and there was no moon to guide them. Drifts of snow rippling across the lake ice had to be driven around, confusing their sense of direction. After a half hour of driving aimlessly about on the flat frozen lake, they realized they were lost. They skidded their vehicles to a stop on the ice.

Father Jungbluth stomped up to the dark hulk of the Hudson. "Doctor, you're going in the wrong direction. You're heading south when you should be going north."

"Oh no. Oh no. To the contrary. It is you who are wrong."

There, in the middle of the lake, in the black night, with the wind and snow hurtling doubled forces against them, the two men stood arguing. Their voices rose and fell as aimlessly as the howling wind. Finally they separated to slam the doors of their respective cars and surge forward to drive for what seemed like endless hours, until at last their headlights picked up the familiar cove that fronted the church. The argument of who was right and who was wrong was never resolved.

Dr. Cormack found the residents of Moberly Lake in a sorry state. He launched a long-term series of treatments carrying on into summer. Back he came, again and again, crashing through the bush in his low-slung Hudson, bringing with him the public health nurse, along with copious supplies of vaccines, ointments, pills, and a large sack of whitewash and brushes. The doctor examined and immunized while the nurse went round to every cabin, ordered the inhabitants out of the house, handed them whitewash and brushes, and said, "Now get busy."

The main problem was scabies, a skin infection caused by mites, although fleas and pinworms were prevalent also.

Dr. Cormack and Father Jungbluth traveled to Kelly Lake, where they discovered more health problems. Knowing that sequential treatment sessions would be necessary, and that the roads were nearly impassable, Dr. Cormack simply ordered (through Father Jungbluth's interpretation) the entire population to move temporarily down to Moberly Lake.

Repeated treks together provided opportunity for serious discussions. Both men were well-educated, but their opinions often differed. Loud arguments resounded through the silent trees as they traveled down trails on horseback, or bounced over ruts in the old Hudson. They argued about the decision of the German General, Rommel, "The Desert Fox." Had he the right to commit suicide because he was condemned by Hitler? Or would it be against Moral Law?

They argued about philosophy, with Father Jungbluth often calling Dr. Cormack crazy and scoffing at his ideas about theology. Dr. Cormack was a devout Catholic and at one time had been determined to become a priest. But there were also many points they agreed upon.

It was a common sight, at any time of day or night, in any season, to see Dr. Cormack driving his beat-up Hudson over the back roads, crashing over stumps, swerving around deadfalls and overhanging brush to come to the aid of a sick Indian who could not be moved out.

On one such call, he drove from Fort St. John through the night. He arrived at Moberly Lake at 4:00 a.m. and administered to his patient. Then, almost in a stupor, he made his way to the church and banged on Father Jungbluth's door. The priest got out of bed, let him in, and went to search for a blanket for him. When he returned, Dr. Cormack was sound asleep in Father Jungbluth's bed.

It made Father Jungbluth smile to think how finicky the doctor usually was about people sleeping in other's sheets. But there was the doctor, fast asleep, snoring softly. Father Jungbluth stoked the fire and pulled up a chair close to the stove, wrapped himself in the blanket, and there he spent the rest of the night.

Dr. Cormack was very much against the current policies of the Indian Affairs Department. He accused it of neglecting the Indians, of not giving them their proper rights. At that time, the Department sent out a list of medicines that doctors were not supposed to administer to the Indians because they were considered too expensive. Insulin was one. It had not long been discovered and was costly. Other medicines commonly prescribed for white patients were not officially available to the Indians. The Department did not want Indians admitted into the hospitals to have their babies; they were supposed to have them by midwives on the reserves (or, like Annie Gladu of Kelly Lake said, "under a tree, just like a cow.")

From time to time, when Father Jungbluth brought in a group of Indians to Fort St. John for annual check-ups and x-rays, he would hear of Dr. Cormack's latest schemes to improve the Indians' treatment. At one point, he offered his services to the Indian Affairs Department as medical advisor for northern Indians and Eskimos. "I'll bet you he doesn't last six months," Braden Herron said to Father Jungbluth. "He won't be able to stand it."

He was right. Dr. Cormack got into trouble almost immediately over the Department's policy of restricting medicines. "If that medicine is good for a white man, it's good for an Indian too," he said, and he quit.

He bought his own airplane, one of those war-surplus trainers that were obsolete immediately after the war because they seemed to swallow gas faster than one could pour it in. On one of his first trips from Edmonton, where he had delivered a patient to the Charles Camsell Hospital, he experienced delays with the weather. He got lost and landed in Peace River, Alberta, with only two gallons of fuel in his tanks. He made another trip with his plane to help search for a lost pilot from Fort St. John, but this was his last flight. The next time Father Jungbluth was in Fort St. John, he found the plane behind the shack with the wings clipped off.

Father Jungbluth also encountered problems with the Indian Department. In one instance, Mrs. Elsie (Prince) Courtoreille was due to have her baby and asked Father Jungbluth to take her out to the hospital. It was feared there would be difficulties and there was no time to ask permission from the Indian Agent. Father Jungbluth warmed up the truck and made the run in to Fort St. John, but it proved to be a false alarm. She spent the night in the hospital and Father Jungbluth brought her back the next day. He then sent in a bill for gas expenses, the usual procedure. The Indian Agent refused to endorse it. No permission had been obtained; no baby had been born. A week later when Father Jungbluth was at another mission, Mrs. Courtoreille went into labor and a radio call was put in to the Indian Department for help. They sent out a plane. When Father Jungbluth returned and was told the story, he sat down and wrote a letter to the Department:

> . . . How can you refuse to pay my small bill of twenty dollars for what I considered an emergency trip, then, with no qualms, pay out two to three hundred dollars for an airplane a few days later? But then, I suppose, paying for a plane makes for good advertising for the great care you take of the Indians, and a simple trip by a missionary's truck is no news.

It was one of the many trips for which he was never paid even basic expenses.

Immediate first aid in Moberly Lake was handled by Harry Garbitt, with Father Jungbluth taking the serious cases out to the hospital in Fort St. John. Quite often Father and Harry would confer: "Is this one serious enough to be shipped out? Should we call in the doctor by radio? Would the patient be able to make the trip?"

When necessary, no matter what the weather, Father Jungbluth would start up his truck. The patient would be bedded down in the caboose, and off they would go. The roads might be covered with a half metre of snow or reduced to boggy ditches of muskeg and gumbo. Often he was followed by a team of horses from Moberly Lake to Jackfish or to Sundance when the roads were especially bad. If he got stuck, they could pull him out.

Sometimes Father Jungbluth would haul his medical patients as far as Sundance. Ernie Pfanner, who hauled mail and freight from Dawson Creek to Little Prairie would then take them the rest of the way to Dawson Creek — if they were non-status Indians. The status Indians had to go to Fort St. John Hospital, otherwise their medical expenses would be refused by the Indian Department.

Whatever the weather or however they managed to get the patient out, the trip had to be attempted. Under such circumstances, death was never a stranger.

One such case involved a young 20-year-old Metis named Johnny Cameron, the son of old Pat Cameron. He had been working as a guide with a hunting party, which can be rough work in October or November. It is cold, often raining or snowing, and one has to sleep out on the ground. For some reason, Johnny became stricken — whether from a virus or a stroke is not known — and he became paralyzed from the waist down. Father Jungbluth took him to the hospital in Fort St. John where he remained for quite some time before they shipped him to a hospital in Edmonton. There they performed surgery on his back, several operations, all to no avail. At that point, his people were ready to clutch at any idea that might give them hope, and so they took him to a chiropractor. He could do nothing. He said the boy had been butchered, the back all cut up, the nerves severed, and so he was sent home. His health then deteriorated to the point where he was completely incapacitated, unable to even pass water. Again Father Jungbluth took him to Fort St. John. He died two weeks later.

Father Jungbluth started up the truck and went in to get the boy, now sewed up in linen and wrapped in a tarp. On the return trip he brought the truck back as far as the road permitted, which was East Pine. There he borrowed a horse from the Maddens and, laying the body across in front of the saddle, rode back through the trail past Jackfish Lake and in to Moberly. The rain came down in a fine mist, soaking him through to the skin; his saddle squeaked with every motion of his horse. The body shifted slightly and he slowed the horse so he could redistribute the weight. It was embalmed and slightly pliant.

"You won't have any trouble with it," the mortician had told him before leaving Fort St. John. "You could have it beside the stove for three weeks if you want to. It will not decompose with formaldehyde in the veins."

All the way home, Father Jungbluth's thoughts ravelled back through the years he had spent working with these Indians. What a hard life they had! But then, everyone had it hard. He thought of his own mother, widowed, suffering the loss of her son; of his friends and relatives back home, now recovering from the ravages of war. The economy was worse there now than it had been while the war was still on.

He recalled coming to Canada, meeting poor little Petit-Jean with his twisted legs, and old blind Sijoli. And the old fellow who had died on his way to Christmas Mass one night — old and half blind, he'd tried to make his way to the church in the snow and had fallen, rolled down a bank and lay there, dying. In church the people were celebrating the birth of Christ and singing Christmas carols. They found him the next day, or rather the dogs did, sniffing out his cold trail and yelping as they came upon the small twisted form, half-covered with snow.

The priest mused on the troubles he'd witnessed since coming to Fort St. John, the poverty and squalor. But still there was always a pot of tea offered in even the meanest shack, and quiet hospitality, the murmur of thanks as he handed them a bright pink and gold holy picture. He thought of the young boy whose body swayed gently in front of him, its covering tarp now darkened with rain, a young boy struck down for no reason, no known accident or disease or willful mischief. He heard, rather than felt, himself cough. Only then was he aware that his throat had become a hard lump, swelling until he could no longer swallow. His face was wet with misted rain. The horse plodded on in the darkening afternoon.

20

On Vacation

*I*n 1949 Father Jungbluth left for France on his first vacation in 14 years.

In Strasbourg he went directly to the Provincial House in the Robertsau, where he intended to stay for the duration of his vacation. The House was central for his travels to family and friends. But he was hardly there a week before he became impatient with public transport. A car was out of the question. Few people had cars in France right after the war; gas was rationed and very expensive. He mentioned his plight to one of the Brothers at the House.

"We had a little motorcycle here, before the war," the Brother replied thoughtfully, "but now it's all in pieces. I don't know if we could ever find all the parts. When the Germans invaded, they requisitioned all our machines, everything. We were supposed to get them back, or get a little something for their rent. Once they got them we never heard of them anymore."

"Where is this motorcycle?" Father Jungbluth asked excitedly. "I want to see it."

The Brother smiled. "Follow me." He walked out to the back garden. "Here we are," he said, sweeping his arms to indicate the entire area. "Some parts are buried here, others you may find hidden in the cellar, or in various parts of the house. We made good and sure the Germans would never find it."

It took Father Jungbluth a week to locate everything he needed. Some parts he never found and he had to adapt them from an old bicycle. He spent his days scraping dirt from rusted pieces of the old French motorcycle, polishing, straightening, repairing and refitting. The Oblate Brothers and Fathers would come out to watch, then shake their heads and go sadly back into the house. The poor little missionary had lost his head in Canada! He would never get that old wreck going. It was nothing but trash.

At the end of a week, the cough and sputter of the engine shocked the House from its quiet routine. Astounded men watched Father Jungbluth roar up and down the back lane on his new machine. They rushed to tell the Father Superior.

"If he has managed to put that thing together, it's his," Father Superior announced, "and the House will grant him the gas for it."

That evening in the main dining hall, Father Jungbluth announced he was going to ride the motorcycle to Lourdes. Had he spoken of using it to cross the English Channel he could not have aroused more excitement.

"Impossible! Too far! You'll kill yourself," the Oblates exclaimed. They looked from one to the other in disbelief. "The bike is much too small. It will not make it over the first hill. What if something happens to you when you are so far away, without help?"

One by one he argued down their protests, even those of the Provincial Superior.

"Then I must tell you," the Provincial said at last, "that I decline all responsibilities for this trip. Going to Lourdes on that old piece of junk! Whoever heard of such a thing?"

"I see no trouble at all," Father Jungbluth said calmly.

The Provincial sat with tightly pursed lips, his objection clearly registered. Father Jungbluth became emphatic. "I mean no disrespect, Father," he said tightly, "but I never thought that you were supposed to have anything to do with it. Nobody has asked you to take responsibility for me."

Silence. Then a slight smile began to show on the Provincial's face. He tilted his head back and sat quietly for a moment, staring at the ceiling, his hands clasped in a prayer position. At last he spoke: "Take care of yourself, Father. We will pray for your safe journey."

From Strasbourg Father Jungbluth traveled to Zurich to visit a colleague in Sierre. Crossing back to France at Belfort, he rode on to Lyon to the shrine of Parais-le-Monial, then south toward Marseille, to the shrine of the Oblate Fathers, Notre Dame de la Garde. In beautiful, sunny weather he roared down the winding roads of southern France, past the homes of the wealthy along the coast to Toulouse. The bike performed admirably, and he took his time.

On his second week, he arrived at the village of Lourdes, nestled at the foot of the Pyrenees. Amidst crowds of the faithful, he visited the shrine. He attended religious exercises: the High Mass, the Hours of Devotion to the Virgin Mary and to our Lord in the Blessed Eucharist. He watched, in the dark balmy night, candlelight processions. He saw the sick from all over the world arrive at the big shrine to be blessed and to pray to St. Bernadette. The power of their faith was awesome.

He continued to Bordeaux, then on to the shrines of the Child Jesus at Lisieux. He obtained a relic from the Convent to take back to his little chapel dedicated to St. Theresa at Moberly Lake.

At Lisieux he also visited with Monseigneur Falaize, a retired bishop who had been a missionary among the Eskimos at Hudson's Bay. From there he traveled on to Orléans, to the shrine of Joan of Arc.

Then, Paris. He rode straight to the Oblate House and there met Oblate brothers from Africa, Ceylon, South America. And colleagues with whom he had studied theology at Liège. In a friendly group they set off to see the sights of Paris. The vacationing priests visited the great Cathedral of Notre Dame, the big church of the Sacred Heart of Jesus located in the colorful neighborhood of Montmarte, majestic above the infamous *boites de nuit* that surrounded it.

"*Paris vaut bien une messe*," quoted one of his companions, recalling the famous words of Henry IV. Indeed, it was a city of inspiration; it was a city to love.

From Paris he rode to Nancy, to the shrine of Notre Dame de Sion; then finally, at the end of one month and a journey of some 3,200 kilometres that took him the circumference of France, he arrived, tanned and healthy, back at the Oblate House in Strasbourg.

Throughout his journey Father Jungbluth kept in daily touch with the Provincial House by sending postcards from the towns where he stayed. He wrote that his trip was going well, and outlined his proposed itinerary for the next day. The worried priests erected on the study wall a large map of France. With each new report, they pushed in stick-pins. On his return he was escorted into the room and shown the map. There, looking like a prickle-bush, was the record of his trip. He laughed when he saw it. Their concern for his safety was genuine. There had been times, although he had not told them, when he'd had to push the motorcycle a couple kilometres to the nearest village, when the clutch control wire frayed or the carburetor plugged. He had slept beneath trees, in fields, in convents and in Oblate Houses, at the homes of friends and in hostels. And he was none the worse for it.

Now back in Strasbourg for the duration of his vacation, Father Jungbluth received many invitations from relatives, friends and local parish priests in Wolxheim and Ernolsheim. As he began to relate stories of his northern experiences, his host would jump up in excitement. "Stop right there! We must invite others to hear these stories." Neighbors would be asked in and sometimes the crowd became so large that they would have to reconvene in the local school or parish hall. There, Father Jungbluth would set up his few slides and begin to tell his wilderness tales.

"A missionary has to go to faraway places, but today such a long journey from the home country to the mission field is not so very difficult," he began. "The endless troubles and extreme hardships are confronted not by traveling, but on arrival!

"I must admit that as I watched Europe's coastline vanish in the distance, a small question assailed my mind: 'Pater Emile, do you really want to go away?' And I know I will ask it again of myself when the time comes to return to my Ice Missions.

"When you have lived for 14 years in the Ice Missions, you are no longer young, you have grown colder, and the spirit of adventure has died down; you know the exhaustion that is waiting for you. However, the love for God and the Souls remains, and this alone counts. Therefore, dear friends, I can truthfully say, 'I am returning when my vacation at home is over, and I am returning full of joy to my poor Indians, although not with a burning longing . . .'"

He felt the audience respond to his honesty.

"A missionary experiences deep happiness when he can see that there is an interest in his work and for his mission field, and when he can answer all the questions put forward to him," he continued. "I have brought slides showing pictures of my poor Indians, showing you how they live, what they eat, how they celebrate their joys and their sorrows."

The lights were dimmed and the projector lit up. There on the screen stood Father Jungbluth, bundled to the chin in a fur coat ("A donation from France!" he explained). The next scene showed a racing dog team, the wild wolf-like huskies straining at leather traces, the Eskimo on the sled looking like a black bear in his voluminous furs. The pictures ranged from summer in Moberly Lake to winter in the high Arctic — scenes he had borrowed from the files of other missionaries.

During the question period, he told stories of the land of ice and snow, of dogsleds and snowshoes, of Indian horses and of wolves that skulked the dark evergreen forests. After these sessions, either he or his friends went around with a hat. Father Jungbluth could never bring himself to talk about money, as the people were still so poor. But the subject always seemed to surface and donations were readily offered. Some gave coins and others promises of steady support for his mission.

Among the first of old family friends he visited was a friend of his mother's, Sister Dosithée of the Congregation of the Sisters of the Cross in Neuhof. He and his mother had often gone there to visit. His mother would insist that he dress properly to show what a gentleman he had become, home now on his holidays from college. One time when they had arrived at the Convent and inquired for her, they were shown a path leading out to the field; there was Sister Dosithée, wearing her heavy old habit, pitching bundles off the big belt of a shuddering threshing machine.

Father Jungbluth sat studying her as she recalled for him the experiences of those "back home" during the recent war. She was now in her 60s, still a strong capable woman. Her habit covered her hair completely, but Father Jungbluth was sure it must be gray.

"Now," she said suddenly, "tell me of your mission."

Father Jungbluth told her of his colorful Indians, his faithful horse, his motorcycle and truck, his new church, of his little enterprises of fixing watches and radios, his invention of the buzz-saw. He noticed her eyes narrow slightly. She began tapping her fingers on the wooden arm of the chair.

"I think you are not telling me everything," she interrupted. "We have suffered here, yes, but you are going hungrier than we are. There's no need for that. How can you go to these missions through snow with a scrap of dried meat in your stomach? When do you ever have time to be a mission-ary with sawing wood and tinkering with old radios?"

"But it's not that bad!" Father Jungbluth protested.

She quieted him with sharp eyes. "I promise you, I promise you here and now," she said slowly, "that from now on you are not going to go hungry. As long as I am alive, we will see to it that you are free to do the job you have been sent overseas to do."

Everywhere Father Jungbluth went in his home country, he found the same response. People were kind and, although they had little enough for themselves, they were more than willing to give what they could. One day he visited an old aunt in Neudorf. As he climbed to the top floor where the family had their small apartment, he could not help but reflect on the poverty that the war had wrought on these people. Cars on the street were dilapidated, with fenders flopping and tires worn bare. People wore old coats; their dresses and shirts had been laundered almost white; their shoes hardly protected their feet from the ground. Inside his aunt's apartment, he noted the sparse furnishings. The signs were everywhere.

At one point during the visit, the aunt called over her young son, whispered something in his ear, and the boy dashed off downstairs. Minutes later he returned clutching in his hand one egg. With a smile the aunt leaned forward and patted Father Jungbluth on the shoulder. "You must eat," she said, and went to the stove. He could feel his face go crimson as the aunt set before him the precious cooked egg, and the family pulled their chairs up to smilingly watch. He would never again have the right to become discouraged.

September came, time to bid farewell. In 14 missionary years, war had torn apart a country, altering the landscape as well as the attitudes of his people. Old friends had scattered. Mother had passed away. In this country, only his past was alive, not his future. The stories had now been told. It was time to leave.

He left Alsace in early fall, when the country was still green and the air still warm. He arrived in Moberly Lake on a windy day in October. Already the trees were bare, and the cold wind whipped from the dark blue lake to rattle the windows of the church. No priest had been brought in to take his place during the six months. An emergency number had been left at the Hudson's Bay store so the priest in Fort St. John could be notified if there were a death or any other emergency. No one had died. It was as if he had never left.

A week back into his labors, he wrote a letter to *Immaculata*, so news would be sure to reach his benefactors. He sat back on his wooden chair, laid his pen upon the paper, and watched in silence as the orange flames licked around the poplar wood inside the stove. His cabin was warm, even though he could see the wall calendar and paper pictures flip out from the wall at regular intervals as gusts of cold wind seeped between the chinked logs. He pulled his chair up to the table. He must give them something light, some color. He picked up the pen.

It is five o'clock in the afternoon and is already dark outside. How short are these fall days in our Ice Missions. Outside the wind is howling and blowing against the tiny window of my small quarters behind the church. It sounds eerie outside. Inside, however, burns a cozy fire, and my friend the Indian Chief sits on the floor between the stove and stool enjoying the warmth of the room. Soon after, I can't believe it, but the good old man suddenly lays stretched out on the floor, sleeping and snoring.

Loneliness creeps up again, and I am really "longing for" the sunshine and warm climate of my homeland, the Alsace, that I had to leave behind once more one month ago. I lean back and remember all the dear friends and supporters to whom I promised to write more often by means of *Immaculata*. Can writing home cure homesickness?

Thank you again for all your kindnesses, and God bless you.

He addressed the envelope and sealed the letter inside, ready for the next mail. He could hear the waves crashing upon the shore, trying to escape from the wind that tore across the lake and rocked the very foundations of his little chapel.

21
Date with the Devil

*I*n the late 40s, a two-way radio system was installed in the Hudson's Bay trading post at Moberly Lake. Scheduled calls were made every day at 10:00 a.m. and 6:00 p.m. to the two other stations, one at the Halfway (operated by the teacher at the Halfway School) and the other at Fort St. John in the post office.

Low-powered and unreliable, the radio was nevertheless a valuable connection with the outside world. As Father Jungbluth was the foremost radio expert in Moberly Lake, the Hudson's Bay factor, Andy Densmore, thought it wise to have direct communication between the post and the church. Father Jungbluth designed a "barbwire phone" (although it had no barbs) from a roll of haywire strung along through the trees connecting the church to the Hudson's Bay store, a distance of 2.5 kilometres.

What looked like a perforated hockey puck attached to coated wires was used for both the earpiece and mouthpiece. It had a "hot wire" attached to the roll of baling wire running through the trees; the wire was wrapped in a piece of rubber, or heavy paper, to insulate it from the ground and the elements. (Bottle-necks were sometimes used as insulators). The second wire was grounded onto a piece of iron hammered a half metre into the earth outside the church. This completed the circuit.

Father Jungbluth would take the mouthpiece in hand and wail a low, "woooo . . . woooo . . . woooo." The eerie sound would waver from the mouthpiece at the Hudson's Bay post to be picked up and answered by the manager or his wife. The barbwire phone was one of the simplest of Father Jungbluth's ingenious communication systems.

He owned a small radio which operated with tubes. "It was," says Father Jungbluth, "the ultimate to get such good reception from those tubes, especially after I extended the band width by opening or closing some variable condensers to include the two-way radio system and some police calls on my home radio."

But he went even further, reasoning, "If I modify the receiver so I can use it as a sound transmission device, I can put another speaker outside, on top of a tree, perhaps. It would be just like a microphone up there. Then, by using the grid of the radio where the sound goes in and is amplified, I should be able to pick up sound from anywhere around. The mike would be much more sensitive than the ear. If sound comes into that speaker up in the tree, and is transferred into a current and carried by the wire to the radio, I should be able to hear people coming; then I can just switch the receiver around so I can talk to them."

He mounted speakers from old radios in trees at various distances from the church. He enclosed the speakers in lard pails, wrapped a piece of tape around the pail so it would be fairly waterproof, then punctured the lid with holes. Some were in three-pound pails, some in one-pound pails, all leaning downward.

He waited anxiously to try out his new communication system. It worked, he knew that. He could hear the sleighbells of the horses over one kilometre away, or the coughing and muttering of the Indians as they trudged down the trail to the post to get supplies. But how could his system be put to use?

One crisp winter day a shy knock was heard on his door at the back of the church. A young Indian woman stood outside. "Hello, Father," she said with head down as if examining her moccasin toes. "Can I see you for a minute?"

It was a cold day and the warmth from Father Jungbluth's little stove fairly blew out the door. He stood back. "Come in," he said. "Come in and get warm."

She stepped barely inside the door, still looking down at her feet. Her face was dark with embarrassment.

"What is it?" Father Jungbluth asked. "What's your trouble today?"

"It's Joe," she hoarsely whispered. "He's going to town."

Father Jungbluth immediately sized up the situation. Her husband, out most of the fall with a guiding party, had come home with a pocket full of money, and the assurance that there was more to be had whenever he wanted it by taking out parties of rich Americans. Joe had been bragging in the post about the money he'd earned. He bought new clothes, he paid his jawbone, he set in his winter's supply of food, and he was now set to blow the rest on a good time in Fort St. John.

"He's packing up now," the miserable wife whimpered. "He's going with his uncle." Her dark eyes blinked rapidly when she told Father Jungbluth what Joe had said to her: "I've looked after you, and now I look after myself. I'm going to get good and drunk and I might not be home till Christmas."

"Can you do something, Father?" she begged. "I don't want him to go to town. He'll be in fights, he'll find a woman . . ." Here she burst into tears, and Father Jungbluth could only think of one comforting line:

"I'll take care of it," he said. "Don't worry. Go back home. I'll take care of it."

After she went out the door, Father Jungbluth sat down at his table to think. It would do no good to go to Joe and beg him to see reason. In Joe's mind, he was acting very reasonably. He'd worked hard, paid his bills, and now he was out to have a good time. Father Jungbluth idly switched on his radio. From out the speaker came a yodelling sound. It was Joe, walking home down the trail. Joe was a singer, and he sure was singing now.

Bending low over the mouthpiece, Father Jungbluth lowered his voice to a deep growl: "Joe . . . Joe . . . Joe!" he began. The singing stopped. "Joe," he began again, "Joe, this is your Guardian Angel." He switched again; still no sound. "Joe, can you hear me, Joe?" Switch. A tremulous, "Yeah?" came over the speaker. "Joe, listen to me. This is your Guardian Angel. The Devil is making you go to town. You have a date with the Devil! Do not go to town, Joe. Do not go to town." He allowed his voice to waver and fall. Then he clicked off.

Joe's wife came by the church two days later. "Joe won't leave the house," she said. "I don't know what's the matter with him. He had a few drinks of home brew at his uncle's just before he was going to leave for Fort St. John, and it made him go funny. He thought he heard the Devil. He wants you to come and bless the house."

Barely hiding his smile, Father Jungbluth got up to pour a little Holy Water into a Coke bottle, and follow Joe's wife up the road to bless their little cabin.

His success led Father Jungbluth to try a similar form of persuasion on his old Beaver Indian friend, Charlie Cryman. Charlie had not been coming to church much lately.

"I'm sorry, Father," he'd say lamely when he stopped in for coffee on his way home from the post. He would set down his back-pack of groceries and let out a great sigh. Then would come the excuse, a different one each week. Father Jungbluth was getting worried. If Charlie stopped coming, so would the other Indians.

Yesterday Charlie had not even stopped in for coffee. Father Jungbluth had put the pot on the stove, then watched through his window as Charlie had stopped, hesitated, then trudged on. Father Jungbluth let him get about half a kilometre past the church before he switched on his speaker.

"C-h-a-r-l-i-e!" he cried in a deep rumbling voice. Then, quickly, like an echo, "Charlie! Charlie!" He switched the receiver over, but there was only silence. He imagined Charlie standing dead in his tracks, looking around, mouth open, eyes darting into the dark forests on each side of the road. Then Father Jungbluth could hear his footsteps starting, faster now, hurrying to get home.

"Charlie! Charlie!" Loud now, an urgent command. The footsteps stopped. "Where are you going, Charlie?" he growled menacingly, in Beaver. "You don't visit the church anymore! Why don't you visit the church, Charlie?" The footsteps quickened into a run, pounding down the road. "Charlie! Charlie! YOU WILL COME!" Then he clicked off the set, stoked the fire to keep the coffee warm, and sat back to read his breviary.

Fifteen minutes later there was a frantic pounding at his door. Charlie burst in, stumbling, breathless, completely rattled. He leaned against the doorframe to catch his breath. "Something . . ." he gasped, "the Devil . . . something speaks to me! Calls me Charlie!"

"Sit down, old friend," Father Jungbluth said kindly. "Let me give you a cup of coffee. Then I have something to show you." He drew up a chair in front of the radio. "Look closely, Charlie. This is what called you. It was done through this machine." Charlie remained silent while Father Jungbluth explained the rudiments of radio communication. "Now you try it," he urged.

They switched on the receiver and waited for trotting feet to sound on the hard-packed road. A quick step — it was *Kokoos*, whose name means "pig" in Cree.

Switching the receiver to transmit, Charlie leaned toward the mouthpiece. "*Kokoos!*" he cried. "*Meonedjedi ki Pikiskwatik. Astam ayamihekamikok!* This is God speaking to you! Come to church!"

They switched it over to hear *Kokoos'* expletives. They could picture the irate Indian whirling around on the road, shaking his fist at the trees.

Charlie began to laugh. "Well, Father," he said, "maybe I don't fool people like you can, but boy oh boy, those Indians shouldn't think that God speaks Beaver with a German accent!"

22
The False Priest of Kelly Lake

*I*n 1952 Father Jungbluth was given two acres of land by Fred Hambler on which to build at church at Kelly Lake.

The Indians wanted to begin immediately. Not knowing how long the enthusiasm might last, Father Jungbluth began construction in the late fall of that year, as soon as the frozen ground could support the heavy loads of lumber and bags of cement hauled in by horses and wagons. Money for the building materials came from supporters in Alsace.

Father Jungbluth was not an experienced builder and had to take impressive steps to keep the Indians' faith in his work. The church was to be a frame building, different from the log church in Moberly Lake, and Father Jungbluth stayed up late at night studying books on construction and hastily sketching out plans for the next day. First he had his crew build rows of fires to thaw out the ground. He then surveyed the perimeter, ordered the foundation ditch to be dug, and supervised the concrete pour. The weather was still fairly mild, although the lake was frozen, and it was important that they hurry to pour the concrete foundation before the frost was too deep in the ground.

With great dignity he measured, by means of a water scale, the level from one corner to another.

"*Nanik-kisik!* Hurry up!" Father Jungbluth urged, running from crew to crew. The steel grey skies could easily release their snow, forcing them to wait out the winter with no roof on the church.

The men sniffed the air, and seemed to sense another message. "Time to go hunting," they said one day, and laid down their hammers. It was time to get their pack-dogs and packhorses ready.

"But . . . you can't! You can't stop now!" Father Jungbluth shouted to the receding wagons.

"The women will finish it," one called back.

"Women? Women?" Father Jungbluth sat down on a sawhorse, his head in his hands. He envisioned crooked nails, injured fingers . . . catastrophe.

The next morning when Father Jungbluth appeared at the work site, he was greeted by his new crew. A middle-aged lady stepped forward. "Do you want us to start putting on the sheeting?" she asked shyly.

Father Jungbluth stared at her in amazement. "Do you know what to do?"

She shrugged. "I guess we can learn."

Father Jungbluth was suddenly ashamed of himself. He knew only too well how hard the Indian women could work. They took over completely when their husbands were away for an entire winter on the trapline or logging. They fed stock, hauled feed and water, chopped wood, looked after the children. Women often seemed able to exist on nothing at all.

He looked up and smiled. "Well, what are we waiting for?" he said. "*Nanik-kisik!*"

The weather got colder. Father Jungbluth and his crew worked in silent haste up on the roof, nailing on sheeting even as small snowflakes swirled around them. With hands stiff from cold, they hauled up boards and carefully crawled to the peak to try to get the roof closed in before the storms hit.

Father Jungbluth was still in bed early one morning when he heard what sounded like a hundred hammers. Were the women up at his hour? The strikes seemed louder, more forceful. He quickly pulled on his clothes and hurried over to the church. Swarming over the half-finished roof was a busy hive of 20 men.

"Hello, Father!" Fred Gladu called from his straddling position on the peak. "We came back."

"Yeah, we thought we better get this work here finished before the snow comes," shouted Narcisse Belcourt.

Bill Gladu squatted on the edge of the roof to roll a smoke. "The moose are easier to track after a snowfall," he said, giving Father Jungbluth a wink. He leaned down to help hoist up a bundle of asbestos shingles.

The decision to name the little church for Ste. Anne, the mother of the Virgin Mary, came quite by chance. Accompanied by some friends from Kelly Lake, Father Jungbluth went one day to see the newly-built church in Grande Prairie. At the same time he took a look through the old church, then being dismantled. On opening the door of a small cupboard under the stairwell, he discovered a discarded statue of Ste. Anne. "Perhaps they don't want this anymore," he thought. "The new churches are becoming wary of putting up too many statues. But it would be just the thing for my little church in Kelly Lake."

Taking the statue out of its dusty hiding place, he approached the Redemptorist Fathers. They gave it gladly.

In June, 1953, Bishop Jordan offered to come again to the wilderness, to bless the Church of Ste. Anne in Kelly Lake. Father Jungbluth went to Dawson Creek to pick him up. There he stood in his beautifully ironed robe and fine shoes. Father Jungbluth groaned when he thought of the muddy trail leading through the muskeg. He had chains and a winch, but after the turn-off from the main road they had ahead of them a rough 32 kilometres.

Halfway in, the truck became mired and they were forced to sleep overnight in the vehicle. The Bishop took the cab and Father Jungbluth wrapped himself in a blanket in the back.

They arrived in Kelly Lake four days late. For the Indians that was no inconvenience. They had readied a feast of the best deer meat and later held a dance in the Bishop's honor.

Sixty-five persons received Confirmation that day in Kelly Lake, among a total population of 120 Catholics.

Celebrating the first Confirmation in Kelly Lake, 1954.

"At one time I was permitted to teach catechism in the public schools," Father Jungbluth relates, "but it depended on the good will of the teacher and the school bus driver. The school principal at Kelly Lake, Mr. Siemens, was very cooperative. 'I know we are not supposed to have any confessional teaching, catechism or so, but I will help you,' he said. And so when we knew the Bishop was coming for Confirmation, we took the smallest catechism we could find and we edited it so there were no terms in there that the children would have trouble understanding, and then the teacher said to the class, 'as a writing exercise, I am going to make you copy this catechism; as a memory exercise, you will learn it by heart.'

"These are the Kelly Lake people I still have, and they are quite attached to their church," Father Jungbluth says. "I would say that it's my best mission, Kelly Lake."

Sometimes Father Jungbluth couldn't help but feel he favored this place, these people. They were so good with him. He recalled his first New Year's with them.

The Kelly Lake people (non-status Cree Indian mixed with English, Scottish and French blood) did not celebrate Christmas as much as New Year's. On this day all the past year's transgressions were forgiven, symbolized by a kiss, and the new year brought in with a clean slate. Father Jungbluth found himself caught up in the celebrations around five o'clock New Year's morning, when he awoke to sleighbells and laughter. The sounds came from across the lake in the vicinity of Milton Campbell's house.

He sat up in bed, rubbing his eyes. The sounds were coming nearer. Pulling on his clothes, he hopped over the cold floor of the log schoolhouse where he was sleeping and looked out the door. A sleigh was crossing the ice, coming toward him from out of the darkness. It was drawn by prancing, snorting horses. Bells jingled from every part of the harness, accompanied by the cheers and laughter of passengers, so many that some were falling off the back. Father Jungbluth was pulled up onto the sleigh by a dozen leather-mittened hands, and was tossed from one person to another, his cheeks soundly kissed and his hand shaken by almost everyone. Even the old men kissed his hand.

"*Otchitchituwikisikaw!*" everyone shouted happily in Cree. "Kissing Day!"

Then they were off to the next house. Another sleigh was added to the entourage, and another. From the final house they turned the horses back across the ice to Johnny Calliou's place. There the people unloaded, the teams were unhitched, and the party began. All the women had brought food: moosemeat stews and roasts, apple and berry pies, bannock, enough food for a week. Out came the fiddles of Celestin, Joe and Isidor Gladu, Leonard Belcourt, Dan and Eugene Gauthier, and the log walls thrummed to music and the rhythm of dancing feet.

So much joy in so difficult a life. Father Jungbluth recalled the time Annie Gladu was attacked by grizzly bears. She and her husband, Isidor, had been at their hunting camp. During the day they would both leave camp, she going one way and he another. Both could then hunt at the same time. She had a rifle (a .32 Special) and a .22, no good for shooting a bear. As she came out onto a little clearing, there before her were four romping grizzlies. She watched them a moment in silence. Her dog's hair stood on end, its hackles a straight brush-line down its spine. It emitted a low growl. One of the bears heard the dog and came running toward them, breaking into a gallop. Before she could fire her gun, the bear was slapping her to the ground, its great teeth ripping at her head. She screamed, then saw nothing. The dog ran about frantically, distracting the other three bears, leading them off into the woods. Then he came back and chased away the last one.

The bear had crushed part of Annie Gladu's skull, ripping her scalp nearly off; just a flap of skin and hair stayed attached. Her arm was broken; one finger was nearly torn off, her hand split up the middle and broken in two places. She sat up, and, blinded by her own blood, untied the scarf from around her neck and wrapped up her arm. Feeling around for her guns, she tucked them under her good arm and began the three-kilometre trek back to camp. No one was there. Fighting unconsciousness, she loaded the .22 and fired a three-shot signal into the air, then lay down on the grass to await her husband.

When Isidor returned, he hitched the horses to the wagon and loaded up his semi-conscious wife for the 19 kilometre trip to Kelly Lake. From there, someone with an old truck took them part of the way to the hospital. Annie lay stretched out in the back, her body jostling over every rut and bump. At Wilkie's they got a faster truck, and completed the journey to Beaverlodge. The doctors reportedly could not give her anaesthetic as she had lost too much blood. They proceeded as she was, conscious of every suture, every ripped muscle and shattered bone. The operation took from nine o'clock in the evening until half-past three in the morning.

"And she still goes out by herself in the bush," Father Jungbluth marvelled. "She's killed lots of black bears since then. She could shoot a moose any day. You just can't stop those women."

The little Church of Ste. Anne became a gathering place used for meetings whether Father Jungbluth was there or not.

It came to be the setting for the phenomenal visit of *"Ayamihewiyinikan,"* the False Priest of Kelly Lake.

The word, *Ayamihewiyinikan,* unpronounceable to the uninitiated, comes from *Ayamihe,* a prefix meaning prayer, and *iyini,* meaning man. Thus the Cree Indians call the priest, *Ayamihewiyiniw,* the Man of Prayer. *Kan* is a suffix meaning false, a substitute for the real thing.

The story was told to Father Jungbluth by Annie Gladu's husband, Isidor, the "patriarch" of Kelly Lake. The story took a long time to tell, the details fragmented by hesitations for silent thought.

"This man came from Grouard," Isidor Gladu said, "and he was one of those happy-go-lucky fellows who are most cheerful when they own nothing, for then they have nothing to worry about. We showed him hospitality, for everyone enjoyed his wit. He had a fine sense of fun. He was good company."

Isidor sat silent for a moment, enjoying his smoke, forming his thoughts.

"This one was a middle-aged man and a non-status Indian, a breed. He played the fiddle with gusto, and brought happiness and laughter wherever he went. Thus he acquired the name of Happy.

"When the Big Day of the Cross (Good Friday) approached, Happy asked me if we would be walking the Way of the Cross. I said usually the priest serves Kelly Lake last, because he lives so far away and has to pray in many other places too. Happy then said, 'But one does not need the Man of Prayer to walk the Way of the Cross!'

"'It is not easy,' I said to him. 'You do not know how our Man of Prayer does it here. He makes us walk from picture to picture, making us stand

and kneel and stand and kneel. All the while he explains what happened to Jesus along the way. On the big pictures we see it all. Many times over he makes us say to Jesus that we pity him and we are sorry. He makes us see that every time we swear, we make the cross of Jesus heavier. Every time we get drunk we swing the big hammer that drives the spikes into His hands and feet. Also he leads us in the long sad song. Like this: *Tatto ka pe nantotamek* — but Happy interrupted me.

"'I know all that!' he said, 'and I can sing better than you.'"

"Did Happy really make the Stations of the Cross with you?" Father Jungbluth asked, interrupting Isidor's soliloquy.

Isidor became angry. "Let me finish, Father! You are just as impatient as Happy who did not let me sing the sad song because he wanted to tell us all he had learned in the mission school and how he hadn't forgotten a word."

Isidor sat back, silent, his dark eyes thoughtful. "'Since you have such a good head,' I said to Happy, 'you could easily lead the Way of the Cross, could you not?'

"'Of course I could!' Happy said.

"'And sing and preach?'

"'And sing and preach!' he said, without blinking an eye.

"'Fine!' I said quickly before he had a chance to back out. 'I will tell all the people that you will lead and sing and preach.'

"There were some neighbors in the house and therefore Happy had to accept. Otherwise he would have lost face, and that is one thing he dreaded. Now from that day on, Happy seemed a changed man. He took long walks in the bush. He would sneak into the church and kneel for hours in front of the crucifix. He looked like a saint. When the big day came everyone, young and old, arrived at the church. There were as many men as women, because all the bad men came too.

"'You must put on Father's black robe,' I told Happy.

"He refused, even though it would have covered the holes in the knees of his pants. I gave him my jacket, not too clean, since one arm was almost gone from the one Happy wore. Happy knelt in front of the altar. His head was tilted to one side. He appeared very holy.

"At three o'clock I lit the two candles on the altar and handed them to Bill and Jack, two no-good boys you had fired as altar boys because they talked and laughed behind your back. This time they did not laugh. They stood where I told them, one on the right and one on the left side of Happy. Wherever Happy went, the boys followed.

"Happy took the cross in his hands — not the big one, but the small one on the altar — and holding it high up over his head, he started to pray, in Cree. And did he pray! He knew every word of all the prayers by heart, and pronounced them much clearer than you do. But, when the time came to sing, not a sound came out of Happy. It could hardly be believed. It took me a moment to realize that something was wrong. Then so he wouldn't lose face, I let go with the long sad song: (The Passion)

> *Tatto ka pe nantotamek*
> *Ka isi kwatakihit,*
> *Jesus ki Manitominow*
> *Ka nipustamakoyak:*
> *Wi nakataweyittatak*
> *Esi kisewatisit;*
> *Kakike wi sakihatak,*
> *Wi nipustamowatak . . .*

"As you know, Father, I have the strongest voice for singing in Kelly Lake. I made the windows rattle. Some women tried to sing along, but nobody could hear them. At last Happy began to preach. At times his voice was loud as thunder, then it would drop so soft like a spring wind. The people could understand every word. No one moved. Even the noisy kids who always disturb the congregation during a sermon were quiet. Their eyes were wide and their mouths open in concentration. No, never, will we forget that sermon.

"Happy stood quiet, looking up at the ceiling for the longest time before he began. Then in a sad low voice, without turning to the people (priests then faced the altar with their backs to the congregation), he said quietly: 'Me, I never had a father. My mother died when I was just a kid. A priest came and took me to a house where there were lots of Sisters. One of them took me on her knee while I was still crying and told me about my Mother, my Mother in Heaven, and that I had got her on the first big day of the Cross a long time ago.

"'I was never so lonely after that. When I lay in bed at night I would think of her, my Mother Mary. The Virgin Mary. I knew She could see me, there in that bed, even though the room was full of beds with kids just like me in them. I knew She cared about me. She could always make me laugh, make me sing, make the music come out of me until it appeared like I didn't have a care in the world. She loved me. She made me free. I am free now to wander and visit or go into the bush by myself for months at a time, or to play the fiddle and sing and make people happy. She is my Mother. I am Her son. We are all Her sons and daughters. We all matter.'

"I had never cried before in my life," Isidor continued slowly and solemnly, "but during that sermon I felt tears come up in my eyes and I had to fight to hold them back. How long did Happy preach? No one could say. But it was dark when he stopped. We could have listened to him all night."

Isidor gave a long sad sigh. "Nobody saw Happy again. The next morning I found my jacket hanging on the door handle. It seems he camped that night at the Horse Lake Reserve and then went on up to Fort Vermilion. A very long way from Kelly Lake."

Isidor's story was done. But Father Jungbluth could not get it out of his mind. That night as he lay in bed he thought it over. "Perhaps," he thought, "the word *Ayamihewiyinikan* was wrong. That miserable suffix, *kan*! Possibly it could be discarded and replaced with the prefix *kitchi* which imparts the idea of greatness, excellence. Thus, by using *kitchi* in front of *okima*, we have the 'really big chief, the king.' And anyone who is a little acquainted with Indian lore knows about *Kitchimanito*, the Great Spirit.

"*Kitchiayamihewiyiniw*, the Outstanding Man of Prayer. But no. We are out of luck there too. By this word, the Cree Indians refer to the Bishop."

He sighed and rolled over to sleep. His last thoughts, as he drifted off, chastised human emotions. It was not right for a priest to have "pets" in his mission, but he could not help but feel a special love for his Indians of Kelly Lake.

23

Moberly Lake School

*I*n 1954, Father Jungbluth added a new dimension to his duties. He became a schoolteacher. He had no training and his English was still far from perfect. Despite this, he found himself the sole professor of 25 Cree and Beaver Indian children.

During the Easter holidays, the teacher in Moberly Lake suddenly quit and a lock was put on the schoolhouse door. Father Jungbluth asked around to see if there was another coming.

"No, there is no one," he was told. "They won't bring a new teacher to Moberly Lake until the beginning of the term in the fall."

Mr. Galibois, the Indian Agent, was not happy about the situation either. He sent Father Jungbluth a letter asking if he knew of anyone who could teach. At that time, Father Jungbluth was championing for a "real Indian school," because "an Indian school was a Catholic school." When Mr. Galibois asked if he knew anyone who could teach, he saw his chance.

"If you can promise me you will try to get a real Indian school — not a public school — I will found my own, in the meantime."

"Fine. Go ahead. And I'll see to it that you are recognized."

It was assurance enough. Beginning immediately during the Easter holidays, Father Jungbluth called in Mr. Paulsen, the local carpenter. He cut the backs off the pews to make benches. They applied special paint to a sheet of plywood for a blackboard. A division shut off the altar from the rest of the building.

Father Jungbluth sent out an appeal for books. Within days he had a reply from the principal of the Blue Quills School run by the Oblates at St. Paul, Alberta, offering books they no longer needed: "If you want them, you can have them. And we'll pay the freight." Case upon case of books arrived: first grade and second grade Catholic readers. They were similar to public school readers but told of St. Francis and the lives of priests such as Father Lacombe, and of the Canadian martyrs, Jesuit priests murdered by Hurons and Iroquois in Quebec. The stories were written for elementary school levels.

At the end of Easter break, Father Jungbluth was ready to open his school. Mr. Galibois arranged through the Indian Affairs Department for his salary as a school teacher. It was, in Father Jungbluth's words, "the lowest salary of the lowest category, $80 a month, I think. I was, after all, not even qualified to be a teacher."

The Moberly Lake "school bus."

Father Jungbluth also operated his own school bus (there had been no school transportation) by fixing up his pick-up truck with seats in the back. Every morning he drove to the river where the Napoleons lived, to get some of their kids; then to the Flat, 13 kilometres up the road, to pick up children from the families there. He didn't go to the West End because they were fairly close. He judged they could walk, but they didn't come at all.

"I had only taught for about three weeks before I knew I needed help," Father Jungbluth admits. "I wouldn't say that I lost control of them, but I had a tough time. You know, when you're not a teacher, it's awfully hard to control kids, to keep them interested so their minds don't wander. The Indian kids at Moberly Lake hadn't had any schooling and were hard to control. They'd do — just what kids do — they'd escape. They went out catching rabbits. They ran away, or else they just didn't come back right away. They'd make those paper airplanes or paper wads and shoot them. Things like that.

"I went around with my truck in the morning, but sometimes I didn't get them. The parents had not gone to school and they didn't see any importance in it to go steady . . . they'd send them tomorrow. What could I do? 'He has a cold.' 'We need him to cut up a moose.' There was no real ambition or real control.

"According to Sister Veronica, who many years later asked me to describe my methods, I didn't know anything. I had not been formed, she said. 'I'm sure you couldn't teach them! They couldn't learn anything like that. That's not the way to teach them how to read.' She had become a teacher by learning how at the university.

"I tried to teach them hygiene too. Outside I had wash basins on benches along the wall of the church, and they had to wash before they went in. I had water in there and that strong, red soap, 'Lifebuoy.' No towels. They just dried themselves on their clothes or shook the water off their hands. They were used to that."

After he had been dragging on in such a manner for three weeks or so, he went one day to Fort St. John and there ran into Father Green. Now there was an excellent teacher! Father Jungbluth told him his troubles and, to his great joy, Father Green offered to come out and give him a hand. He did very well, helping out for three or four weeks. Father Green taught and Father Jungbluth observed how he did it:

"That man had special talents to control them," Father Jungbluth recalls. "All he had to do was stay in the middle of the room and stretch his head up and look around for silence. I didn't have that. I felt like taking their heads and knocking them together."

As summer came nearer, it became more difficult to keep the children in school. One bright day around one o'clock in the afternoon, Father Jungbluth heard a great commotion outside. The kids stretched their necks to look. Some left their seats and ran to the window.

Outside, with a team and wagon, was Rossie Napoleon. It was such a nice day that he thought he would get some of the kids and go rabbit hunting. Father Jungbluth stood outside on the step, his arms crossed in front of him, as if to brace himself against an attack.

"What do you mean by coming here in the middle of the day?" he demanded of Rossie. "You have no right to do this! These kids are under my care during the school day. Come back at three o'clock and you can have them."

There was no point in that, Rossie said mildly, slapping the reins to scare the flies off the horses. He was here now and he wanted them. Father Jungbluth had to make a stand. The kids were crowding behind him, looking with big eyes, waiting to see who would win. Neither man wanted to lose face in front of them all. If Father Jungbluth gave in at this point he would lose control completely.

The two men faced each other in growing anger. Suddenly Rossie jumped down from the wagon and began to take off his coat. Father Jungbluth leapt over the step railing and broke off a willow switch. And then, both men stopped. Rossie looked at the children and at Father Jungbluth. He jumped back onto the wagon, turned the team around, and left. Father Jungbluth faced the wide-eyed and now silent students.

"Come back in and sit down," he said. And they did, clearly disappointed with the outcome.

Elmer Davis of Moberly Lake was one of Father Jungbluth's students. "I remember going to the Indian Catholic school here before we got the other one," he recalls. "Father taught us. He used to be mean inside the classroom, but as soon as the lessons were over he'd give us candy. But inside, boy, it was a different story. I don't think our parents really knew what was going on. Nobody would go home and tell them that he was mean and bad."

Elmer's wife, Victoria, also remembers Father Jungbluth's school. "I don't remember too much about what we learned inside, but I remember how we used to play house, outside, in the bushes down by the lake. Father used to give us little dishes and things. But it was hard to go all the time, every day."

Father Jungbluth finished out the term, and the holidays started. During the summer he heard that the school board in Dawson Creek was not too pleased to have a Catholic school operating in Moberly Lake. Before September, an announcement was made that the school board was intending to reopen their public school in Moberly Lake in the fall. They requested a meeting with the entire population, to be held in the old schoolhouse.

The meeting opened by the Chairman asking, "Do you want a public school here, or don't you?" Then he named the advantages: "There was never any transportation for the school children here before, and the transportation you have now is illegal." (It was true: Father Jungbluth had no licence to haul students). "If we reopen the public school you will have a real bus. Also, lunches will be provided at noon, and there will be new sports equipment. The school will be extended to have more classrooms, and have not only one teacher but two and possibly three."

Father Jungbluth, in the audience, knew then and there that he would lose his school. Still, he planned to put up a fight.

Mary Gladu was there, an Indian woman whose children went to Father Jungbluth's school, and Father Jungbluth watched in pleased amazement as she suddenly stood up and said, "I want a Catholic school." Up to then it had only been referred to as a "private" school. "I want a Catholic school," she said, "because in a Catholic school the children learn their religion. For them their religion is more important than anything else they can learn in a public school."

The representatives from the school board in Dawson Creek — who had come in three cars — looked at her, then at each other.

"Probably they thought that I had coached her," Father Jungbluth says, "but I hadn't. Absolutely not. She was quite a forceful woman, that one."

Reverend Ivan Golding spoke, the resident minister from the Church of the Nazarene. "The Indians deserve just as good a school as the white children," he said. "They should not have an inferior school. I therefore opt that we reopen the public school."

"You know," says Father Jungbluth, "those fellows from Dawson Creek were not Catholics and they were not too happy that I had a school. They thanked Reverend Golding, but for Mary Gladu there was no thanking at all.

"Anyway, they couldn't exactly close my school, tell me right there that my school didn't exist anymore. When September came, the day of the opening, there were two buses: a big bus and my truck with some benches in the back, going to the same houses, trying to get the same kids. One trying to beat the other.

"For quite a while many of the Indians stayed faithful to me. They came with me in my truck, and I had them in school. But slowly one, then another, went in the other bus. Finally I had practically nobody left. I kept on going anyway. I had to send in my attendance report to get paid, but by then Mr. Galibois had turned against me. When I told him the public school was getting active, he'd say, 'Oh Father, don't worry so much! Even if they build that new school they've promised with bricks of gold, they will not get our kids.'

"So anyway, he didn't do anything, and in the fall, in October or the beginning of November, Mr. Galibois came to see me with an official. I assumed he was the Indian School Inspector. Attendance had fallen to maybe five children, from up to 25 in the beginning. I showed them the scribblers and so on. They were nothing to be proud of, and I knew it. Finally when they finished looking at everything, we had a little meeting in the back of the church and they gave me the news: 'Your school is closed from today on.' Then, to my astonishment, they added, 'We have made arrangements with the public school board in Dawson Creek. They are willing to accept all the Indian children that we can send them. The Indian Department will pay them a pro rata grant, so much a head.' So that was the end of my school.

"It was fun. I guess I gave them a run for their money, and possibly it resulted in them getting a much better school. From then on they got fairly good teachers. After a time the lunches were dropped, but the bus service stayed and also the sports equipment, and a kind of recreation ground that they leveled nice, all that stayed. Later they decided to have only grades one to four or five there. The others were bused to Chetwynd. That's still the arrangement now."

The picture is not black and white. Elmer Davis describes the grey area, the change of systems that greatly altered the progress of the Indian children, to a point where many dropped out: "When the new school started, I had to start all over again. They made me go back over A and B and C. I was about nine when that new school opened in Moberly Lake, but they said I'd only been to the Catholic school before and this was a different kind of school, so they put everybody back to the beginning. Anyway, I didn't last too long. I went trapping instead. When I was about 12 years old, I just quit school."

Elmer's memory treads softly into the past. "Father was always good, though," he adds in conclusion. "If you were stuck he'd help you . . . all the way. He's part of us here."

24

Tomslake

$\mathcal{F}$ather Jungbluth's next assignment involved not his "children of the forest," but the war-ravaged people from Sudetenland, a region located on the slopes of the Sudetes Mountains in Czechoslovakia, on the borders of Bohemia, Moravia and Germany. Due to the Treaty of Versailles in 1918, the people found themselves citizens of Czechoslovakia. The Munich Agreement of 1938, however, gave Sudetenland and other Czech areas to Germany; some were deported back to Sudetenland where they tried to leave, but others were allowed to emigrate as refugees.

In January of 1939, Canada sent a cable to the London representatives of the Sudeten German Refugee organization saying that it would accept physically fit families who were suitable for land settlement, as long as they had $1,500 per family in addition to transportation costs, which was eventually realized through contributions from Great Britain. The money was sent first to the Canadian government and then to the Canadian Pacific Railway and Canadian National Railway to arrange for suitable areas; the CNR allotted the settlers spaces in north-central Saskatchewan; the CPR chose the Tupper area of the Peace district of British Columbia.

"They were clean, hard-working people, fully civilized," Father Jungbluth says, "and they had somewhat of a hard time adjusting." Most of the Sudetens had been tradesmen and professional people; many were doctors, lawyers and storekeepers. They found farming tough.

The Tupper settlement, on a block of land known as the Gundy Ranch, had been renamed Tomslake. The Sudetens had first built small log houses measuring 5 m x 5 m or 7m x 7 m with lumber floors. They then graduated to shiplap buildings, 4 m x 5.5 m, built in groups of 15 or 20. The men had elected a council and assigned leadership responsibilities: one man to take care of stables, one for fields, one for machinery, one for building, and so on. Women and girls labored in the fields, picking roots; others were assigned as builders.

When the Sudetens first arrived in 1939, Father Jungbluth had ridden in on his horse to visit the colony. But it was Father Horne, a Redemptorist priest from Dawson Creek, who originally took responsibility for the spiritual needs of the Sudetens and for building the church. The Sudetens helped a little with the construction, but seemed without much fervor. Father Jungbluth again rode out to the colony to witness the blessing of the church by Bishop Langlois. He sat at the back, listening, as the Bishop stood

Tomslake settlement, 1939.

up and praised the Sudetens for their faith, and stressed how they were to keep that faith in Canada.

"The Sudeten men were absolutely not church-going people," Father Jungbluth relates. "All they were interested in was seeing that their women went to church. The men never went. They seemed to want a church built at Tomslake, but soon it was in disarray. They didn't come to church, and they put forth no effort to keep it up. Finally, after some years, the Redemptorists gave it up altogether, and the Bishop was not too happy about that. He was far away, and to him any parish was worth great effort to keep going."

There was a change in leadership in the parish of Dawson Creek about that time, and the Redemptorists gave the parish over to a diocesan priest, Father Turgeon. As he did not know how to speak German, and the people of Tomslake still spoke mostly German or Czechoslovakian, Father Turgeon turned to Father Jungbluth for help with the Tomslake mission.

Father Jungbluth went out to look over the situation. The church was a mess. Moisture had seeped up the walls; on one side the boards were so rotten that he could press his finger into them. The adjacent parish hall had collapsed, caved in under snow. Father Jungbluth called on his Indians for help.

Arriving back at the church with his chief carpenter, Fred Letendre, the Testawich family from Pouce Coupe and others from Kelly Lake and Moberly Lake, he set about making repairs. Men from Tomslake also helped. The combined crew used lumber from the old parish hall to repair the church and some from the old garage to make a good classroom. The church had no steeple; the bell was sitting directly on the shingles. Father Jungbluth and Fred Letendre constructed the steeple at their shop in Moberly Lake, hauled it to Tomslake and set it up.

The graveyard had also fallen into neglect, although the individual graves were well cared for. Father Jungbluth went around finding helpers to rebuild a good fence. "What a shame it is," he said to the residents of Tomslake, "to allow horses access to your graves."

A good crew turned out to rebuild and paint the fence. "Perhaps that is how to get them more interested in their church," Father Jungbluth thought. On summer evenings, he would see the farmers coming with horse and wagon, hauling milk-cans filled with water to pour over the flowers that decorated the graves. The stones traditionally carried pictures of the deceased. The people of Tomslake, cruelly ripped from their homeland and old traditions, came faithfully to respect the graves of elders who had brought them.

Father Jungbluth employed his electronic skills to lure the Sudetens to church. A powerful amplification system was installed in the belfry, over which he played records of traditional German hymns.

Father with master-builder Fred Letendre.

But when he tried to bring the men into the church itself, the trouble began.

"Perhaps their reluctance was a result of the way the Redemptorists handled them," he thought, recalling what one of the former priests had told him about a wedding in Tomslake. The Redemptorist Father had urged the bridal party to be sure to be at the church promptly at two o'clock. The time arrived, but no wedding party. It was raining, and the Father looked anxiously at the darkening skies, afraid he would have trouble getting back to Dawson Creek over the rutted roads. He became peeved. An hour passed, and two. Angry and upset, he began locking up, but as he was going down the steps, he beheld a strange sight coming down the trail. As it neared he identified it as a big tractor pulling a car. Inside the bespattered car, its windshield coated with a thick layer of mud, sat the bridal party. The Father stood on the steps, arms crossed, viewing the entourage with disgust.

"In this shape," he cried in a loud voice as soon as the tractor motor had turned off, "you are not going to come into the church! You are late! I have locked up already."

The people, stepping gingerly from the muddy car, looked to one another in dismay. They had done everything possible to get here. What was the matter? Could they not be married?

"I will marry you," the priest said, tight-lipped, "but not inside the church. You must be married right here, on the porch." And there he conducted the ceremony.

"That was a bad mistake," thought Father Jungbluth when he heard the story. "That turned them away."

And then he did the same thing himself.

The occasion was a funeral at Tomslake. Father Jungbluth had observed that the people rarely came to church except for funerals, and then everyone came. Funerals therefore provided him with an excellent opportunity to talk to the entire community, to try to convince them to come to church on a regular basis, and take an active role in the upkeep of the buildings and the church yard. He watched happily as trucks rolled up the road toward the church. Entire families jumped out and gathered in friendly groups in front of the porch. This time the men did not turn the trucks around and drive away. This time they stayed, captured by duty to their dead.

Father Jungbluth rang the bell, announcing that the service was about to begin. The pews began to fill, but again only with women and children and a couple of men who always came. No one else entered. Father Jungbluth sent out two altar boys.

"Tell those people out there it's time to begin. Tell them to come in right away," he said.

The boys returned. "They say 'go ahead.'"

Father Jungbluth then sent out two of the old men who were sitting stiffly at the back of the church. They came back, alone. "They said you should start."

Father Jungbluth now became angry. He strode down the aisle of the church and flung open the door. "You can come in now," he said to the men standing out on the grass. "We are ready to start."

Nobody moved. It didn't concern them. They looked around at each other, then down at their boots, or off across the flat fields. Father became incensed.

"What kind of Catholics are you?" he shouted to them in German. "You come here but you won't come into the church! What are you coming for at all?"

No response.

"Fine!" Father Jungbluth's voice went strangely quiet. "Then we will have the funeral sermon out here."

No one moved. Perhaps if one had gone inside the others would have followed, but they just looked at each other, and stood. Father Jungbluth reentered the church to conduct the Mass, then strode down the aisle and, standing defiantly on the porch steps, he delivered the sermon.

When the service was over, the people formed a little procession with the cross-bearer in front. In that traditional manner they walked slowly to the graveyard, the little bell tinkling the *funeral clas*: a ring, then a two-second hesitation, then another soft ring. They did that well, lining up in proper order, but that was it.

After the funeral, Father Jungbluth stayed for dinner with one of the families he usually visited.

"I guess I was too harsh," he said ruefully.

"No, no, you did right," they assured him. "Those people wouldn't have come in anyway."

But Father Jungbluth's relationship with the people of Tomslake seemed to change from that day on.

"I lost my appeal to them because of that. Fewer and fewer came, and the earlier camaraderie was gone. They seemed now sullen and resentful, attending Mass only out of religious duty."

He regretted many times losing his temper; it had been a bad mistake. Over the seven years Father Jungbluth was in charge of the church at Tomslake, only a few families remained faithful. Soon the collections didn't even pay his gas for the trip. He decided to drop it from his circuit. The Dawson Creek diocesan clergy kept it for a while, but finally told the people that if they wished to attend church they could come in to Dawson Creek.

In the 1960s the little church stood abandoned and neglected, except for the care given the surrounding graveyard.

One day Father Jungbluth mentioned to some student mission helpers, called "Frontier Apostles," the need for a good bell at the Moberly Lake church. "There is a nice bell at Tomslake," Father Jungbluth recalled. "The Redemptorist Fathers gave it to the church there. But it's just sitting."

One night the Frontier Apostles drove out to Tomslake, removed the bell from the belfry and hauled it back to Moberly Lake.

But Father Jungbluth was never happy with the Tomslake bell hanging in his little log church in Moberly. For one thing, it was not properly installed and never swung right; if pressure were applied to lengthen the swing, the rope broke. Also, it was a railroad bell and emitted a sharp clanging sound. He finally asked that it be taken down and the original small bell be reinstalled. It hangs there still.

The Tomslake bell, like its church, is no longer cared about. It rests, forgotten, covered with dust and cobwebs, in a storage shed out in the bush.

VIBRATIONS OF PROGRESS

25

The Big Father

*B*ishop Fergus O'Grady, OMI, ordained Bishop of Prince Rupert on March 7, 1956, seemed a progressive sort of man. He was in charge of over 214,000 square kilometres of British Columbian territory — including Father Jungbluth's missions — and in a very short time he had established 13 Indian schools in that vast area. He then appealed to Frontier Apostles from all over the world to come and help him in his work. Young men and women responded by the hundreds.

Bishop O'Grady visited Father Jungbluth's mission at Moberly Lake, and liked what he saw. When Father Jungbluth told him of the blunder they had made by building the Moberly Lake church 15 centimetres over the property line, Bishop O'Grady had hesitated not a minute. "We must buy more land! Find out who owns the property next to the church. Tell the owner we want it for a boys' camp."

"A boys' camp? What's this?"

"It's a perfect idea," the Bishop said, surveying the wide beach and the forests that encircled it, "and this is the perfect spot. We'll build a camp overlooking the lake. Boys will come from all the schools in the province. My Frontier Apostles will help run it."

Father Jungbluth was able to obtain a parcel of land from Pete Thiessen. The church now owned a total of 305 metres of lakeshore, about 8 hectares reaching across the main road and up the hill.

The area was quickly developing. A new road would soon join the developing town of Little Prairie to Moberly Lake, and there was speculation that a railway would pass through Little Prairie.

"I want to spend more and more time there, in Little Prairie," Father Jungbluth said to Bishop O'Grady. "Moberly Lake can be a secondary mission. It can hold its own. It won't change too much."

"Then you must look for land in Little Prairie!" was the Bishop's quick response.

At last Father Jungbluth had the sympathies of a Bishop who saw potential in his remote mission territories, but sometimes Bishop O'Grady's ideas frightened him. Father Jungbluth cringed when he recalled the Bishop's latest instructions, given at the annual summer meeting. Each missionary was instructed to confront each Catholic person within his mission field, rich or poor, church-goer or not, and ask for a percentage of income, over the next two years, for building churches and schools.

The priests were all speechless. Most were missionaries of extremely poor areas. Father Jungbluth looked over at Father Hettrich of McBride. He looked back in distress, encouraging Father Jungbluth to step forward and say something.

Father Jungbluth stood up. "Most of us present have missions without any income," he said bravely, "and the people we serve have not the slightest income either. We cannot possibly ask our poor Indians for money. They are poorer than all of us together!"

The Bishop seemed impressed. He closed his eyes in concentration. Then, in a clear voice he said, "Yes, the Indians of your missions must also have the opportunity to help finance the building programs for churches and schools in their country. You have to point out to them that such is a great honor and that they should give joyfully."

Father Jungbluth sat down silently.

He returned to Moberly Lake in a state of depression.

On the following Sunday he read in church the letter outlining the Bishop's demands; then he preached accordingly, telling his poor Indians of the expectations of the Bishop. After Mass he came up with a specially created prayer on the same theme. And then, he was compelled to go from cabin to cabin, from hut to hut, begging for money.

He started off by visiting the "richest" of his poor congregation.

"Yes," the man said, "the Big Father is right. Each one of us must help and give whatever he can. I will give 10 dollars, and the same sum each month." Father Jungbluth was speechless, but before he could thank him for his generosity, the man went on: "I do not own any money, though, but I have a good name and will borrow the amount. Just follow me and you will see."

Father Jungbluth followed the man to the trader's store and went inside. Trying to hide his red face as he pretended to inspect a display of canned goods, he had to listen to the begging words of the Indian, promising the trader that for the loan of 10 dollars he would bring him all the furs he could trap. After five minutes the fur trader handed over the money. The Indian, excited with his success, ran up to Father Jungbluth and, in a loud voice, cried, "Take it! Here is the money for your Bishop!"

The next parishioner was supposedly the second richest man in Moberly Lake. He also had no money but owned an old alarm clock which he presented to Father Jungbluth.

The third man he approached for money was able only to tell of his good intentions. He promised he would set out trapping the coming winter. Meanwhile, Father Jungbluth should inform the Bishop in advance to expect a money gift when he had sold his furs.

That was it: he had 10 dollars collected from his Indians, a little more from some Metis of Kelly Lake, and a bit more from white Catholic settlers in the area. He had just posted the modest amount to the Bishop's administration when the "richest" Indian paid him a visit.

"For three weeks now a parcel has been waiting to be collected by me, containing a new dress for my daughter so she can go to school in the fall, and one pair of warm socks for myself," he said matter-of-factly. "It will, however, only be handed out to me when I pay its value of 12 dollars. Otherwise the post office is returning it to the sender, and this is today. I have already been to the fur trader, but since he lent me the money for your Bishop he would not give me any more. I think it is your turn now, Father, to give me 12 dollars as I have given you 10 dollars for your Bishop."

Father Jungbluth looked down at the floor, rubbing his head in exasperation. "Oh, dear, oh dear . . . such prospects there are . . ."

On November 21, 1956, he received a letter from Bishop O'Grady thanking him for the small amount that he was able to forward. Then, as if in afterthought, the Bishop added: "You told me of all your good friends and benefactors back home in the Alsace, in Switzerland and in Lothringen, who helped you to build your church in Kelly Lake. Please tell them of our great needs within our whole district. Tell them too that I am hoping to grant you a vacation to Europe, providing I receive the permission of the General Mission in Rome."

Father Jungbluth closed his eyes for a moment, thinking of going home again after nearly eight years. He continued reading: "During the time of this vacation you will have plenty of opportunities to find alms for our missions here to help finance our building projects, especially for your planned church in Little Prairie."

Father Jungbluth folded the letter and placed it in his record box. Then, drawing forward his writing pad, he began to list the promotional materials he would need to take with him to Alsace.

Father Jungbluth in front of Moberly Lake Church.

26

The White Faces Have Spoiled Our Nature

$\mathcal{F}$ather Jungbluth made his second trip back to Alsace in 1957. This time, however, his promotional paraphernalia was more sophisticated than the simple slides he had taken in 1949. He borrowed a 16mm projector from Carl Shubert of Fort St. John, and set about making up his presentation. Fact was mixed with fiction, time spans of no consequence, as he unashamedly spliced himself into any space where he could be fit, using as a base the film *The Law of the Yukon* produced by a missionary from Whitehorse. He also doctored the fine Eskimo film, *Inuk*, which showed Eskimos killing a great white bear, or poised over seal holes in the Arctic ice. These were interspersed with scenes of Father Jungbluth sawing wood or loading school children onto his truck. The result was an engineering masterpiece.

He wrote ahead to an old friend, Rene Halmenschlager, with whom he had studied in Florennes, Belgium. Mr. Halmenschlager set out to visit the parish priests in the surrounding villages and booked several parish halls free of charge. He then visited the mayors of the small villages, using his position as mayor of his own village of Valff, and put up notices throughout the towns announcing, "Father Emile Jungbluth, an Oblate Missionary from the Polar Missions."

Father Jungbluth was amazed to see how France had recovered. Instead of a small hand-built motorcycle, he was now given an old Hotchkiss, a huge car manufactured in England with the steering wheel on the right side. It started with a crank — the starter had long ago quit — and the worn old motor roared like the loudest diesel. It was so large he used it as a traveling motor home; it easily carried his cameras and projector, his Indian memorabilia, his clothing, and his bedroll. Canadian citizens still received a cut rate on gas, and he was the only one who could afford to run the big car.

He found it easy to visit with the people who came to hear him in the parish halls. He had built a reputation during his vacation home in 1949, and continued the interest through stories he sent regularly to *Immaculata*. The people were eager to meet him again, and hear in person the wonderful stories.

"It is not only my Indians who are extraordinary in my missions," he told them. "There are some interesting white people too. I'll tell you of an incident that will never be forgotten by those who witnessed it:

It happened at Easter. It was a beautiful sunshine morning — Easter Morning can be very nice — but the roads were still drying out (that means they were in very bad shape). While we were sitting there waiting for all the people who were supposed to come, we heard, louder and louder, some kind of a special noise. We looked at the sky and no plane. The noise was inexplicable! Then we heard trees crashing and we wondered if there was a big wind. But no, everything was quiet. The youngsters ran about looking and suddenly we see a big machine coming on the road. The road at that time was not wide, just enough to let a wagon through or possibly a pick-up. Trees were crashing down on both sides. The big machine pulled into the church yard and on it sat two mud-covered figures. They stood in front of me and all my Indians and began to peel — off came their big gloves, boots, coveralls, everything. Two beautiful gentlemen emerged, fully dressed for church!

They were two brothers, Ernest Purschke and his brother (who later became a diocesan priest), and they were working for a company that was exploring for oil. They heard there was a Catholic church in Moberly Lake and they wanted to attend Easter Mass and do their Easter duty, so they left at three o'clock in the morning from the north, toward the Peace River, to come in the only way possible, on a big D-8 Cat. They had to make their own road part of the way.

It shocked the Indians. They had never seen a machine like that before. It literally chewed up their forests.

At another gathering he told the story of his own efforts to reach the church for Easter. It happened in the early 1950s. He was living in Moberly Lake, but had been to Fort St. John and was caught in a late spring blizzard, as deadly as any in mid-winter.

Toward the end of Lent he had been called to help out with confessions at his previous mission in Fort St. John. On leaving, he had promised his Indians in Moberly Lake that he would be back in time for Easter, even if he had to crawl. They laughed at the image, and he departed in his truck.

On the return trip, the road was a sheet of ice. Not a single gravel stone protruded; again and again his truck spun in circles toward the ditch. The wind came from the north, pushing heavy clouds across the sky. He had passengers, too, a 16-year-old Indian boy and a young woman with a child, all just released from the hospital.

After several hours traveling they reached a forest road. It was covered with a fresh layer of snow, giving the impression that not a soul had touched it during the long winter. He stopped the truck, enshrouded by a dancing snowy whirlwind. Why on earth had he taken on passengers? Alone he would only have to look after himself. If they got stuck out there, far from any help, what then?

"We'll have to turn around and go back," he said to his passengers. The Indian woman started to cry. "I want to go home!" Father Jungbluth turned to consult the young boy.

"I'm good with snow shovelling and making large fires in the snow," said the boy, "and I want to go home too."

Father Jungbluth threw the truck into gear.

The weather turned colder and the snowfall heavier. Suddenly the engine gave a strange sound, the vehicle took a leap forward, and, though he pumped the gas pedal, it slowed and stopped. The boy got out and lit a fire, while Father Jungbluth tried to figure out what had caused it to stall. A small ice particle had closed the gas line, not uncommon in the sudden change of temperature.

"Why didn't I add alcohol to the gas to prevent such a problem?" he chastised himself. "But . . . alcohol is expensive." Now he had to crawl underneath the truck, rub the hose off with a cloth, blow into the gas tank until his face became blue, suck on the fuel line taking a quantity of gas into himself, and finally get the truck started again.

The snow continued. They took turns shovelling, pushing, finding the holes and filling them in. The young woman put her baby down on the seat and helped as much as she could. In the end they made it to a Metis' cabin. Aroused from his sleep, the man lit a fire and fed the weary travelers dried meat and strong tea. Fetching their sleeping bags and blankets from the truck, he spread them around the stove.

Next morning it looked worse outside. The snow was so high they could hardly force open the cabin door. Father Jungbluth's truck was completely covered. They sat down and discussed possibilities. The Metis had the best idea: leave the woman and child behind in the cabin, where she was half-way home anyway; Father Jungbluth could borrow his dogs and sleigh. The young boy's help would be needed to move the dog-sled up the three-kilometre hill. He would then return to the woman and child. Only the Metis and Father Jungbluth should try to reach the next cabin, about three or four hours away.

This plan was accepted by all. But the snow was so soft that the dogs plunged in up to their necks. In order to keep going, one man had to make a trail with snowshoes while the other walked behind and pressed the sled down to keep a balance. The Metis, more used to snowshoeing, was the guide ahead of the team, while Father Jungbluth stumbled behind. He felt he could barely cope, and he was glad to see the dogs getting tired so that the Metis had to slow down.

The Metis showed no signs of exhaustion when they finally arrived at the hut. The cabin was only occasionally used by trappers and was in very poor condition. Wind and snow whipped in wide open cracks in the loose log walls. Although Father Jungbluth was fatigued, he could hardly sleep as the storm raged on, a good part of it inside the cabin.

"In the morning my blankets were covered with snow," Father Jungbluth said to his spellbound audience. "Had I camped outside under a spruce tree I am sure I would have slept better than in that draughty place. I was frozen

stiff and hardly managed to get up. But my thoughts were in Moberly Lake
and it was already the Saturday before Easter! The Indians of my mission
would be waiting.

"The words of the Metis brought me back to reality: 'Father, we cannot
make it today with our dogs. The snow is too wet for them. I will find a
horse where they winter not far from here. Then you can ride on to Moberly
Lake. You are much too stiff to walk on snowshoes.' I agreed to everything.

"And so it came that I found myself some hours later riding an Indian
pony amid the everlasting snow storm. I had to leave behind my altar and
all other bags. One good day's ride should get me home to Moberly Lake
the same night."

He paused for a break. No one moved.

"At first all went well," he continued. "I was in high spirits and the horse
did its best. Approaching the foothills of the Rocky Mountains, where
Moberly Lake is situated, I noticed deep drifts and fresh-fallen snow. The
little horse could hardly lift its legs high enough for the next step. I jumped
down and took the lead. It was hard work, sinking myself over the knees
in snow and pulling the creature forward so it didn't stop. 'If we could only
make it to the hilltop, the way down might be easier and it is only 10 more
miles [16 km] to go.' But the nearer we came the deeper got the snow. I had
to use a stick to keep the horse going.

"I suddenly did not feel good anymore and was sweating all over, from
fatigue or from anger, I didn't know. I only knew that the pony and myself
were at an end. It was high time to find a shelter for the night, as there was
no returning. I knew of a trapper's shack somewhere nearby which would
be better than nothing.

"We made it, but the shack was in ruins, without windows or doors. A
damaged roof sank in at a frightening angle. There was no stove and no
wood, so I used part of the roof for a warm fire on the earth floor. I had
nowhere to shelter the pony. When I looked out it had not run off in the
bush, but stood head down, motionless on the same place I had left it. Not
even the snow was shaken off that was piling on its back. I tried to pull the
poor creature into the hut, but at the very sight of the fire it resisted. It did
not even bother eating the sparse grass I found for it. It was just too tired
and exhausted.

"I found in my pocket some chocolate, a piece of dried meat and some
bread, more than enough! Then I found an empty tin, rusty and filled with
mud. I cleaned it out with snow and melted some for water and thereby
stilled my thirst. I wrapped myself in an old blanket, smelling of horse
sweat, and settled down near the fire, sleeping far better than the night
before. I had to get up now and look after the fire and the horse.

"Morning approached. I heard only the howling of the storm. Back home
I saw the church and the choir and the ceremonies of the Easter Mass, with
the many ministers and their candles and incense bowls; here there was

nothing but rotten walls. I imagined the choirs singing with masterful voices fourfold; outside there was only the groaning of the trees straining under the burdens of snow and the powerful winds.

"It was already the evening of Easter Monday when I heard dogs barking in the distance. It sounded to me as beautiful as a thousand church bells! In order to be found in the wilderness I hurried and put damp wood and lean grass on the fire. This created a big smoke which climbed into the sky and gave a sign.

"When I was found by two boys, I must have looked like an escaped convict, with my four-day beard and smoke-blackened face. On seeing me they laughed their heads off. But soon I was seated in the sled, one boy staying behind because of the horse and the other bringing me on a fresh trail the quickest way back to Moberly Lake.

"Do you believe, my dear friends, that the Indians had pity for me? On the contrary. They only laughed. To them being delayed by a snowstorm means lack of experience. Pointing up to an airplane flying above, one made a comment: 'The white faces who speed so masterfully through the skies above their heads, should rather learn first how to cope with the snow in the forest.'"

Father Jungbluth accepted their jeers with good humor.

"In the end," he concluded, "everything turned out well. We had Easter with all its celebrations one week later. Almost all the Indians either stayed on or returned from their homes back to the church, and I am sure that God was just as pleased as I was to find so much simple devotion and faith among the children of the woods."

He stopped, wondering if he should bring up a subject that must be on at least a few people's minds. Then, making his decision, he told, in a sad low voice, the epilogue:

"Most probably my cousins and lots of horse lovers will want to know what happened to the little horse. It is hard for me to tell you, but the horse did not make it. It died. It was so exhausted that it was not able to accept any food, and it became stiff and froze to death. When I mentioned the horse later to the Indians, they only lifted a shoulder as if to say, 'It served, and it died. That is all there is to be said.'"

Some in the audience were crying, others sat silently, staring off into adventure-memories of their own. A friend, Father Fuchs, circulated among the audience with a hat, and, as Father Jungbluth stood at the front accepting the applause, he saw with astonishment that the hat was quickly filled to the brim.

It took him a long time to get to sleep at night. The undulant sound of applause seemed to roar like an ocean, keeping him awake for many hours after the lights had gone off in the Oblate House in the Robertsau.

"Pater Emile, haven't you been already stationed for 22 years in the Ice Missions?" The comments of a dear old aunt, with whom he had visited, rang in his ears. "And don't you think this should be enough as you grow older? Don't you think," her voice persisted, "that it would be far better to stay here now and be *ein Herr Pfarres* — a parish priest — instead?"

The thought, until she had uttered it, had never entered his head. He had quickly answered her with a question of his own: "Why do you not stop working? You still labor in the fields. After so many years you should sell all your cattle and look for an old millionaire and go live in his castle!"

"Oh!" she had laughed, "that's nothing for me anymore."

And Father Jungbluth had replied, "Exactly. Life in this country, in spite of all the comfort it will offer, is nothing for me anymore."

For the return trip, he made arrangements to fly. The airplane was huge. Two flight attendants in succession led Father Jungbluth into the vast interior and seated him at a comfortable club chair facing a small table. Loudspeakers gave instructions on the safety and comfort offered by this particular plane, and the flight attendant demonstrated the use of safety belts and window exits. Father Jungbluth listened nervously.

"*S'Wasser hat keine Balken* — the water has no beams," he thought miserably, as he pictured this mammoth bird flying through the night sky above the bottomless oceans. "If we go down, we go down . . . there is nothing to catch us."

Flying through the black skies he thought of the changes that had occurred over the last few years. Alsace was again prosperous; cars hummed through the streets and people scurried to jobs that brought them more and more opulence. It was becoming the same at Moberly Lake. The entire Canadian North was developing. How he hated all that noise! Where only three or four years ago small Indian ponies had pawed undisturbed throughout the winter in fenceless pastures, huge bulldozers now raided the hills and valleys. Where bears used to hibernate in hidden dens, now diesel-driven machines dug mercilessly into the ground. The cleverness of the fox was now a mockery when confronted with the blinding headlights of a truck. All too often one came across a bloodied pelt flattened on the road.

His Indians too were shaken by the vibrations of progress. Lately each time they came across a young mineralogist searching their territory, looking at stones and knocking on rocks, they had come to feel that they were being expelled from their hunting grounds. The government was attempting to uncover resources — oil, gas, coal. These were the new gods now, and the people, instead of looking to the heavens for evidence of their charity, now sought them deep in the earth.

"Perhaps," he thought, "there are some blessings to be derived from civilization: better roads, health care, electric power. But . . . Moberly Lake will not likely be touched by those things for a long time to come. I will be using kerosene for many winter nights yet."

Moberly Lake looked exactly as when he had left. He was greeted cordially, the Indians showing no resentment at having been neglected. He did not expect that they would.

Nothing ever seemed to change in Moberly. The old people looked the same as when he had first met them. Their hair was still as black and their laughter as strong as it had been 10 or even 20 years ago, when he had first journeyed by horseback out from Fort St. John. Nothing had changed. But . . . why did the people sometimes look at him strangely and caution him against setting out in the winter alone?

One night, the winter after he returned from Alsace, a fierce snowstorm raged outside, colder and more intense than any he could remember. The snow that blew against the little windows at the back of the church in short sharp gusts was dry like powder, as fine and clean as white flour. Father Jungbluth put another log into the gas barrel stove, and settled down next to the fire to read the breviary.

Suddenly the door blew open and in stumbled a snow-covered man, his good friend, Chief Dokkie. His dark weathered face was surrounded by a white aura of ice and snow, his beard gleamed with ice crystals, and his nose had frozen into a shiny cone. Without a word he moved next to the warm stove, rubbing his legs, belly and face. Then he settled down on his heels and, with solemn ceremony, stuffed his beloved pipe. Only then did he speak, in his native Beaver:

"Man of Prayer, I must tell you something, and what I have to say is true. The white faces have spoiled our nature with all that bombing, and that is why there are these days more and severer snowstorms than in previous times."

Father Jungbluth closed his breviary and leaned nearer to the chief.

The ice on his beard and face had thawed and the beautiful aura vanished. His wrinkled leather-skin face told of a very hard life, of wind and snow, of cold and hunger. Through the smoke of his pipe, the old eyes looked into the past. His breath came heavily and Father Jungbluth leaned closer to catch his words as he began again:

"I tell you one thing, today's world is crazy. Nature has become as bad as mankind, and it is certain that the Great Spirit is angry too. For never in the old days was the snow so deep and heavy as now.

"The ice is thicker and harder than it used to be, and now I need twice as long to cut a hole in it. Why do the white faces nowadays make such clumsy axes so that one can hardly lift them, as is the case with mine? The snowshoes too are now heavy like stones on my feet . . . and, Man of Prayer, did you notice how people lie today? For instance, the trader told me it was only 30 degrees below zero outside, but I am quite sure that is wrong, for it is colder today than when it was 60 degrees below!"

Tired now from his philosophizing, the old chief settled full length down on the floor next to the stove and sleep came over him. Father Jungbluth filled up the gas barrel stove with more wood and put a kettle on. He watched the sleeping man, wondering how old he might be. This one might easily be 100 years old . . . or perhaps just 80 or so. Father Jungbluth remembered that he looked just the same age when he had met him first 13 years ago.

"It's strange," he mused, "but why do old people, no matter if they're white or Indian, never admit that not the world has changed, but only they themselves?"

Content with his conclusions, Father Jungbluth picked up the breviary once more, but then the chief opened his eyes. He looked at Father Jungbluth for quite a while, even resting on his elbow to get a better glimpse, moving his head from right to left and back again. Then, half-closing his clever small eyes, he said, "Man of Prayer, you once mentioned that your name means 'young blood,' but do you know that you are almost without hair? And that at times all of your teeth fall out of your mouth? And that your face is full of wrinkles? Do you realize that you are quickly aging?"

Deeply shaken, almost annoyed to hear such words, Father Jungbluth got up to look closely into a new mirror. Indeed, he hardly recognized himself.

"It is true," he said slowly to the chief. "Today everything seems to be upside down. Before the war, we got only good mirrors, but this new one here seems to be made not from the best materials."

He sat down and silently refilled their mugs with hot tea.

27

Little Prairie

When Father Jungbluth first traveled through Little Prairie in the mid 1950s, he said Mass in the school. He used the teacher's desk for his altar, carefully moving the line of books from the desk to the clean floor. One day he forgot to put the books back, and that was that. The teacher wrote the school board in Dawson Creek saying church services were an inconvenience. However, if it proved absolutely necessary, he would allow services for a $5 rental and clean-up fee — more than the collections.

The next day, Father Jungbluth searched for a building that would do for a church, and secured an empty workshop from Ed Boulton, who worked for a company that was building the railroad.

Land was the next item, and Father Jungbluth had a piece of property in mind: four acres on which Fred Letendre was squatting. Fred had made application to buy the land but the government still owned it. Father Jungbluth offered a deal: Fred would relinquish his rights to the land for a reasonable sum, in return for permission to stay until he had found another place. Father Jungbluth promised him a job building the new church, and would buy him a little house and the lumber to renovate it. The next day they went to the land office in Pouce Coupe to make out the formal transfer papers.

Paul Demeulemeester hauled the old workshop over to the property, and Father Jungbluth began to use it as a church and dwelling whenever he stayed over in Little Prairie. At first he had only 15 parishioners. They gathered in the little workshop, on unplaned wooden benches, talking excitedly of the future of the town growing up around them.

The new church building was progressing well. Every evening Father Jungbluth and Fred Letendre would have dinner together at the hotel and discuss the next day's plans for the church, drawing it out on a paper napkin. Then Fred would go straight back to work. He had no car, so he stayed on the job. He had no tools, so Father Jungbluth provided them: a skill saw and hand tools. Fred was a good carpenter, and fast.

Father Jungbluth's excitement at their progress was reflected in his letter to *Immaculata* dated July, 1959:

> I just received the April edition of *Immaculata*, this dear little blue paper, and I was so excited to find a printed picture of my new chapel of Little Prairie, the photo being taken when the roofing was not quite finished.

Today I will send you the latest pictures of the almost-completed new mission church. Now, what do you think of it? I must confess I am mighty proud of it, though it is only a very little church, so modest that it is not comparable with the churches back home in the Old World . . . the church I have just built in Little Prairie is made of rough wooden boards, which I obtained from the sawmill. In order to preserve the boards from moisture and rot, I covered them completely with black tarpaper. It is practical rather than nice, and later when I should have the financial means I will surely cover it with shiplap and paint this chapel with an attractive color. I am naming the new church, "Our Lady of Peace."

Chetwynd Church,
"Our Lady of Peace."

In March of 1958, Premier W.A.C. Bennett rode the first Pacific Great Eastern Railway train into Little Prairie. The town was established as a divisional point for the railway, and housing was constructed for its employees.

In the summer of the following year, paving work started on the Hart Highway, beginning with the East Pine region where once Father Jungbluth had stayed with the Maddens. Instead of climbing steep hills through Sundance Lake to Jackfish and then to Moberly, the road cut straight through Wabi Hill, and Little Prairie was no longer isolated.

When Frank Oberle moved to Little Prairie and started a Chamber of Commerce, Father Jungbluth was one of the first members. He became Public Relations Chairman and in charge of membership drives.

Little Prairie resident and long-time mayor, Ernie Pfanner, recalls: "Father Jungbluth kept the Chamber of Commerce club going. Where nobody else would have taken the time to sell memberships, he did it. And it didn't make any difference if you were Catholic or not Catholic — the whole community admired him. Not because he was a priest or religious or whatever — it was just his personality."

The Chamber of Commerce also sponsored the first newspaper, edited by George Peck. In the first issue of March 12, 1959, he summarized all the news events of Little Prairie. The summary was timely. In July, 1959, Little Prairie ceased to be. The provincial government announced "an official renaming of the Little Prairie Post Office to Chetwynd", effective immediately. The Chamber of Commerce was asked to organize a Chetwynd Days Celebration to be held early in July. The people were speechless. Who was "Chetwynd"? Why was their town suddenly losing its name? Delegations went to Victoria to protest the change, but the government would not reverse its decision. Father Jungbluth sided with the protesters, but was away on a trip when the final "celebration" of the name-change occurred. Ernie Pfanner's truck, in the Chetwynd Days parade, carried a coffin, over which a banner flapped in the wind. "REST IN PEACE, LITTLE PRAIRIE," was its mute protest.

By 1959 Father Jungbluth was established as an oldtimer. On July 10, the Chetwynd *Chinook* gave him front page coverage.

"FATHER JUNGBLUTH OBSERVES 25TH YEAR!"

Editor George Peck was a man who took great stock in summaries:

Father E. Jungbluth is this year observing his 25th year in the priesthood. A councillor well known by his parishioners and friends throughout the Peace River country, he has built a reputation of his concern for native welfare and devoted attention to those under his wing. At a banquet in the Father's honor on Wednesday evening, an overflow attendance recalled stories of his courage and efforts throughout the space of the Peace and the time of his stay in Canada.

. . . With a quiet humor, the Father relates such hazards as having his saddle horse swim the Halfway River while he was towed behind, hanging onto the horse's tail. Or when he changed to motorcycles and fell off, he says, every half-mile as a result of the muddy, sandy or icy roads. Or he will tell you of the old Model A which he called "Eileen" . . .

In Chetwynd, few pass Father with less than a nod, a salute to the respected elder. We all remember the line from Abou Ben Adam:"List me then as one who loved his fellow man." Father

Jungbluth's love for his fellow men has been illustrated by 25 years of intense and devoted attention, but "Youngblood", the translation of his name, perfectly describes his remarkable and continuing energy in the service of his fellow man.

Father Jungbluth was presented with a gift of a great reclining chair and two strong men to move it into his little workshop-shack behind the Our Lady of Peace Church. He watched incredulously as they labored to hoist the thing inside. The chair filled his small living room. He couldn't get to his desk. The next day he asked their kind permission to return it for a smaller one: "Otherwise," he said, "I will have to build a house around it." In its place he bought a small brown chair, which he set in the corner and reserved for guests. He was not yet ready to recline.

28

The Competition

$\mathcal{F}$ather Jungbluth was a man who believed in advertising. His letters home to *Immaculata* promoting his "far North" missions brought dividends, and he also advertised his missions throughout the Peace area. A local artist painted a picture of the Moberly Lake church on the door of his truck, above the words, "R.C. CHURCH, MOBERLY LAKE, B.C." He installed speakers under the hood of the truck, powered by the battery, from which he played music at top volume produced by a little record player resting beside him on the seat. Whenever the truck hit a bump the record would skip.

Tape machines came into the mass market, and Father Jungbluth bought Moberly Lake's first. He purchased a big transformer and hooked it onto the battery, transforming the 6-volt direct current to his 115 alternating current. He then sat down at the organ, and within a few minutes heard a perfect replay. The transformer was kept in the cab of the truck, which Father Jungbluth parked close to the church steps. The only problem was the risk of running the battery down, as the little machine took a lot of power.

For the new church in Chetwynd, he purchased a set of loudspeakers which he installed instead of a bell in a tiny roof-rider on the peak of the church roof. The editor of *Immaculata* sent him recordings of Strasbourg Cathedral bells, which he played to the amazed population. His congregation loved the new machine, crowding in to hear it, filling the church.

At Moberly Lake, people were shaken from their sleep by Sunday morning wake-up music resounding from the truck speakers as Father Jungbluth made his rounds to pick up the children for church. Then, to encourage those who lived nearby, or put a spring in the step of those who dawdled on the trail, he plugged the tape recorder into the lard-pail tree speaker system. The finest sound of all was at the church — the voices of the Indians themselves recording "The Kyrie" in Cree, or "The Passion," or perhaps a country and western song in halting English. Everybody came for this new show. Tommy Napoleon brought his tom-tom; old Nancy, who knew some traditional Cree songs, sang them in her soft quavering voice.

But Father Jungbluth's system could not compete with the long-reaching powers of communication possessed by another "Man of God" residing in Moberly Lake, the Nazarene minister, Reverend Ivan Golding. Father Jungbluth made a difficult trip from Fort St. John to Moberly Lake one year to prepare for the Christmas Midnight Mass celebration. On his arrival, he found that Reverend Golding was also planning a Christmas Eve celebration, more in the form of a concert and party. Father Jungbluth went to visit him, to explain how their two services would create a conflict for the Indians.

"I know that you in your church don't celebrate the feasts that we have. You don't celebrate Easter or Good Friday, and especially Christmas — it's just a day like any other day — so couldn't you put your Christmas celebration on another night? As you know, that is the night the Indians come to me and they're all prepared; they go to confession and all that. I came from a long way, and I would like to keep them, as it has been in the past."

Reverend Golding thought for a minute. "Uh huh. Yes, I could . . . but I want to consult the Lord first. Can you come back in 10 minutes?"

"O.K., 10 minutes, 20 minutes, I'll be back," Father Jungbluth said.

"Perhaps the Good Lord will tell him he'd better be a bit more charitable now," he thought as he trudged down the road toward his own little church. When he returned, Reverend Golding had received his answer from the Lord: he should not change the date.

Shortly before midnight, Father Jungbluth was surprised and pleased to see a large group of Indians hiking down the road to his church. Clutched in their hands were little bags of candy and nuts that Reverend Golding had given them earlier. They were a bit late — no time for confessions — but they managed to take in both celebrations.

Reverend Golding, a tall, handsome man molded in the style of the old "fire and brimstone" preachers, was also bent on saving "Mister" Jungbluth, and lost no opportunity to castigate the "harlot church." He wrote Father Jungbluth letters. He liked him, he said. Mister Jungbluth had always been good to him and treated him in a civil manner. "But," he added, "the Roman Catholic Church is not a Christian church! It does not uphold

Mass at Moberly Lake, B.C.

the gospel. They do not preach salvation, just redemption through purgatory and there's no place after death. When a person dies in sin, he's lost to eternity . . . and in this you are serious!"

"Also," he stated in another letter, "salvation comes through Jesus Christ, not the Virgin Mary. When you have a broken bone, you don't go to the hospital, and ask for the doctor's mother, do you? No! You go to the doctor!"

Although the Indians in Moberly Lake were 90 percent Catholic, they still listened to Reverend Golding, brought him fish, attended his church when they were so persuaded. And occasionally one was buried in his public graveyard.

"He means well for us," they said, "and he's been here a long time. Life wasn't easy for him either."

29

Moccasin Flat

*W*hile the village of Chetwynd was encouraging settlers, it was ignoring a group of people in its midst. They were not status Indians, but people whose Indian blood severed them from white society, whose white blood severed them from Indian society, and whose general lack of industry severed them from any society at all. They hung on the fringes, living in shacks so deplorable that at a distance they looked like beaver huts. Father Jungbluth would visit them to see how they were doing, to ask if they had enough wood or if they were out of meat.

The sights that greeted him often made him sick.

The shacks were located about one kilometre from the village, in an area called Moccasin Flat. Most were constructed from cardboard and tarpaper, torn and flapping in the wind. The doors were frames of board and cardboard. To enter, one lifted this contraption and set it aside, then turned and lifted it back into position.

On entering, Father Jungbluth had to wait a moment for his eyes to adjust to the gloom, and his nose to the smell.

"How are you coming?" he would ask in Cree. "Are you still sick?"

He might make out forms of men lying down, one on a bed and one on a couch of sorts, on which had been thrown parts of old car seats, pieces of foam rubber and old rags to make it soft.

"Why are they always on their backs?" he would wonder. "Only the women ever seem to get up and do anything."

Sometimes when Father Jungbluth arrived, all were drunk. He would open the door, size up the situation and back out. There was no use staying; they couldn't even talk.

Occasionally he would be phoned: "Please, Father, take my mother to the hospital. She's sick." Or: "Can you take us to the Frenchman?" That meant to Girard's Store, for groceries. So Father Jungbluth would pull up in his truck — and later in his old Dodge car — and two or three of them would pile in. One old lady, when she was drunk, could not hold her water. She never changed, so the urine dried on her and made a stench that caused Father's eyes to water. Then he would go home and get out a bucket of hot water and disinfectant to scrub off the car seat. But . . . somebody had to do it. Somebody had to take an interest in them.

There was no road to Moccasin Flat. To reach it by car you plunged down a small ravine and up the other side. The Indians, no matter what the weather, would try to get their cars through. Often the car would slip backwards or sideways, and roll over. Father Jungbluth was constantly after the Chamber of Commerce to build a little bridge so there wouldn't be so many accidents. At first Frank Oberle, president and founder of the chamber, bucked Father Jungbluth in his attempts to assimilate the Metis, or to help them establish permanent residences within the village.

It's not our business, Frank Oberle said. We don't want a bridge there; we didn't build the settlement, and so therefore it's not our problem. But Oberle later became interested in the local Indian problem and thereby redeemed himself in Father Jungbluth's eyes. Oberle became Mayor of Chetwynd, and took another look at the Indian situation. He became their advocate and the instigator of an uplifting program for Moccasin Flat. Frank Oberle tells how it began:

> The town was being organized, water and sewer systems and streets being laid out, and suddenly the Indian problem resurfaced. White people were buying lots and the Indians were being forced to move away, another 200 or 300 metres down the road. The problem was, they used all the facilities — the schools, recreational facilities — they really made more demand on the infrastructure of the town than anybody. So it occurred to me that you can't forever push these people back. We should find some way to allow these people to participate.

> As a result of the Hellyer Task Force in the 1960s, the government brought out a policy whereby people who were living in substandard housing would be eligible to move into rental accommodations built by the government. The idea was that the federal government would pay 75.5%, the provincial government, 12.5%, and the municipality, 12.5%. The municipality would manage the houses and get the tax revenue from them; also it meant these people — who were using our facilities anyway — would be brought inside the town limits and we'd then get a per capita grant from the province.

Father Jungbluth was involved all the way, examining the plan for 30 houses to be built on Crown land. Then Frank Oberle had a better idea: instead of the government building rental units, why not let the Indians themselves help in building these houses, and let them own the houses? Instead of subsidizing rent, the government could subsidize the payment.

Frank Oberle traveled to Ottawa and convinced Ron Basford, then Housing Minister. The Chetwynd Project is now Section 40 of the Housing Act.

Disagreement between Father Jungbluth and Frank Oberle surfaced with the selection of the people who would live in these houses. Oberle and the Council felt there were some people who did not deserve any kind of break. Father Jungbluth felt that the people in the worst houses had the most acute need. The town was not too happy about any of it. Father Jungbluth pushed.

Although the Indians wanted to handle it on their own, they agreed that they should have some financial guidance. Dr. Lennox was appointed chairman of the committee. He sympathized with the Indians, sharing Father Jungbluth's attitude. But, as time went on, the Indians started speaking against Dr. Lennox' decisions, saying he seemed to favor some families over others. First it was decided that an applicant must have "Indian blood" to get a house. That was cited as discriminatory against whites, so the restrictions were removed. Few whites applied.

The political battles fought over the Indians of Chetwynd were not resolved with the housing project. Another rift between Father Jungbluth and Frank Oberle was over the loss to the Indians of a community hall worth around $300,000. Frank Oberle relates the background of the "perfectly legal heist":

> The Indian houses were built for $14,500 apiece, and when the project was completed there was some money left over. I got some more money from the Secretary of State, and a community hall was built for the Indians' use. Father Jungbluth held a kindergarten there and catechism lessons, wakes and funerals, but it was open for all kinds of community uses.
>
> But after a few years, the building fell behind in taxes. I was in Ottawa then (as the elected Progressive Conservative Member of Parliament for Peace River South), and the problem was eventually addressed to me. I went to Council on two occasions, and Father went with me both times, to try to sell them on the idea that they should not levy a tax on a centre like that because it was a 'cultural centre,' like a church, or a community hall. Anyway, they just nodded their heads and said they'd think about it, but they never did think about it. When the crunch came, there was about $9,000 owing in taxes. The Indians were up at the Village Office, negotiating with the Mayor at the same time as the work crews were down there jacking up the building and moving it down to the airport. It's now the Chetwynd Air Terminal building. For a $9,000 tax bill, they got themselves a $300,000 building. There should be a lawsuit over it.

"These Indian people were here long before we came," said Oberle at the Chetwynd Industrial Days Celebration, "and they can't cope with all these things. If I were still the Mayor here in Chetwynd, I would immediately tax all the churches, because people now have to come to their Member of Parliament, not to their priest, to get any help. The government looks after everything now. So why should the churches get a free ride? If the church had been on the ball, why would the town repossess the building? Why didn't the priest go in, get some activities going, hold the bingos there, help the people integrate and assimilate into the town? Everything falls apart when a politician leaves town."

Father Jungbluth wasn't at the meeting, but one of the Sisters took Oberle to task and said, "That's illegal, taxing a church!"

Oberle replied: "Look, if we, Father Jungbluth and I, had only done what was legal, this town would never have been on the road."

Frank Oberle now speaks about the falling out: "I guess Father got really mad at me and that's why he didn't invite me to the opening of the new church that was built in Chetwynd many years later. He invited my wife, Joan, but not me. Father Jungbluth was always my strongest supporter; in fact, if it hadn't been for him, I wouldn't have ended up in politics, but we always fought. We still do."

Father Jungbluth summed up the success of the Moccasin Flat Improvement Project, some 15 years later:

"Some of the houses are in good shape, some are not. I was scared when the engineer left, because the Village Council kind of lost interest in the project. So right now, I don't call it a ghetto yet, but there are some youngsters in there who are pretty wild.

"I call on those people yet, a little bit, but not much. I have so much trouble getting up their stairs. The stairs are all wrecked in the back, the rail is gone and I have to scramble up by holding myself on the rough stucco wall. When they see me, they come and help me.

"A certain number even come to church."

30

"In the Meantime, I Got Old"

*I*n February, 1960, Father Jungbluth wrote a letter to *Immaculata*. He was flat on his back in the Dawson Creek Hospital, "a sort of humiliation for a missionary of the Indians working without interruption for almost 26 years in a most severe climate without once being sick."

He did not tell them that his health was not always what it should be. His back bothered him, and some mornings he could barely get out of bed to start the fire in his small cold shack. At times his knees and legs hurt so much he could hardly do the proper genuflections before the altar. He thought of the old sacristan back home who, once retired, took to his bed and never rose from it again. The idea had appeal.

A month earlier he had traveled south of Chetwynd into the Rocky Mountains, out toward the Sukunka. This overland trip could only be made in early winter, when the creeks and muskegs were frozen but the snow was not too deep.

He spent the first night in a small Indian camp, where he met the illustrious Monsieur Larose. In his letter to *Immaculata*, Father Jungbluth explained:

> M. Larose is a French-speaking eastern Canadian, who has lived for a long time in the wilderness without any intention of going back into civilization. He trims his hair with a knife once in a while when it reaches almost to his mouth, and they say he only changes his clothes when they are in rags. I might say he does not smell like a rose, and therefore is not easily identifiable by his name. The Indians tell me he prays the Rosary every day, and I was happy to see him at my service, peering at me through a part in the long fringes of his hair, his eyes reflecting the small flame of the coal-oil lamp. I hope I measured up to his expectations.

Father Jungbluth wanted to proceed on with his journey, but by three o'clock in the afternoon grey clouds had formed, puffing over the hills like smoke signals. Father Jungbluth went to Larose's hut to ask his opinion about the weather. M. Larose came out, sniffed and peered in two directions. Then, pointing with one hand to the sky and the other to the ground, he murmured, *"Demain matin, neige profonde —* tomorrow morning, lots of snow."

Father Jungbluth had to be back in Moberly Lake by Sunday. There were about 100 kilometres yet to go. Even if he had to drive through the night, he must risk it. Half an hour later, the first snow fell. Thick wet snowflakes dropped straight from the sky, at first softly, then faster and faster, covering the windshield until the wipers could no longer move. He opened the window and leaned his head out, but the headlights could not penetrate the white flurry that danced in the black night.

He drove slowly, and for two hours all went well. The greater part of the journey now lay behind him — and the best part of the road too — but he was in high spirits thinking of the people he would see at church, the men who would ask him about his trip and what he would tell them. "No problems. Everything went fine." Deep in his daydreams, he did not notice the high speed at which he was traveling. There was a sudden bang, and his head hit the windshield. The Madonna, held on the dash by a magnet, had fallen to the floor, and the vehicle did not seem level. It didn't take long to find the cause, and he cursed himself for his daydreams. While barrelling down the snowy road, he had failed to notice an iced-over creek. His right front wheel had crashed down into the water. The ice embraced it firmly and a little trickle of water seeped up around the tire.

There was no time to lose. He had tools, but the wind, which had whipped up during his reveries, was blowing him off his feet. The boards he tried to shove under the wheel slipped on the ice. Then he too slipped, and freezing water immediately penetrated every layer of his clothing. Nevertheless he continued working, and was surprised to feel moisture on

Father Jungbluth in his truck

his forehead and a stickiness over his body. He was sweating profusely, even though the temperature was at least 20 degrees below zero.

It took two hours to drag the truck out from the creek, and even then his problems were not over. The steering wheel would not turn, nor would the wheel which had broken into the ice. The brakes, too, were completely frozen. With his axe he tried to break off icicles that formed around the wheel, but nothing helped. He made a fire, but the wind was too strong. Even warm wet rags did nothing to thaw the frozen wheel; on the contrary, the rags themselves froze instantly.

Finally it occurred to him to pour hot water from the radiator over the frozen wheel. It worked.

He put chains on the back tires, remembering several fairly steep hills yet to climb. He drove very carefully now, praying the Rosary and calling on St. Christopher for assistance. He was so tired that he felt quite sick.

After what seemed like hours, Father Jungbluth reached the more-traveled road, still two hours from Chetwynd. Twenty-five kilometres later he was flagged down by a man waving a flashlight. His beautiful new sedan had slid into the ditch, and his wife and two children sat huddled inside. Could the shabby old truck, which had barely enough energy to haul itself up the hills, pull out this big car? Using boards and chains, and a lot of body heat, Father managed to pull the sedan back onto the road. The delay took an hour.

It was four o'clock in the morning when he pulled into the yard of Our Lady of Peace Church in Chetwynd and stumbled from the truck. And it was still dark outside when he heard someone knock on his door. An old Metis, who lived with his wife in a temporary shelter behind the church, was knocking to tell Father Jungbluth it was time to say Mass. As he pulled his aching body from his bed, he heard the Metis say to a parishioner outside: "I knock at his door, I knock at his window, and still he doesn't open. He really must be lazy."

When Holy Mass was over, Father Jungbluth sat on one of the church benches to say a prayer of thanksgiving. His head was on his chest, and he was nearly asleep when he felt, rather than heard, someone beside him. It was the old Metis, waiting for the cup of coffee that he had been promised after Mass.

"Good bye. Go now," he said to the Metis. He heard the old man walk out of the church, and, as he passed a window, heard him mutter in Cree, "This Father is indeed lazy. And furthermore, he is a miser, too."

Father Jungbluth had often worked through the night, but this time he felt different. His back was throbbing with pain. He stumbled to his bed and slept, but every time he awoke daggers shot up his back making him cry out and causing him to break into a sweat.

On the third day, he realized he must do something. He dressed and went outside. The truck was a wreck; the rear axle needed a spring replacement.

One thought still needled him: he must be in Moberly Lake on Sunday. He would not tell everything that had happened. He would only admit to some problems.

Sunday passed in a blur of pain. By Monday he was incapable of moving. The Metis sent for a white man, who immediately transported him in his car to the Dawson Creek Hospital. The doctor's prescription included 10 days of bed rest. He was to stay flat on his back, not getting up even to read Mass.

The Bishop chose this time to make a visit to his missionary. He flew up from Prince George and, hearing that Father Jungbluth was already in Dawson Creek, he hurried over to visit. Father listened quietly as Bishop O'Grady circled round his bed, clasping his hands in excitement as he reeled off his plans for Chetwynd. It must have a Catholic school, with Sisters to teach. And a small church hall. And, oh yes, Father Jungbluth was to officially consider Chetwynd his principal residence. And buy more land! The Bishop wasn't pleased with the location of the church. He thought a church would be better located higher up, on a plateau overlooking the town and the industries that were making Chetwynd grow and become the industrial capital of the North.

Father Jungbluth turned in his bed and looked out the window at the white snowflakes hitting and melting, hitting and melting. With great sadness, he realized the Bishop was right: Chetwynd was growing rapidly. It's increasing population, in direct relation to the decrease at Moberly, gave him a clear view of what was happening to his beloved little mission by the lake.

In the summer, the people of Chetwynd sometimes came to Mass at the little log church, making a picnic of it, enjoying the quaintness of the church and the solitude of the surroundings. But the Indians didn't like it. They stayed away, more each Sunday.

"I'm tired, Bishop," Father Jungbluth said softly.

The Bishop nodded. "I'll be back tomorrow. You take care of yourself."

Father smiled weakly and closed his eyes. Old images floated in front of his eyes, of sports days at the church after Mass, three-legged races and spoon races, Elephant Walk and Duck Walk competitions, and games. Father Jungbluth had offered prizes of puzzles, rubber balls or magic slates to entice the children to attend. When the race was finished and the winner was announced, Father Jungbluth would ask him to come up and present himself. The child would be handed the microphone and he had to say, "Thank you, Sisters!" or "Thank you, Father!" The speakers would be mounted on top of the truck so they would be even louder than usual. The parents would come for Mass, and quite often everyone would bring lunch. Everybody shared. All the food was put on a big table, and there would be a fire for a wiener roast. Adults joined in a game too: a tug-of-war with a big rope. They always saw to it that the rope was a poor one, and there was a big laugh when it broke.

Father Jungbluth's Moberly Lake

There were baseball games. The Indians had helped him build a kind of ball diamond next to the church. There wasn't enough room to make it standard size, but they flattened the land, took the bush out, picked the stones, and it served the purpose. But the Indians didn't get too well organized themselves. "And too," he thought, "I got old in the meantime. One can't help it."

Father Jungbluth sighed and tried to shift his body to a comfortable position. He turned his head and stared across to the bed of an old man, whose snoring filled the room with unsteady tremors. He again closed his eyes and invited sleep. Instead, his subconscious offered him memories of other noises: the wild yelps of Indian children in Kelly Lake on spring days, as they raced across the fields going nowhere. They reminded him of young colts crisscrossing the pastures, happy to have the snow gone and a chance to test out their longer legs.

In Moberly Lake he remembered dances in the winter would provide money for the rodeos of summer. The dances were held in a great log hall that was there no longer. People donated their help to build it. Music was provided locally by Pete Leo (West End Pete) and Simon Redhead or one of the Paquettes on violins, and Archie Walker with the guitar. Everyone would go — but Father Jungbluth. Kids went along with the adults and crawled under benches to sleep. No babysitters. No booze. The odd time there were rumors that there had been some home brew around, but nothing too serious would result. That was before the road came in.

Slim Garbitt (son of Harry) was the head guy at the dance hall. He had donated nails and other materials to build the hall. Slim was gone now, too. One of the sad Moberly Lake funerals.

At the rodeos, people from West End (the Beaver reserve) would donate their broncs. Fred Napoleon from East End (the Cree/Saulteaux reserve) had the most cows, so he would donate cows for the wild cow rides. There were no cows there anymore. No place to keep them. Too many highways. The fences had fallen down, or were cut down with tinsnips.

Father Jungbluth remembered announcing rodeos. He would set his loudspeakers on the hood of the truck, crank up the volume and, taking a deep breath, begin the two-hour sessions of announcements, jokes, stories, orders, threats to end the event if the people didn't show up . . .

"And here comes Marvin Desjarlais on a horse called Mother-in- Law!" he'd yell, over the cheers of all Marvin's relatives. And the chute would open and there would be the horse, Mother-in-Law, not making a move. The people would laugh!

He could not remember the Indians laughing much lately. Now he was more and more a witness to their sorrows. He was kept busy making out Pledges. Just last week he'd had another one. He had answered a knock on his door, and there stood an Indian woman, her hair dishevelled, her face swollen and tearstained.

"I can't live with him anymore!" she cried.

Father Jungbluth backed into his shack. "Come in," he said.

She had edged inside the door and sat down on the brown chair. "He told me I was chasing him out. But he promised me he would come with me to see you, and that he would take the Pledge not to drink anymore."

He had taken them both into his office — the front room of his two-room shack in which there was a large desk, filing cabinet, an old couch, a heater and the brown chair. The man was still pretty much under the influence — he was drunk, in fact — but there he sat, swaying slightly, promising.

"I know I promised not to drink before, Father," he said, "but I couldn't stand it. This time I want to take the Pledge — maybe the three-month one."

So Father Jungbluth had written out a Pledge, placing the Church stamp at the top, and the date. Underneath, he carefully wrote: "I promise to God and to the Virgin Mary and to Father Jungbluth that for three months I will abstain from all alcohol, so help me God."

And he let the man sign it with his "X". Then, for good measure, he made the man promise, but not in writing, that when it was over he would take another three-month Pledge.

A week later the wife had come again, shaking the paper in her hand. "Here is the paper! It's no good at all! Last night he came home and he said, 'I can't stand it anymore.' So here, Father, you have the Pledge, he broke it already."

Father Jungbluth knew who had given him drink; one of the white men in Chetwynd. He knew who it was. But the husband had become so abusive that his wife had phoned the police — and Indians don't usually do that. The police had come and loaded him up. All they could do was take him into the jail and let him sleep it off overnight.

"Did he hit you?" Father Jungbluth asked the distraught woman. "Do you want to put a charge against him?" No, she didn't want to cause any trouble. He sighed.

Sometimes the wives came to see him, black and blue, and sometimes they had been drinking too. When he abstained, she abstained. There they'd stand, both of them, heads hanging. Father Jungbluth would get angry. They'd kneel in front of him, clinging at his legs. "Oh, Father, I am bad! I am bad. Help me, help me . . ."

So he would write out a Pledge and take it into the church, and give each one of them a candle to hold in their hands. He made them promise right there, in front of the altar, "I promise to God . . ." When they had signed it, Father Jungbluth would fold it up and put it under the altar.

"It will stay there until the Pledge is finished, if you have not been drinking," he would tell them in a solemn loud voice. "BUT," and his voice would clap like thunder, "if you drink, you know what I will do?"

In a dramatic gesture, he would grab the Pledge from under the altar and hold it over the lighted candle in the man's hand until it started to burn. "That's the way I'm going to burn it! That's the way you are going to burn in Hell!"

Well, he had to scare them sometimes. Perhaps he could create a turning point.

Father Jungbluth shifted in his hospital bed and stared at the ceiling. He had tried to help them assimilate into town life. He'd taught them about banks, and the importance of saving their money, until the bank manager approached him and begged, "Please, no more Indians. They open an account, we do all the books, and then they just come and take it all out again the next day!"

He tried to keep a stock of used clothing for the Indians: coats and boots and school clothes for the children. He moved his supply into a little shed behind his shack, and laboriously sorted everything into sizes. But the Indians were not impressed. He would send them in to get what they wanted, but when he went in later, everything would be all mixed up. They took what they wanted and just messed up the rest, even though he told them pointedly to put everything back into the same boxes. They thought they'd take this one, but then they'd find something better, and the first thing was just thrown aside. After a while he didn't let them in anymore. He told them to wait outside and would go in himself to find something. He wasn't left with such a shambles, but the Indians were not always happy. They couldn't be sure they had the best.

Ladies' clubs sometimes had sales — 10 cents for any item — but the Indians were now better off. They were not interested in these bargains. The final solution was to cut off the buttons and zippers, put them in jars and sell them; they made more money that way, and the buttons were bought immediately. But otherwise he couldn't get rid of his piles of sweaters and skirts and coats.

Now the Indians were mad about bingos. Father Jungbluth didn't like the game on moral grounds. "It doesn't make the people better," he thought, still staring up at the hospital's white ceiling. "In fact, it encourages that kind of gambling spirit that many people have, that idea of becoming rich. They spend too much money, money which might belong to the poor people, money which belongs to their family. Instead of keeping good care of their kids, they go to bingos, trying to get rich quick." His thoughts turned blacker: "They have not the right to expose themselves to the chance of losing money! They are not supposed to take such a risk. If they can't afford to lose five dollars, bingo is not justified."

Everyone in Chetwynd was having bingos. First the men of the Legion, then the Auxiliary, then the Elks and then the Royal Purple. According to the law you were supposed to hold bingos only once a week, but the way around that was to shift the source. And then the Indians started, and there were not enough days left, so they had one on Sunday. In their Indian hall. So now every Sunday was taken.

Sometimes one of the Indians would come and tell him, "Father, here's a dollar. Pray that I would win at bingo!" So he would pray, but sometimes the Good Lord didn't always hear his prayers.

Father Jungbluth's roommate stopped snoring, jolting him back from his reverie. Where was he? Oh, yes, in the hospital, flat on his back where he would remain for another eight days or so. He thought of the cold, hazardous journey that had brought him here, of not paying heed to the forecasts of Monsieur Larose, who lived in the mountains and had enough sense to stay home when the weather dictated. Monsieur Larose was not affected by civilization. Let it come — he would surely move farther and farther back into the mountains. It would not destroy him.

Father Jungbluth's thoughts drifted now, as he sank into sleep. "Let God long protect the Monsieur Laroses of the world." He foolishly thought of the skunk, whose scent drives others away, and of the bear, whose sour smell and gruff demeanor keep at bay the curious tourists. His Indians were becoming too civilized, that was the problem. They were using after-shave lotions, the young boys and girls all carried plastic combs and wore brightly colored shirts and dresses and shiny pointed shoes.

His dreams were slide-flashes of clothing of all descriptions and colors and sizes, falling into boxes marked in his own painstaking hand, "child's small, child's medium, child's large." And in his dreams, the Indians were laughing at a joke he did not understand.

31

Dog Days

In 1962 the Second Vatican Council was convened by His Holiness Pope John XXIII. Its theme was "renewal." The popular new Pope called on all believers in any faith to come together "to strengthen the positive aspects of their faiths."

Ecumenism was not a new idea to northern missionaries. The harsh climate, the distance between homesteads and camps, and the primitive and hazardous methods of travel brought people together in a natural way. Father Jungbluth had spent many hours riding along forest trails on horseback accompanied by Miss Monica Storrs, the Anglican missionary who lived in Fort St. John. But it was true that the Catholic Church promoted rules that often got in the way of friendship with those of other faiths. For example, a Catholic was not to enter a church of another religion except to attend a wedding or funeral. Ecumenism was, for the most part, positive.

But other changes wrought by Vatican II caused the Church, in Father Jungbluth's eyes, to weaken. Latin was gone. The altar was turned around so the priest faced the congregation. Rules on dress were slackened. It was no longer considered necessary for a priest to wear the white alb. Some wore just a suit, or a windbreaker, with the little stole draped over the shoulder.

"Our Bishop was a little bit lax," says Father Jungbluth. "He didn't communicate all the latest changes authorized by Rome and we sometimes read of them first in *La Voix*. Sometimes I'd ask our Bishop and he'd say, 'Well, if *La Voix* gives permission, I give it too.'

"I was conservative with the changes when they came so fast, but I hadn't been perfect myself. Sometimes in the old days I said Mass in the teepees when I didn't have everything along with me. The old missionaries, I am sure, did that too. We had many permissions among the Indians. I took my own liberties.

"In those days everything didn't make sense. You were supposed to wear the maniple on your left wrist, a kind of hand-towel. It was a ceremonial thing. I didn't do that. You were supposed to always have an altar stone along that contained the relics of some saint. It was a nuisance to take that on a motorcycle or on horseback, but still I always took it. It was a piece of marble and weighed up to two pounds [907 g], and was 6" to 8" square [1.8 x 2.4 m]. When it broke you had to get another one, and have it consecrated by the Bishop.

"I didn't use any English when it was forbidden. Later on, the intimate part of the Mass — the consecration — was still supposed to be in Latin while the rest was in English. Some priests who were more aggressive started to disobey that. 'Why should I say that in Latin?' they said. 'People have the right to understand what we say.' But that was not my stand. I would say that regulations and laws were made to be obeyed, when you can, except when they interfere with practicality."

Finally the day came when all of the Mass could be said in English. When Father Jungbluth made that announcement, a principal man on his Parish Council was so overjoyed that he took Father's big Latin Missal and said he was going to rip it in two. Father Jungbluth was appalled.

"That's not definitive!" he yelled, lunging to retrieve the book. "And that's a blessed book! Don't you dare to do a thing like that."

Father Jungbluth was not happy with the eagerness many of the new priests displayed for the radical changes. In his eyes, they had become "city-slickers," shunning the clerical collar, the alb, the very uniform that separated men of their calling from the man on the street. At a meeting of priests in Prince George, he spoke out about it.

"We should give witness at least to being priests by wearing our collars," he said, conscious of the anguish of Father Hettrich who was sitting near him, miserable over the new look of most of the priests around them. "The police have their uniforms, a judge has his uniform, why shouldn't we have our uniform when we are in the function of priests?"

But as time went on, Father Jungbluth adjusted . . . slowly. "Had I been with the other priests in the province and could have studied the changes and discussed them, I probably would have understood," he said, "but being in the North, it was different."

He was one of the last to stop regular wearing of the collar.

The changes affected both priests and congregations. With greater frequency, the subject of birth control was raised. "Why can't I just use my own conscience?" a parishioner asked Father Jungbluth.

"A conscience is not a law," he replied slowly. "It has to be formed, with your own intelligence. If the Pope makes a declaration, you have to obey it. If he says that birth control is not natural, it is not to be used, there is a reason for that."

"But Father, I already have six kids! I'm afraid for my health to have any more."

"Many deceive themselves when they say, 'It is for my health,' or 'for regulating the periods,' or 'so I will not have to use any birth control instruments.'" he had answered. "In these cases, all I can say is 'pray that the Good Lord will help you.'"

He did not look directly at the woman. He was very uneasy, but he continued.

"Pray that the Good Lord may give you enough generosity and willingness to follow His law, so that you would know what is proper, so that you would not offend Him seriously, so that you would be willing to observe the Law of God no matter what hardships."

The woman looked down at her lap. Following her eyes, Father Jungbluth, too, noticed the hands that rested there. The nails were broken stumps, the knuckles of the fingers rubbed raw, likely from scrubbing laundry for six children and two adults on a scrub board in an old tin tub, using homemade lye soap. Well, what could he do? The right answer, of course, might be to tell her to abstain from the marital act. But then . . . if they abstain from the marital act, it might break up the marriage, if the husband insists on his rights and so on.

"The question has never been fully perfected," Father Jungbluth said lamely. "Never."

Still the woman did not rise to leave. There was something else.

"What about sterilization?"

"That's a mutilation!" Father Jungbluth jumped up and began pacing the room. "It could only be condoned for health reasons, if an organ is diseased. But if your doctor says, 'this woman, if she has another child, might die . . .' There is another alternative — and that is abstinence."

The woman now rose to go. Father Jungbluth looked out the window.

"Thank you, Father," she murmured.

Father Jungbluth turned, then wished he hadn't. The woman's lips, held tight for control, began to tremble. As she turned to go through the door he saw, to his great sadness, that tears were welling up in her brown eyes and running down her cheeks. He turned back and looked out the window once again, until he could tell by the sound of her footsteps that she was far down the path.

Priests were changing, and nuns were changing too. Gone were the long habits, the veil. He sometimes wanted to chastise them, to cry, "Carry your veil, at least!" but he was afraid they would turn to him and say, "Mind your own business. What do you know about the uniforms of women?" They were able to talk back now. "Where is your cassock?" they might say to him. "Where is your collar?" Even the Bishops didn't talk about it anymore.

Then there were other things, like meatless Fridays, fasting at Lent and Advent, all the Holy Days they used to observe, the Assumption of the Virgin Mary, the Immaculate Conception Feast, all these things were taken away. One had the right to observe them, but they were not necessary. Some priests were very upset. And many began to leave the priesthood.

"The Church is going to the dogs!" Father Jungbluth would think morosely, then quickly chastise himself for such heretical thoughts. "No, no, that's a bad thing. I shouldn't think that. Just . . . well, it's lost its fervor."

One night, in this period of greatest torment, his telephone rang shrilly, scaring him, bringing him out of his bed and onto his feet. The telephone rang only a few times each month, and it still frightened him each time. He answered tentatively.

"Hello?"

"Hello, there! This is Freddy."

"Freddy? What Freddy? Who is that?"

"Are you awake now, or are you still sleeping?" the voice asked, laughing. "This is Pater Bruckert, Pater Alfred Bruckert, Order of the Oblates of Mary Immaculate, the Parson of Peace River . . . come on, old boy, don't you know me anymore?"

"Ah, it's you, Freddy!" Father Bruckert, his old friend from Alsace, his fellow seminarist in Berthécourt. They had studied Cree together in Grouard. "You are indeed alive? I have not heard from you in years!"

Father Bruckert was now the parish priest in the town of Peace River, Alberta, (formerly Peace River Crossing), approximately 480 kilometres from Father Jungbluth's mission. Speaking quickly during the long-distance call, they agreed to meet the following week and together go back to visit the missions at Fort Vermilion and Eleské. This trip back in time would perhaps enable him to recapture the magic, the sense of adventure and worth.

Fort Vermilion looked the same from a distance. As they approached they noted a new church, and an expanded hospital. But there were the old missionary buildings, just the same as 30 years ago . . . and the Indian school and the house of the Sisters. They were heartily welcomed and spent a day going through the buildings, talking to the residents. Father Jungbluth's mind flipped back through the decades. The smells of the old mission house, the wood-burning furnace, the chalk-dusted classrooms, the campfire smell of the old Indians who had taught them their first halting words in Beaver — all returned to his memory. Thirty years, gone so quickly.

"Jungbluth, don't dream!" called Father Bruckert. "We have to move on, you know."

They traveled out to Eleské, and marvelled at Father Mariman's fine grotto. Suddenly they burst out laughing. Above Father Mariman's grotto was his hand-written sign, "DRINK OF THE HOLY WATER OF THE GROTTO." Beside it the Health Department had posted another sign, "WATER CONDEMNED."

Atop the old chapel in a little wooden tower hung the bell donated by *Immaculata* readers in Strasbourg. Inside the church stood the little harmonium. Father Jungbluth walked over and uncovered the keyboard. He pulled up a chair and ran his fingers lightly over the keys. Music filled the hall. He pumped the dusty pedals and began playing a medley of hymns that once had brought the Indians out from their huts throughout the settlement. He could see again old blind Sijoli, his busy fingers alternately tapping time to the music and scratching in his hair. He laughed out loud, remembering.

On the way back, Father Bruckert told stories of Peace River. It was a growing town and he loved it there. He had never gone back to Alsace. When it came time to take his 10-year vacation home, he had refused to go. Father Bruckert was silent for a moment. "I am afraid that if I go, the Bishop will take my Peace River away from me. He'll put someone else in there, and when I come back, I'll be sent to some remote place out in the bush."

They came at last to Peace River, and Father Bruckert invited him in to view the church he had built and enjoy a glass of wine before he journeyed back to Chetwynd. Father Bruckert had installed a small room divided from the interior of the church by a glass wall. Mothers could take crying babies there to quiet them or feed them in private. Father Jungbluth remembered how often he had said Mass to a congregation of Indian mothers who sat before him calmly suckling their young.

He walked with his friend out to the waiting truck.

"Good bye, and good luck," he said simply. Father Bruckert nodded, and their eyes met in farewell.

It started to rain as Father Jungbluth neared Dawson Creek, and by the time he reached the town limits, it was coming down in a white sheet. At the side of the road stood two young Indian boys. They were from Moberly and he knew them well. Father Jungbluth stopped the truck and they climbed in, shaking off the water like wet dogs. The heat of the truck took the chill off the day, and they began laughing and telling stories.

"Do you remember when we just had horses at Moberly Lake, Father?" asked one of the boys. "Remember Fred Napoleon had two white horses, Little Silver and Big Silver? Boy, they were a good team."

"I sure do," Father Jungbluth replied. "He pulled my old Model A out of the river more than once. It was before there was a bridge across the Moberly River. When the water was too high to ford, I'd toot the horn and finally Fred Napoleon would notice. I had to put all the stuff on top of the car and take the carburetor off and plug it with rags, and I'd crouch on the seat, while Fred Napoleon pulled my car across with his team. The water came in through the bottom way high, high. I told him to avoid the big rocks.

"On the other side I put the carburetor back on, pulled the sparkplugs out and cleaned them and turned the motor over a few times. I took the oil plug off underneath and let the water drain out. When I felt there was no water anymore I closed it up quick. I'd work on it for three-quarters of an hour or so, and I had the car going. With the Model A, you could do anything. It was a '29 or '30 coupe."

The boys sat quietly listening. The windshield wipers slapped out a steady metronomic beat. Father Jungbluth talked slowly, not so much to them as to the darkening rain-blurred road ahead.

"It had big wooden spoke wheels, the Model A. They got ruined going through those rough roads — they don't last forever. During the war I

204 Direction of Time

couldn't get tires for it anymore, so I put V-8 wheels on it. It was a bit tough because they didn't fit properly, but I put some washers on behind to build it up and I had lots of power then."

"I remember, Father, you used to go so fast!" one of the boys interjected. "One time you gave us a ride and you went so fast. Someone said you'd been drinking."

Father Jungbluth gave him a sidelong glance. "It had lots of power," he continued, "but the car rode lower with the 16-inch [40 cm] wheels and it wasn't quite as handy to go through the potholes as it was with the high wheels."

The rain slackened and the clouds on the horizon seemed to be breaking. A hit of red sunset appeared over the Rockies.

"I remember at Kelly Lake," Father Jungbluth went on, "the car had those running boards and I had two or three Indians on each side hanging onto the door with the windows open. I drove up and down the roads, advertising that I was there over the loudspeakers, and of course they liked to go fast. The road was rough, rocks sticking out a little bit all over, but we went, and there were all kinds of dogs around. The Indians kicked at them to get them out of the way, but they didn't succeed. When we came back we saw we had killed two dogs. There they were, lying on the road. Two nice big dogs, pack dogs. And the Indians who had been standing on the running boards didn't even know we'd hit them! They looked and said, 'Did we kill them? I didn't notice it.' Big dogs. I was sorry for them because they were good dogs, and a pack dog at that time had more value than a horse."

They were coming to a hill, and the road was slippery from the hard rain. In front of them they recognized the one-ton truck belonging to Reverend Ivan Golding.

"Look at him slide!" Father Jungbluth cried.

They followed at a distance as the big truck fishtailed up the greasy hill. Father Jungbluth finally stepped on the accelerator, knowing that to lose speed on this hill would be disastrous. They would slow, spin out, then begin to slip and slide back. As they neared the big truck, a painted sign across the back of the box declared: "AT THE END OF THE TRAIL, YOU WILL MEET GOD."

They could see the wheels of the big truck start to spin. It began to slide back toward them.

"Watch out, Father!" the boy shouted. "Reverend Golding's going to help us meet God!"

Father Jungbluth swerved around the struggling vehicle and they made their way slowly up the long hill. The boys sat back, grinning and high-spirited in the excitement of the near mishap.

When they reached Chetwynd, he dropped the boys off and drove over to the post office to pick up his mail. He was walking, head down in the rain, when he heard someone call his name.

"Father Youngblood! Yeah, you!" He did not recognize the man. He stopped.

"Yes, I am Father Youngblood. Who are you?"

"Your church is going to the dogs! Do you hear me? You have nothing left anymore. It's going to the dogs."

Father Jungbluth put his head down again and continued walking.

"Even your Pope says so!" the man taunted. "Don't deny it. He says the Church is not what it should be." Just before Father Jungbluth turned his head and walked on, he saw the man stick out his tongue at him. From the corner of his eye he could see people standing, shocked by the raving stranger.

Long after he picked up his mail and returned to his shack, the man's words echoed about his head. "Your church is going to the dogs. You have nothing left. It's all gone . . ."

He sat down on the brown chair and held his hands out to the small heater. He felt like a relic from another time, without defence against the cold winds that blew from ever-changing directions.

32

The Youth Camp

*I*n 1967, Bishop O'Grady's farsighted plans began to take shape. Father Jungbluth started work on a summer youth camp at Moberly Lake. He used the property to the east of the church, purchased from Pete Thiessen; all he needed was money to put up a dormitory and cookshack, and volunteer staff to help run it. Local clubs gave their full support, and soon the camp materialized.

Situated perhaps 30 metres above the lakeshore, there were two main buildings: a dorm and a dining/recreation hall. The dorm was divided into two wings with a meeting room in the centre. The building was heated by wood, with a little stove in each partition. The indoor washrooms had sinks, mirrors and cold running water.

Across from the dorm, overlooking Moberly Lake, was a combination kitchen-dining area and recreation room. The high-pitched roof, facing the lake, supported a wall with a row of windows reaching from one end of the building to the other. Inside was a storage room, eating area and kitchen, for which Father Jungbluth had designed a hot and cold running water system that gave perpetual trouble with its varying pressures.

In the trees behind the dorm were wooden outhouses. The Frontier Apostles recruited from the cities to run the camp found these difficult to get used to. They seemed always crawling with spiders, or housing bees that came buzzing up from the holes at inopportune moments. Bats clung in high dark corners and hornet nests buzzed with excitement each time the door banged. In the dark of night, when these creatures could not be seen, they were even more frightening. The wind moaned through the tall poplar trees, echoing cries of wild things that lurked beyond the flashlight's beam . . . or spirits of the dead, still protecting the nearby graveyard.

Down the hill, closer to the water and near the church, rested the "white elephant," a silver trailer unit received from Peter and Paul Demeulemeester. Father Jungbluth had divided it into four small apartments which housed the Frontier Apostles and the Sisters. Down from the trailer, at the water's edge, were three small sparsely-furnished cabins. These also provided rooms for the Frontier Apostles or visiting priests.

The log church was a delight to the young Apostles. Old-fashioned pictures of Mary, Mother of God, and the Sacred Heart of Jesus (painted by a friend of Father Jungbluth's from Florennes and presented to him at his first Mass) had adorned the interior for 30 years now. They seemed to belong to a time long past. In back of the church was the room where Father Jungbluth had lived for 12 years, containing a narrow bed, a crucifix, coat hooks and a wood stove. To the right of the church was a storage garage, housing an old boat that looked more like a bathtub but still managed to float. This was Father Jungbluth's "rescue boat," a mandatory piece of equipment insisted upon by the Department of Health.

Behind the conglomeration of buildings lay the graveyard, overrun with long grasses and wildflowers. Purple fireweed, pungent clover, pink wild roses and Indian Paintbrush almost covered the little peak-roofed houses built over the graves.

The youth camp was run primarily by Carl Forsberg, a man who gained Father Jungbluth's immediate respect for his energy and his extraordinary ability to whistle. Assisting him were volunteer priests, Sisters, and Frontier Apostles from the western provinces.

A letter from one of the earlier Frontier Apostles, Mrs. Claire Stitsen (nee Kieser), recalls the first years:

> In the summers of 1968 and 1969, St. Albert High School in Alberta asked for volunteers for the Summer Youth Apostolate in Chetwynd and Moberly Lake. Father Ducheneau from St. Albert organized us as a group and gave much of his time helping out, preparing us to teach catechism for one to two months in some of Father Jungbluth's missions.
>
> We traveled from Moberly Lake to Chetwynd daily, teaching catechism and preparing the children for First Communion. We assisted as staff at the youth camp. We helped in sports, cooking, and with transportation, as many of the children had to be transported to and from catechism class. They knew Father was on his way when the loudspeaker atop his vehicle resounded music for miles.
>
> Father's love for children showed through and through. He treated them as though they were his own. He always had a smile on his face. Father Jungbluth is a special priest — one of a kind.

Michelle Brissette, another Frontier Apostle, worked at the camp in the summers of 1975 and 1976:

> I guess I have to admit it, I was afraid to meet Father Jungbluth. The first time I'd even seen his name was in reply to my application for summer work with the Frontier Apostles. His writing was very prim and proper, rather "old country" style. It left me wondering what type of person expressed himself in this manner. As time went on, I grew afraid and more afraid of meeting him, until the day finally arrived — June 26th.
>
> Thank goodness for the moral support of my family as I stepped out of the car into the churchyard, to be greeted by a warm smile and an arm around my shoulder. With that, it was into Father's shack — pardon me, rectory — for refreshments.

During the first couple of days, I learned quite a few things about Father Emile. First, he was a real packrat. I couldn't believe the stuff he had in his shed beside his shack in Chetwynd. In one shed he had everything from fancy dishes to homemade snow-shoes. Once when we were driving, he saw two Indian girls, and he made some comment as to how good-looking they were. I looked at him. He grinned and said he was a man before he was a priest.

On my third day in Chetwynd, I saw a different type of Father Jungbluth — not the usual "get up and go" one. He woke me up to tell me that he had received a phone call. One of his best friends, Father Holmes from Fort St. John, had died. I didn't realize until then how much compassion, love and loneliness Father had.

To sum it up, Father is simply a priest and a man. He restored my faith in the Church.

The youth camp was a daring experiment; it required money, dedication and ingenuity. Father Jungbluth was everywhere at once, overseeing the catechism lessons, planning activities, procuring equipment (bales of old sleeping bags purchased on sale, donations of soccer balls, baseballs, bows and arrows). It took a great deal of time, and sometimes Father Jungbluth — now a man of 60 years — felt it was more work than he could handle. Then, almost imperceptibly, enthusiasm for the camp dwindled. His Indians, the ones he thought would most benefit, were the first to drop away.

"The first year it was open, our kids went to the camp," says Elmer Davis, one-time chief of the East End band at Moberly Lake. "They camped over there for 14 days. It was free. The nuns ran it, and Father gave orders to the nuns. Then they had those helpers — Frontier Apostles — from all over the place. They used to come to church and some of them could play the guitar. But after a while our kids didn't want to go anymore because there were too many different kinds of people — white kids. They were shy with all those other kids there." Then, he adds with a wink, "You know how Indians are — they're shy."

Ernie Pfanner of Chetwynd, whose daughter, Carla, worked at the camp, remembers the problems:

> The local people didn't support it, so the Welfare paid to send kids in. There was friction right away. There were kids whose parents were paying, and welfare kids who didn't have to pay, and local Indian kids, and there was friction. I don't know if they tried to separate the Indians from the whites, if that's where the fights started, but there was just too much of everything: paid campers, welfare kids, Indians, whites, Catholics and non-Catholics, and it didn't work out.
>
> It hasn't been used as a church camp now for years. Different groups rent it for a week or a weekend, but as far as the Church

itself goes, they don't run it, except for a two-week intensive catechism course for local kids.

Father was really unhappy about it closing up.

Father Jungbluth looks back on the project, with pride at its successes and a noncommittal shrug at its demise.

People thought I was foolish to build the Moberly Lake Youth Centre, and I was taken aback when the children did not respond as well as we had hoped. They like now to go rather with their families in the modern trailers and campers, and that is as it should be. In my days, families did not have money to go away, and a camp was a very nice thing to have; so this is better, I suppose. It is good that children now can have enjoyment with their families.

(In 1968, Father Jungbluth was presented by the Chetwynd Chamber of Commerce with the Citizen of the Year Award, partly because of his work with the Moberly Lake Youth Centre, but also because of his contribution to the community in general, as a member of the Hospital Board and the Ambulance Service, Knights of Columbus, the Royal Canadian Legion and the Chamber of Commerce.)

33

The Sisters

$\mathcal{F}$ather Jungbluth at first rejected the notion of Sisters as pastoral assistants. But he couldn't deny his own limitations. The uneven ground around the Moberly Lake church held a thousand holes, and he was always losing his balance. The Sisters could be his legs; they could hold catechism classes, religious upgrading classes, encounter sessions, perhaps get his census cards up to date. He asked the Bishop about it.

"The Sisters of St. Joseph in Hamilton, Ontario, would be the most likely candidates," the Bishop suggested. "I'll be going there soon. I'll speak to Sister Marina and ask her for Sisters to help."

Father Jungbluth next met Bishop O'Grady at a dinner in Fort St. John.

"Well," he asked impatiently. "Well? Did you get me a Sister?"

The Bishop smiled, and said nothing. Father Jungbluth badgered him throughout the meal. But the Bishop was always preoccupied with the person next to him, or across from him.

At the conclusion of the meal, the Bishop stood up. "I have an announcement to make that pleases me very much, and will certainly please Father Jungbluth here beside me." Father looked up sharply. "I spoke with Sister Marina, and she has seen her way clear to sending a Sister to help Father Jungbluth in his parish work. Sister Gemma, who is schooled in nursing and has pastoral experience, will be coming to assume the duties of pastoral assistant."

Father Jungbluth wrote the following day.

> Dear Sister Gemma,
>
> We are very happy that you have accepted to come to Chetwynd as a parish worker. Although Sister Marina told me that you could commute between Dawson Creek and here until you get a companion, my Catholic men are making plans that you may be comfortable here. Also, my Bishop promised to buy you a new car. To find out what kind of a slave-driver I am, write to Sister Margaret or Sister Anne, or to the Sisters in Fort St. John. Sister Marina says that we can expect you by middle of August, so, welcome, Sister!
>
> Sincerely yours in OL (Our Lady), Emile Jungbluth, OMI

Sister Gemma's letter of response contained a bit of news that sent Father Jungbluth's hair flying. She was planning to change her name back to her given name of Barbara Kernick, another concession allowed by Vatican II. Father Jungbluth's letter was in the return post:

"You can't do that! I've already introduced you as the 'Gem of Chetwynd.'"

Sister Gemma read the letter with trepidation. "Oh no," she thought, "I don't even know this man, but I have the feeling that I had better not do this." She left her name as Gemma, and the Gem of Chetwynd she became in Father Jungbluth's eyes.

Sister Gemma arrived on the 12th of August and at first commuted the 96 kilometres from Dawson Creek, as the little house in Chetwynd was only partly finished.

"When I first came here, Father Jungbluth wouldn't look at me or talk to me," she recalls. "If he wanted to know anything, he would direct it through Sister Anne of Dawson Creek."

Sister Gemma was first struck by Father Jungbluth's accent. When he talked about Brother Vince, who had just made his vows, it came out: "Brother Wince with his wows." She burst out laughing. Her mirth was contagious, and it wasn't long before Father Jungbluth was laughing too, and talking to her excitedly about the house, which he called, "The Dollhouse."

"Just after I arrived," says Sister Gemma, "the Catholic Womens' League had a kitchen shower for me. They told Father he couldn't come, it was just ladies. Well, he drove around town while it was going on, and finally got so curious that he just had to come in. He had to be part of everything."

Sister Gemma was just what Father Jungbluth needed. She was young, in her 30s, and full of fun. She had curly light brown hair, smiling grey eyes and fine white teeth. She seldom spoke without a smile. She was a big woman, and enjoyed her food as much as her fun. She responded to Father Jungbluth's scoldings by staring him straight in the eye, and carrying on. She simply ignored his bossiness.

"People in the community sometimes didn't understand," Sister Gemma says. "Some people thought I was being awful to him. But he knows and he understands. If I had agreed with him on everything, I would have gone stark raving mad. And he likes a good fight."

On a trip to Dawson Creek they talked about the role of Sisters. There had been an article in *Time* magazine about a Sister who had defied the Pope, and about womens' ordination.

"The Sisters aren't what they used to be," Father Jungbluth stated firmly. "They used to be in the hospitals, and they used to teach school, and they aren't doing any of that stuff anymore."

Father Jungbluth with Sister Gemma and Sister Veronica
(left to right)

"O.K.," she said. "Good. Then I'll phone Sister Anne tomorrow and tell her I want to go back to Hamilton Hospital; they need nurses. I'll work again in a hospital. You don't need me here."

"I didn't say that!" he said hotly.

"Well, you're saying the same thing."

"That's different. That's different."

"It's not different. You're just relating it to your situation here and you understand that, but you don't know what's going on in other places."

"Oh, yes I do. I see it all clearly," he said with finality.

They drove along in silence.

"You don't think women in the church should be ordained, do you?" Sister Gemma said, still piqued.

"I never said that. There's lots of jobs women can do much better for the Church than men can."

"Like what?"

"Well, cleaning the church, for example," he said, hiding his mischievous smile.

Sister Gemma's foot slammed down on the brake, causing them both to lurch forward. They spoke not a word for the next 80 kilometres.

Sister Gemma attended three services each Sunday: in Hudson's Hope at nine o'clock, in Chetwynd at eleven o'clock, and at Moberly Lake at half-past one. As often as possible, they traveled out to Kelly Lake. Although a priest from Hythe was now assigned to that church, Father Jungbluth still liked to say Mass there whenever the roads were passable, or on special occasions like Easter and Christmas.

Sister Gemma's first Christmas at Kelly Lake was the subject of her Christmas letter to her friends and associates "back east." She described how they had gone out to Kelly Lake on Boxing Day after the Christmas service. They first drove around the lake, Father Jungbluth and Sister Gemma, with Sisters Veronica and Bernadette, playing a John Denver Christmas tape; whenever they passed a house, Father Jungbluth called over his microphone, in Cree, "Father's here! Come to church! Father's here!"

The church was brightly lit, flanked by cars and pickups parked haphazardly throughout the yard and down both sides of the road. Father Jungbluth heard confessions behind a curtained booth in a back corner; a bazaar-like buzz surrounded a table on which were displayed religious articles for sale; choir practice, with an Indian girl practicing the chords to "Country Roads," was being held at the front of the church; over all this activity was the friendly chatter as people entered and moved over to the pot-bellied stove. Every so often someone would throw in a chunk of wood from the pungent-smelling woodpile stacked behind the stove. Children ran everywhere.

A party followed the celebration of Mass, and there were gifts for the children.

After everyone had left, Father and the Sisters retired to the little "rectory" beside the church for their supper. Sister Veronica held a pot of ice over the woodstove, trying to melt enough water for coffee.

"They all gave me hugs and kisses today," Father Jungbluth commented. Then he added with a wink, "It must be because I'm 70 now."

It was 12:45 a.m. when they finally got back to Chetwynd.

Sister Veronica, who maintained that Chetwynd was to be her last assignment before retirement, shared the "Dollhouse" with Sister Gemma. She performed her duties thoroughly, but did not challenge Father Jungbluth's attitudes; that she left up to the more aggressive, and decidedly favored, Sister Gemma.

Together the two Sisters despaired over the hazards of their jobs: the dogs that terrified Sister Veronica; the sometimes erratic temperament of Father Jungbluth; the harsh climate and the raw town.

Sister Gemma came to regard Father Jungbluth as the father she never had. Her own father had died when she was young, and she found Father

Jungbluth's scoldings and admonishments both heartwarming and irritating. He became jealous so easily; all she had to do was spend too much time laughing with a group of young people and he was glowering from the doorway. "Come on. Get your coat. We have to go now."

She had the youth and energy that he thought would never leave him.

Father Jungbluth, in his later years, became more and more sensitive about his age. He simply would not divulge his birth date.

"You're like the Indian, the guy who was at Prince's house for the funeral," Sister Gemma chided him. "Every time I hear his age, he's going up. He's over 100 now, for sure he's over 100. But some of the Indians say to me, 'How old is Father Jungbluth?' and when I say, 'I think he's 70 . . .' they say, 'Oh, he must be older than that. He's got to be nearly 100.'"

Father Jungbluth's face reddened with annoyance. "What does it matter how old I am?" he grumbled. "It's nothing. Nothing. Unimportant."

One day, to settle the matter, Sister Gemma sneaked a glance at his drivers licence and, although the card was smudged and frayed at the edges, she was sure the birth month read "5" or "9", May or September. She took it for a "5".

On Tuesday, May 2, at Mass time, Sister Gemma was the only one in attendance. But slowly people started to come in. Repeatedly the door opened and one or two people would sneak inside, tiptoe up the aisle, genuflect, and take a seat in the old handmade wooden pews. Father Jungbluth looked puzzled. He turned to Sister Gemma, who sat below him in the front row.

"Why are they all here?" he whispered hoarsely. "There's never more than one or two." He stepped down to mingle, asking people why they had come so unexpectedly.

"Oh, we just wanted to come to church," was their casual reply.

Soon the church was filled. Sister Meinka played the organ, and the congregation sang. Don Teslyk and another boy came in to be altar boys.

"What are they doing here?" Father Jungbluth demanded of Sister Gemma. "Why is everybody coming? It's only Tuesday!"

Two Brothers, Tom and Maynard, had arrived that day to work on building an addition to the "Dollhouse." Finally, at the homily part of the Mass, Father Jungbluth decided that the reason everybody was there was to welcome them . . . even though nobody knew they were coming. He started on a long sermon about one who'd made his 'wows' and the other who hadn't yet, and he got them all mixed up.

At the end of the Mass, Sister Gemma stood up. "Now, let's tell Father why we're here," she said. She turned to Father: "You can take off your clothes in here while everyone sings 'Happy Birthday.'"

"My clothes?" he said incredulously. "Why?"

"I mean your vestments!" laughed Sister Gemma, red-faced as the congregation roared.

"But . . . it's not my birthday!"

"It is so! I saw it on your drivers licence."

They argued a while, in front of everybody, and finally Father Jungbluth stamped off to his shack to rummage through his filing cabinet for his birth certificate. He was right. It wasn't his birthday for four more months. The "9" had been correct, the 2nd of September.

"Well," said Sister Gemma lamely, "now that everyone is here, we might as well have a party." They did.

Instead of celebrating Father Jungbluth's birthday again in September, the town got together to celebrate the 50th anniversary of his vows. Father Mariman came, bringing with him a song he had written on the bus, a song containing no less than 25 stanzas, finished as he arrived at Father Jungbluth's door in Chetwynd. The theme was a play on Father's name, "Youngblood." He sang it for the congregation, verse after verse, interspersed with the chorus after each.

The two Sisters provided Father Jungbluth with the renewal he so badly needed. They looked after church supplies, washed the linens and pressed them to perfection, visited the sick, administered to the distressed, and taught catechism and religious upgrading. But most of all, they made him laugh.

When the Sisters had been in Chetwynd for four years, the Mother House thought it was time for them to move on: Sister Veronica to retirement in Hamilton, and Sister Gemma to a new, challenging parish in Red Lake, Ontario, where her experience in the North would serve her well. They put off discussing the matter as long as possible. Sister Gemma enjoyed her work, the people and the area. Most of all, she loved Father Jungbluth. How could she leave him? He had come to depend on her, and she on him. He now showed respect for her judgement. They were partners.

She paced her living room, looking up each time she passed the portrait of Jesus that hung on the wall. The eyes seemed to follow her. "What shall I do?" she begged.

"You know I've been asked to go to another parish, Father," she told him quietly one day.

"Of course, of course," he said quickly. As when she first moved to Chetwynd, he wouldn't look at her.

"And I think I must obey." They looked at each other quietly. Sister Gemma's eyes filled with tears and her body shook. She turned away. She could hear his breath rasping, but he said not a word.

In church at Moberly Lake the next Sunday, Father Jungbluth broke the news to his congregation.

Outwardly he expressed little emotion over Sister Gemma's departure. A few Sundays later, in the Moberly Lake Church, he casually introduced the two new Sisters.

"Now I guess all have met our new Sisters here, Sister — how should I say — Ignatius, the white one there, and then we have Sister Doreen, the small one over there. Sister Doreen is mostly doing Sister Veronica's work, and Sister Ignatius will take the place of Sister Gemma, and that's a hard place to follow, you know. The footprints of Sister Gemma are deep — I do not know for what reason — but anyway, she will have quite a time to fill such a big imprint in our parish . . ."

The new Sisters did try to fill the positions vacated, but they had a hard time. Sister Ignatius — called "white one" by Father Jungbluth because of her white hair — had spent most of her life in the city. In Father Jungbluth's parish, she was expected to assume such duties as keeping the barrel stove in the Moberly Lake Church burning at an even temperature by adding wood and adjusting the dampers at crucial moments, with Father Jungbluth giving advice loudly from the pulpit. "Pleasing Father" became more difficult as time went on. Sister Ignatius was not in Chetwynd two months when she took sick and had to be moved back to Hamilton. She was replaced by Sister Mary, just evacuated from Guatemala. But Sister Mary was not happy either, and soon received a transfer.

34

The Winter Years

*F*ather Jungbluth had become "an interesting character." He had been places, met people, and suffered hardships that ranked him as a pioneer. In 1977 he received a medal and an award from the Queen, sent via Rideau Hall in Ottawa:

> On the occasion of the 25th Anniversary of the Ascension of Her Majesty the Queen to the throne, the accompanying medal is presented to Reverend Father Emile Jungbluth, 1952-1977.

He held the document in his hands and surveyed the walls of his small shack. Where could he hang it? He finally found a nail on the wall of his bathroom.

Although Father Jungbluth's wit and intellect remained as strong as ever, his health was deteriorating.

"See this bump here?" he asked a visiting friend, pointing to a stomach protrusion that was not round, like a distended belly, but bumpy, like a bag of rocks. "Well, that is an artificial bump. I had an operation, a gall bladder operation about five, six years ago. They took the stitches out, and that evening the nurse cranked me up for the meal, and all of a sudden I felt something tearing. The whole thing opened again. So, they pushed the emergency button and the doctor came quick, running, and the next day I had this big bump here."

His hands, once so deft they could machine tiny pieces for a Swiss watch, were cramped with arthritis, and his grip was weak. He opened the boxes of his watch repair kit and looked at their contents: the Seitz stacking tool, the set for calibrating balance wheels, the Swiss pocket watch hand assortments, a box of mainsprings . . .

"Junk," he said to himself, "just junk. It means nothing anymore."

His Jesuit training still served him well: head over heart, practicality over emotion. He had never owned anything, had never become attached to anything. He had sold his horse, Katie, the moment she became impractical to keep. He had a cat once, a nice little cat, in Moberly Lake, but it disappeared one night and that was that. He never went looking for it.

Father Jungbluth was over 70 now, and more defenseless than he'd ever felt in his life. "Some people feel that because we are priests, we have a certain aura around us that must be maintained," he mused. "I don't pay enough attention anymore to the atmosphere. I can no longer hear so good, and I have to ask questions. And I can't walk, so I have to hang onto things. How can I be solemn? I cannot, in this way, hope anymore to weave a spell of solemnity."

It did seem, as he got older, that he was more often accosted by the world's oddities. One morning, as he walked into the Chetwynd Hotel for breakfast (provided by the proprietor without charge), he was approached by a strange-looking man with unkempt hair and the light of lunacy in his eyes.

"I need money," he said, standing so close that Father Jungbluth could smell his breath. "I need funds for the City of God."

"How do you mean, 'the City of God'?" Father Jungbluth asked, trying to edge past."

"The City of God that's described in the Revelations!"

"Gosh, I don't remember. There is something like that, perhaps, but . . . impossible! Don't even consider it. I have no funds for such things. I could not ask my Bishop for money for such a thing."

"Well," said the man, "in that case, I guess I'll have to look somewhere else."

"Yes, that's right," Father said heavily, sinking into a chair, "that's right."

But the man puzzled Father Jungbluth. These were no longer isolated occurrences. Sometimes people came to the Sisters' door, drunk, when Father Jungbluth was not around. On occasion they were given something to eat, and told others. That brought a procession, Indians as well as whites. Even some Eskimos.

"Well," thought Father Jungbluth as he handed two dollars to the bedraggled looking beggars, "I finally got my Eskimos."

One autumn night there came a sharp knock. He got up from his desk and opened the door. A young man stood in the shadows.

"I want a bed for the night!" he said sharply.

"Gosh, I don't have any beds for you," Father Jungbluth said, adjusting his glasses so he could make out the man's features. "I don't have any beds here at all, in fact."

"I want a bed tonight."

"Where did you come from?"

Suddenly Father Jungbluth heard a snap, and felt a knife blade under his chin, the tip poking his throat. He tried not to swallow. A moment of panic passed, and then he felt deadly calm.

"What do you do that for?" he asked quietly. "What do you want?"

"I want a bed."

"That's not the way to obtain a bed. Where do you come from?"

"Jail. Ever heard of the place?"

"Oh? And have you been to the police?"

"Yes. They won't give me a bed. There's no welfare here. Can you give me a bed somewhere?"

"No, I cannot do that, with the knife here. If you threaten me like this with a knife, you don't get a bed." Father Jungbluth looked the man in the eyes. "This is not the way to act," he said firmly. He began to feel tired. He was standing on tiptoe in an attempt to raise his chin above the scratching knife point. The man's hand twitched. "You've been in jail," Father continued, "you don't want to be there again. You will end up there again."

Slowly the knife pulled away. Father Jungbluth plunged his hand into his pocket and brought out three one-dollar bills. The man put out his hand.

"Just a minute," said Father. "I will give you some money, but, because you threatened me with a knife, you can have only a portion of what I have here."

Slowly he extracted one of the dollar bills and put it back in his pocket. He held out the other two.

"This is enough to pay for a bed in the hostel, in the bunkhouse thing behind the hotel. Now, go."

The man mumbled something, then turned and left. Father Jungbluth shut the door, and sat down heavily on the brown chair. Perspiration stood out on his forehead. His hands were shaking. He rested a moment, then walked over to his desk and phoned the police.

"Yes, we know the guy," the officer said. "He was here earlier, but we didn't think he was dangerous, so we sent him over to see you."

Father Jungbluth lay that night for a long time without sleeping. He thought of all the years he had spent with the Indians. Never had an Indian struck him, or threatened him. Was this, then, what was called "civilization"?

Was this progress?

The next day he drove out to Moberly Lake. Driving down the winding road past the Indian cemetery, he parked his old green Dodge in front of the log church of St. Theresa, and went inside. The church was cool and quiet. The white pillared altar, trimmed in gold, shone cleanly in the shaded log interior. The altar still held artificial flowers that had once been a bride's bouquet. The statues of the Virgin of Lourdes and the Sacred Heart in each corner still quietly watched the comings and goings of congregations.

He walked down to the water's edge, and lowered himself gingerly onto a large rock. The water of Moberly Lake shone blue and black and silver as waves lapped the shore, pushing with uneven rhythm against the pebbled beach. Directly at his back leaned an old grey poplar tree. Its half-dead roots clumped above the ground like an arched octopus, with only thin tentacles of living fibre securely fastened onto the rocks. Behind him, beyond the bluff of trees, lay the smooth dirt road, its dark ribbon forming the lower line of his view of the church, framed by a gap in the trees.

"My roots are like those of the big grey tree here," he thought, "partially buried in this rough soil, just far enough to give some sense of stability. Like this tree, my body too is greying. We both bend more each year, from wind and snow and the weight of years. And oh, gosh, I grow weary."

He stood up, clutching onto the twisted tree trunk for support and slowly made his way back up the incline and onto the trail to the Indian cemetery behind the church. He had an appointment to keep.

His name was Theophile, but everyone called him Tofel, an old Indian who helped with funerals and kept the cemetery in order, considering this the task of his life. He was cleaning up the yard and hacking eagerly at the lean frozen grass, the weeds, the wild rose hedges. They had to be removed quickly. Tomorrow, eve of All Souls Day, the Indians would be coming to the cemetery to sing their sorrowful songs and to bless the graves of their dead.

"Hello, Father!" Tofel called. He leaned on his scythe, waiting for Father to make his way up the hill.

"I am so glad you have come, Father," Tofel said, in Cree, "for I would like to know what to do with the little hut on top of William Calliou's grave. Shall I remove it and burn its old boards?"

The two made their way through the high brush over to William's grave. For his own benefit, as much as for Father Jungbluth's, Tofel reminisced aloud:

"William was one of the first we put to rest here. And for you, Father, it was your first funeral in Moberly Lake. Do you remember, it was in the summer of 1937." Tofel noticed how the old priest let his hand glide over his bald head to protect it from the cold. "Yes, Father, at that time you still had lots of hair, when you came from far away on horseback. Now you look much older, and only want to drive by car." The two men smiled at each other.

Tofel went on talking as they moved to William Calliou's grave. "William was not born over here. He came from down south near Lac Ste. Anne, where he learned to pray. When I was still young myself I remember him telling me always of a black-robed man. He meant a 'Man of Prayer,' one like you. And he often assured me that he would not die before he could see such a black-robed man again. He must have been 100 years or so!"

Tofel stood very straight and looked over the rippling waters of Moberly Lake. "Ah, Father, did you know it was me who asked for a black-robed man for this old William? I went to the fur trader myself and asked him if he could write the Bishop. And then you arrived. William was so happy for it. Two days later he died, peacefully, and then it was you, Father, who decided where his grave should be.

"It was then when you told all of us that we should bury our dead not any longer underneath a tree, but here in this burial ground. I will never forget your angry face when we placed this little hut instead of a cross on top of William's grave. I remember then that you were not capable of understanding our Indian language as well as you do today. And you did not understand us properly. We could not understand you either. But one thing I knew, that you were of the opinion in those days that such a hut on a grave was a sign of superstition. Later you came to understand us better and said nothing against this custom. But the hut is now falling apart and mostly rotted. Father, please say, shall I remove the rest of the hut and burn it?"

Father Jungbluth was moved by the memories brought back by Tofel, memories of his first eager missionary years. Today this tombstone did not signify to him superstition, but a dignity. "Do not touch it," he said. "Allow it to die on its own."

Tofel began working again. Praying in silence, Father Jungbluth passed the long rows of graves. Almost 100 Indians buried here. And none died without his blessing. Not once did he come too late for a dying. There were the graves of the adults, and there, at the south end, the graves of the children who went innocent into the heavens . . .

As Father Jungbluth drove back to Chetwynd, he thought of the graveyard in Moberly Lake. Indians were peacefully buried in sacred earth, which once belonged entirely to them. He was sure their souls were in God's Eternal Kingdom. No! His work was not in vain. He knew it. God knew it. And he felt only gratitude that he had learned to understand these cultured and dignified people.

He slept more soundly that night than he had for a long time.

35

Direction of Time

"We are building, intending to build, a new church," Father Jungbluth announced to Father Mariman, who had come by bus from Meander River, Alberta, to visit. Father Mariman looked out through the doorway of Father Jungbluth's rectory to the back of the present church.

"That is very nice," he said, "but what about this one? It still looks alright to me."

Father Jungbluth followed his gaze.

"I'm not excited about it, the new church," he admitted, "but I guess they have to have it. They say I'll have a few years in the new church. I hope I'll be dead by then. I've built so many buildings — I don't feel like going to all the trouble it will cause." He turned from the doorway, and sat down heavily at his desk. "Of course, it's different, this one. It's being built by a contractor."

They bent their heads over the blueprints while Father Jungbluth explained the layout.

"When do they hope to have this finished?"

"Oh, if everything goes perfectly, if there's no holdup, which practically never happens, we could possibly be in it by next Christmas. But, I don't think we will be."

They sat in silence looking at the plans, then through the open door of Father's shack to the little white painted church of Our Lady of Peace.

"You are getting older, Mariman," said Father Jungbluth bluntly, "and yet every year you come here, you still wear that old suit, the one you wore coming over on the boat from France in 1935! How long do you think it will last?" He tugged at the distended pockets that hung on each side. "Look here, the pockets are all misshapen and bulging, like you've got them stuffed with apples."

"Eggs."

"Eggs? I don't believe it."

Father Mariman reached into his pockets, and withdrew a wrapped piece of bread folded over some cheese, and a smudged boiled egg, still in the shell.

"Oh my gosh!" Father Jungbluth stood up and looked at his friend. "Oh my gosh, Mariman, you still play on your poverty!"

Father Mariman smiled and began combing his hair with a tiny plastic comb. The teeth were mostly gone, and the plastic looked scratched and old.

"And where did you get that thing?" Father Jungbluth demanded.

"I found it on the road," Father Mariman answered nonchalantly, putting it back into the breast pocket of his suit.

"We are relics, Mariman, you and I," Father Jungbluth said slowly, sitting down again. "Look at us . . . and look at this." He passed his hand over the blueprints.

"We are relics, Mariman, you and I."

For all his reluctance to build the new church, Father Jungbluth participated fully in its construction. But he never liked the plan. There were no windows. The nearest thing to a window was a long strip of amber glass that would allow a streak of sun to shine onto the altar. Nor did the adjoining hall have any windows. It was ultra-modern, following the stark geometry of the church building.

"The windows are too high," he complained, "and furthermore, it looks like a Disney World production. Mickey Mouse should come walking out of there." The contractor listened politely. "They sacrificed the inside to the looks of the outside! It's too high! It's too big! It's too dark! No, no, I don't like it at all!"

One day in the fall a big wind came up and blew the half-built structure over. The walls collapsed. Father Jungbluth took the news calmly.

The architect restructured his drawings, the contractor increased his bracing, and the church went up again. This time the walls remained. Soon the outside was finished, the windows and doors installed. Carpenters, electricians and plumbers scurried through the buildings, accomplishing, with their modern tools, feats that Father Jungbluth never dreamed possible. They installed an electronic amplification system for his Strasbourg Cathedral bell-ringing records and built a high tower that allowed his recordings to resound over the valley.

The day of the dedication, October 18, 1981, the sun shone gold over the Peace valley. A stiff wind rattled dried leaves that still clung to the trees, making dancing contrasts of orange and yellow against the grey trunks.

The church's exterior of diagonal cedar was fronted by a plain white cross, rising high above the square belfry that housed the modern sound system. Recorded music swept over the windblown land. Eight Knights of Columbus, resplendent in costumes with black pointed hats trimmed with white osprey plumes, lined up to form a guard. Father Jungbluth watched.

Bishop O'Grady walked solemnly around the circumference, sprinkling the walls with Holy Water, stepping gingerly over the bits of board and construction paper. After the ceremony came the speeches. Father Allan Noonan, OMI, Provincial Superior of St. Paul's Province, took the stand:

"We look upon Father Emile as one of the last of the great apostles, one of the last of the great missionaries," he said. "He has something inside of him that inspires us in our wish to reach out to those who are most in need."

When it was Father Jungbluth's turn to speak, he seemed to gather his forces. With a wide smile, he stepped up to the microphone, and was immediately taken aback by the thunderous roar of applause. He stood smiling and red-faced until it finally subsided.

"Such applause!" he said, looking flushed. "I certainly don't deserve it. The contractor who built this place certainly would agree with me that I don't deserve it, because he put up with a lot."

The people strained their ears to catch his words. His smile grew wider and his voice stronger as he went down the list of helpers. Then, picking out people whose features he could distinguish in the audience, he told little stories about them. They cheered in anxious concern as they watched the little priest reach for the microphone stand to correct his balance, or hesitate a moment over a name. The church was new, but their priest was not.

Father Jungbluth moved into the "Disney World" rectory and attempted to carry on. But it became obvious, first to himself, and then to those who attended his services, that he could not much longer keep up the pace of serving four churches.

In the spring of 1983, the rumor began: first one, then another, until Father Jungbluth could no longer claim that they were only rumors. He was going to be put out to pasture. Everyone said so. Resigned from his post. Moved away. Other priests came to visit him, and from them he picked up the details, even the fact that Father Conway, formerly of Dawson Creek, was being brought in to replace him.

"It's all because of this new church and fancy rectory!" he thundered. "If they had left me alone in my little shack, with that little church built by the Indians and myself, then no one else would even want to come in here. But now look what's happened! They built this big church — which came with a big burden of debt, mostly paid off by my benefactors in the old country — and it's so fancy that they will have no trouble now replacing me here. I knew it would happen."

He sat down and dashed off a letter to the Provincial Superior, Father Noonan, with whom he spared no words. He was not going.

Father Noonan wrote in response:

> Thank you for your letter of March 12th . . . I realize too that it is difficult for you to even consider moving out of Chetwynd. You have become very much a part of the local church. We do not see you retiring — I hope that you never retire — but there does come a time when we need to slow down and move into a less demanding type of situation. We see you very much a continuing part of the church and the ministry in the Peace River area. You can continue to be a great help to us by working out of Fort St. John as part of the team there. This allows you to remain in the area that is very much a part of your life, and to continue your ministry but not with the responsibilities that you now have.
>
> It is not going to be easy to replace you — we can find someone who will be able to do the work, we hope — but no one will ever replace Emile Jungbluth.
>
> We will continue to pray that the appointment will not be a difficult one for you . . . you pray too that we will find an Oblate who will be able to work in Chetwynd and Tumbler Ridge.
>
> God bless and pray for the provincial.
> *Allan F. Noonan, OMI, Provincial*

When the final official letter arrived from the Provincial House, dated May 18, 1983, it contained no surprises. Father Jungbluth sat at his desk, his head bent toward the window, and read:

> I want first of all to thank you for your work in Chetwynd — no one can ever replace you in this work.

"Ha!" he said to himself. "First they butter you up and then they let the knife fall." He read on:

You are so much a part of the area, and loved by all the people. It is very difficult to see anyone else in your boots!

"Good. Then let me stay in them."

However, this is to tell you officially that you are being appointed to Fort St. John, B.C., as assistant to Father Ray L'Henaff, the new pastor, effective August 1, 1983.

"To do what — watch T.V.?"

The main reason for the move is concern for your health — we love you too much to leave you any longer in a situation that is becoming too difficult. Father L'Henaff is delighted to have you come with him . . .

"No doubt."

. . .and the Bishop has approved your new assignment. We missed you at the Congress. You have many more years of service to God and the Church. You have a great gift of presence to the Indian people especially, and you will be of great assistance to Father Ray as he moves into a new responsibility.

Sincerely in JC and MI
Allan F. Noonan, OMI, Provincial

Father Jungbluth took off his five-dollar spectacles purchased at Kresge's and rubbed his eyes. His vision seemed to whirl out of focus. He stumbled from the wooden desk chair and flung himself into the big new velvet recliner, furnishings of the "Disney World" rectory. He leaned back and closed his eyes.

He had done what he had always wanted: worked in the harshest missions, with unspoiled people. Perhaps he had been inspired in the beginning by the fantasies of Karl May, or the harsh romantic life of Father DuChaussois, but he had been brought down to reality. He recalled that first winter with Father Mariman in the attic at Eleské, studying the Beaver Indian language by coal oil lamp. He had done it . . . all. And now it was over.

He looked down at the letter in his hand, his last Obedience. Then he folded it carefully, and put it back in its envelope. Taking up his pen, he scrawled, "No need to answer" across the front and threw it onto a corner of his scarred oak desk.

He made the announcement himself, and his congregations were hushed in disbelief. They looked down at their hands, aging too.

*A parade in Chetwynd was not complete without
Father Jungbluth. Country music was amplified through
speakers mounted on the roof of his green Dodge.*

The people of the parish rallied to give him a farewell party. They arranged for Sister Gemma to fly in from Red Lake, Ontario. They filled the hall with well-wishers: white, Indian, and Metis, from all the towns and reserves in the Peace. Telegrams were read from Mr. and Mrs. Frank Oberle, Member of Parliament; from Mr. and Mrs. Don Phillips, Member of the Legislative Assembly; a message from Sister Meinka; one from friends Marcel and Marie LaMarre. A speech was made by Mayor Lasser of Chetwynd, who presented Father Jungbluth with a framed picture of Chetwynd at night, taken from the great hill — a familiar sight.

The Native Association representative, Phillip Gladu, presented him with a gift of handmade moccasins. "Just a little gift to show appreciation," he said. "He's helped us a lot, in a lot of ways, and I congratulate him on his retirement."

Father Jungbluth picked up the tanned moosehide moccasins and put them to his nose. Breathing deeply, he smiled and then held them high in the air. "Aah!" he said. "Exactly the smell I like!"

Amy Gauthier, representative for the East End Saulteaux band, made an emotional speech, recalling many of the couples Father Jungbluth had married, dating back to the late 1930s. "I am certain we shall never again receive such a priest as Father Jungbluth," she said, tears in her eyes.

Eventually it was Father Jungbluth's turn to take the stand:

"It is nice for you to give me a nice celebration for getting rid of me," he said. "I am happy to see so many of you here — especially the Kelly Lake people, stand up please! Yes, and the people here from Dawson Creek, Progress, Fort St. John, Hudson's Hope, Mackenzie, Moberly Lake, all over.

You know, I said to Father Noonan, 'What's the matter with you? I love it here! I can stand it for another year or two,' but you know how these bosses are — they never listen to the workers.

"So, I go. But I will come back to visit, as often as I can, as often as they let me out. Now, I think Sister Gemma wants to say something."

Sister Gemma took the microphone. "I can hardly express my happiness — and my surprise — at being here tonight. I only found out Monday that I was coming. But it means very much for me to be here.

"I worked in the parish with Father Jungbluth for four years, and during that time, he became the father of my life. My own father died when I was young, and I did not know, until I met Father Jungbluth, how much I needed someone strong and wise and beautiful in my life. Thank you, Father. Thank you."

The applause broke, standing applause, and the hall was filled with the cheering and clapping of hundreds of well-wishers, many with tears in their eyes. Father Jungbluth sat, smiling, as they sang in choked voices, "For He's a Jolly Good Fellow." He looked around at all the beloved faces. He'd baptized nearly all of them, married many of them, counselled not a few; sometimes he'd dealt with them harshly, sometimes he'd just listened, but he knew them, each and every one. They pleased him greatly.

Father Emile Jungbluth, OMI.

Epilogue

*I*n May of 1969, the Provincial Oblate House had sent Father Jungbluth a form to fill out to allow an update of records. The form was headed:

BIOGRAPHICAL DATA ON EMILE JUNGBLUTH

Beyond the basic statistics of "place of birth," "education," and so on, were questions pertaining to the missionary's progress. Father Jungbluth's form was returned as follows:

Any degrees, special courses, qualifications?
No degrees. No special qualifications. No courses.

Any relatives who are priests, religious, or otherwise notable?
None.

Membership in non-Oblate organizations?
None, except small civic clubs, etc. (Chamber of Commerce, Indian Friendship Club, etc.)

Special achievements either prior to or subsequent to ordination/ profession?
Started a club, built a church, won an award. No special achievements. Speak Cree adequately, Beaver haltingly; know some French, German, English.

Built mission churches at Eleské, near Fort Vermilion	*(1936)*
" " " at Moberly Lake	*(1939)*
" " " at Kelly Lake	*(1953)*
" " " at Chetwynd	*(1958)*
Rebuilt church of Sudeten immigrants at Tomslake	*(1957)*
Built Moberly Lake Youth Centre	*(1967)*
Man of the Year Award, Chetwynd	*(1968)*

Any other newsworthy angles?
Not much I can think of.
Sorry, I have no picture of myself.

The first edition of *Youngblood of the Peace* was released in the fall of 1986. The author loaded 600 copies of the book into her car, picked up Father Mariman in Edmonton, and together they journeyed to Fort St. John to celebrate the "launch" of the book.

Father Jungbluth was waiting impatiently for them on the lawn of the rectory. Then, apparently satisfied, he began autographing the entire shipment. The Fort St. John chapter of the Catholic Women's League sponsored the celebration, which was attended by over 200 people. "Youngblood of the Peace Gets Tremendous Send-off" stated the *Alaska Highway News*, and indeed it did. All 600 copies sold, along with orders for double that number. The two Fathers told stories of the past, and visited with friends who had come to wish them well.

The author subsequently wrote a stage play based on the book, which was presented at the Fringe Festival of Plays in Edmonton in August 1987. The play, too, was attended by Father Jungbluth and Father Mariman, who at this time were residing together once again in "Placid Place," a retirement home for Oblates in Edmonton.

Then, in December 1987, the Chetwynd *Echo* newspaper carried a black-bordered article headed, "Pioneer of the Peace Goes Home.'" Father Emile Jungbluth, OMI, passed away on December 17, 1987. Services were held in Edmonton, Alberta, Chetwynd and Mission, B.C. He was buried in the Oblate cemetary in Mission.

Father Césaire Mariman continued to work diligently on his last personal mission: a translation of the gospel to the Beaver Indian language. He had almost completed his goal when he died on February 6, 1989. He is buried among his beloved Beaver Indians above the grotto he built at his first mission, Eleské.

On June 21, 1989, *The Alaska Highway News* informed residents that the Oblates were ending their 125-year mission in Fort St. John. Father Ray L'Henaff, the last Oblate of Mary Immaculate to serve in that area, was being transferred to Burns Lake.

Reminiscing on the history of Oblates in the Peace area, Father L'Henaff made reference to his former room-mate: "Father Emile Jungbluth typified the old way and the classical idea of what it meant to be a missionary," he said.

The churches built by the Oblates still stand, and some are used fairly often, although there seems to be a vibrancy missing in the services. Perhaps one remembers the mystery of Latin; the poetry of myriad Indian languages singing the Kyrie or the "long sad song," the Passion: *Tatto ka pe nantotamek* . . . Perhaps one recalls the funny accents of the old priests, and the old-world atmosphere that permeated their little missions in the bush, where the Oblates went to serve "the ones who were the most abandoned."

About the Author

Shirlee Smith Matheson was born in Winnipeg, Manitoba, and has since lived in every western province. After she married Bill Matheson in Lacombe, Alberta, he took her for a trip to his home town of Peace River. "I absolutely fell in love with the area," she says. Proving the adage, "If one drinks from the Peace he will always return," Shirlee, her husband and two daughters moved to Hudson's Hope, some 500 kilometres upstream on the British Columbia side of the Peace River, where they resided for nine years. While living in Hudson's Hope, Shirlee became familiar with the people and territory of Father Jungbluth's mission.

Shirlee is an alumna of the Banff Centre's writing program, and winner of a number of awards, including first prize for historical writing in a competition sponsored by the British Columbia Historical Federation in 1983. More recently, she won the 1990 Roderick-Haig Brown B.C. Book Award and the 1990 Alberta Culture Non-Fiction Award for *This was our Valley* (co-authored with Earl K. Pollon, published by Detselig Enterprises). Her articles and short stories have appeared in magazines across Canada and into the United States; as well, she has written novels and stage plays for adult as well as juvenile markets. She presently resides with her family in Calgary, Alberta.

Printed in Canada